Lecture Notes in Computer Science   1326

Edited by G. Goos, J. Hartmanis and J. van Leeuwen

Advisory Board: W. Brauer   D. Gries   J. Stoer

Springer

Berlin
Heidelberg
New York
Barcelona
Budapest
Hong Kong
London
Milan
Paris
Santa Clara
Singapore
Tokyo

Charles Nicholas   James Mayfield (Eds.)

Intelligent Hypertext

Advanced Techniques
for the World Wide Web

 Springer

Series Editors

Gerhard Goos, Karlsruhe University, Germany

Juris Hartmanis, Cornell University, NY, USA

Jan van Leeuwen, Utrecht University, The Netherlands

Volume Editors

Charles Nicholas
University of Maryland Baltimore County
Department of Computer Science and Electrical Engineering
1000 Hilltop Circle, Baltimore, MD 21250, USA
E-mail: nicholas@csee.umbc.edu

James Mayfield
The Johns Hopkins University, Applied Physics Laboratory
Johns Hopkins Road, Laurel, MD 20723-6099, USA
E-mail: james.mayfield@jhuap.edu

Cataloging-in-Publication data applied for

Die Deutsche Bibliothek - CIP-Einheitsaufnahme

Intelligent hypertext : advanced techniques for the World Wide
Web / Charles Nicholas ; James Mayfield (ed.). - Berlin ; Heidelberg
; New York ; Barcelona ; Budapest ; Hong Kong ; London ; Milan ;
Paris ; Santa Clara ; Singapore ; Tokyo : Springer, 1997
  (Lecture notes in computer science ; Vol. 1326)
  ISBN 3-540-63637-4

CR Subject Classification (1991): H.2

ISSN 0302-9743
ISBN 3-540-63637-4 Springer-Verlag Berlin Heidelberg New York

© Springer-Verlag Berlin Heidelberg 1997
Printed in Germany

Typesetting: Camera-ready by author
SPIN 10545719   06/3142 – 5 4 3 2 1 0   Printed on acid-free paper

Preface

James Mayfield[1] and Charles Nicholas[2]

[1] Johns Hopkins University Applied Physics Laboratory, Laurel, Maryland, USA
[2] Department of Computer Science and Electrical Engineering, University of Maryland Baltimore County, Baltimore, Maryland, USA *

The papers in this volume grew out of contributions and discussions held at the Workshops on Intelligent Hypertext, which were held in conjunction with the 1993 and 1994 Conferences on Information and Knowledge Management (CIKM'93 and CIKM'94). The theme of the CIKM conference is the interaction between the fields of artificial intelligence, database management, and information retrieval. With their emphasis on intelligent systems for managing information, using the hypertext metaphor, the two Workshops on Intelligent Hypertext were consistent with this theme.

In the years since the workshops took place, the World Wide Web has achieved enormous success. Indeed, for many people, the Web is the only hypertext system they have ever used or even heard of. With this in mind, the editors invited several of the workshop participants to prepare chapter-length papers based on their workshop contributions, with special emphasis on how their results apply to the Web now, or might apply to versions of the Web that appear in the future.

Bieber describes his experience with creating a Web version of the August 1995 issue of *Communications of the ACM*. He points out that the although rich semantics for hypertext links is a familiar idea in the hypertext community, the Web in its current form does little to support this. In particular, no tool to aid authors in adding semantic information to their links is available, making this process laborious and error-prone. Bieber goes on to describe a browser in which semantic information *about* a link, e.g., what sort of relationship exists between the current document and the one being linked to, is presented. One of the important lessons to be learned from this effort is that producing a well-designed hypertext document of non-trivial size is still a significant effort.

Brusilovsky discusses adaptive hypermedia, in which the hypermedia system adapts to its individual human users. This idea goes beyond the idea of "preferences," standard in contemporary browsers. Adaptive hypermedia includes adaptive content, in which different users may see different versions of what is essentially the same hypermedia document, whether that document is an ordinary Web page, for example, or perhaps an annotation or index document. Adaptive hypermedia also includes the notion of adaptive navigation, in which some users see links that others do not. Brusilovsky addresses the

* Supported in part by a Sabbatical Fellowship from the United States Department of Defense.

question of how adaptive hypermedia might be evaluated, and he discusses many example systems.

Gobbetti and Turner describe the Virtual Reality Modeling Language (VRML), and explain how 3D documents may be implemented using VRML and the Web. They present an overview of VRML's historical beginnings, implementation issues, and sample applications. Of particular interest is the "Virtual Sardinia Project," in which geographic information, including satellite images, are used to create a VR model of the island of Sardinia. This model can then be explored with a VRML-enabled Web browser.

One component of intelligent hypertext systems (or indeed of intelligent systems in general) is the degree to which the system adapts (or can be adapted) in order to better serve its users. Kay and Kummerfeld describe their PT system, which builds and maintains a model of each user. For new users, this process begins by PT asking them questions about their background knowledge in computer programming. As the system runs, this user model is updated, and information derived from it is used to generate customized documents, and to customize navigation between documents.

Kent and Neuss argue that World Wide Web search should be carried out by exchange of meta-data, not (as is now practiced) by exchange of the data themselves. They suggest that *formal concept analysis* can provide tools for representing the semantics of hypertext documents, which can serve as meta-data. *Conceptual linkage* in their formulation is the overlay of relationships among the concepts represented in documents onto an existing hypertext link structure. *Conceptual browsing* is browsing along the lines of such an overlay. Conceptual browsing represents a midpoint between traversing the links that are part of a document (*e.g.*, by clicking on a WWW link) and using a global indexing scheme (*e.g.*, by searching the WWW with AltaVista or HotBot). The techniques they report apply both to the structuring of local hypertexts, and to guidance of the user through such a structure.

Mayfield presents an overview of two-level models of hypertext. For a hypertext system to be considered intelligent, it can be argued, requires that the raw data be augmented by some meta-data structure. The purpose of such meta-data is to organize the information so that it can be accessed more easily. Several forms of meta-data are possible, and Mayfield describes a variety of two-level hypertext systems.

In their chapter on the TELLTALE system, Pearce and Miller present their work on the scalability of information retrieval techniques in a hypertext context. TELLTALE is a hypertext system that provides similarity matches between documents (much as traditional information retrieval systems do). But it is integrated with a hypertext interface in a way that greatly improves the speed and ease with which a user can explore the information space. For example, three statistics-based similarity measures are available to the user for controlling how dynamic hypertext links are created. TELLTALE's two main scaling techniques are 1) the use of n-grams (sequences of n contiguous characters) as retrieval terms in lieu of more traditional word-based terms; and 2) the distribution of meta-data about the documents in the collection across several machines. The former adds scalability in the types of documents that may be included, while the latter aids scalability in the number of documents indexed.

The notion of meta-data in hypertext emerges several times in this volume. One specific proposal is presented by Wang, Ghaoui, and Rada, who discuss the use of semantic nets as domain models for hypertext systems. Of particular interest is the issue of how to maintain the consistency (of both meaning and style) of a set of hypertext documents created by many people. As Web content becomes more dynamic, the need for techniques to understand (and control) what material exists, and where it resides, will increase. The MUCH and RICH systems described in this chapter are important steps in this direction.

Rus and Subramanian describe an architecture for intelligent software agents, and argue the suitability of such agents to discover and use information distributed over a network. These agents are intelligent in the sense of being able to examine data, make plans in response to the data, and perform actions according to these plans. Agents are endowed with "sensors" and are capable of making sophisticated analysis of documents at different levels of detail. The agents are mobile, and migration from one site to another is one possible action. Rus and Subramanian describe the formal underpinnings of their system, and discuss its operation in detail.

Table of Contents

List of Contributors

Michael Bieber
Institute of Integrated Systems Research,
New Jersey Institute of Technology,
University Heights, Newark, NJ 07102-1982 USA

Peter Brusilovsky
Human Computer Interaction Institute,
School of Computer Science,
Carnegie Mellon University,
Pittsburgh, PA 15213 USA

Claude Ghaoui
CMS, Liverpool John Moores University,
Liverpool L3 3AF, UK

Enrico Gobbetti
Center for Advanced Studies,
Research and Development in Sardinia,
Via Nazario Sauro 10,
09123 Cagliari, Italy

Judy Kay
Department of Computer Science,
University of Sydney, Australia

Robert Kent
Department of Electrical Engineering and Computer Science,
Washington State University, Pullman, WA 99164-2752, USA

Bob Kummerfeld
Department of Computer Science,
University of Sydney, Australia

James Mayfield
The Johns Hopkins University Applied Physics Laboratory,
Johns Hopkins Road, Laurel, MD 20723-6099, USA

Ethan Miller
Department of Computer Science and Electrical Engineering,
University of Maryland Baltimore County, Baltimore, MD, 21250, USA

Christian Neuss
Technische Hochschule Darmstadt,
Fachgebiet Praktische Informatik,
64289 Darmstadt, Germany

Claudia Pearce
U.S. Department of Defense,
9800 Savage Road, Fort Meade, MD, 20755-6000, USA

Roy Rada
Department of Electrical Engineering and Computer Science,
Washington State University,
Pullman, WA 99164-2752, USA

Daniela Rus
Department of Computer Science,
Dartmouth College, Hanover, NH 03755, USA

Devika Subramanian
Department of Computer Science,
Rice University, Houston, TX 77005,
USA

Weigang Wang
GMD-IPSI, Dolivostr. 15, D-64293,
Darmstadt, Germany

Enhancing Information Comprehension Through Hypertext

Michael Bieber

Electronic Enterprise Engineering Program; and
Hypermedia Information Systems Research Laboratory
Institute of Integrated Systems Research, New Jersey Institute of Technology
University Heights — Newark, NJ 07102-1982 USA
telephone: +1 201 596-2681; facsimile: +1 201 596-5777
email: bieber@cis.njit.edu; URL: http://megahertz.njit.edu/~bieber/

Summary. We discuss the process, issues and lessons learned in designing and implementing the World Wide Web (WWW) version of the August 1995 special issue of the *Communications of the ACM* on hypermedia design. The vast majority of WWW authors rely on the text of the link's anchor to provide 100% of the semantic information about the destination and purpose of the link. Yet, following a link often takes the reader out of the current context. We discuss remedying this by providing semantic link labels and other information about a link's purpose and destination, so that readers can evaluate whether to follow a link without having to select it.

1. Motivation

People and organizations have embraced the World Wide Web (WWW) in part because it so dramatically facilitates information access [2]. WWW system builders have begun to take advantage of the tools the information retrieval field has developed. In contrast, builders of WWW servers and browsers (e.g., Netscape) have not incorporated tools to exploit lessons learned by the hypermedia research community. It seems obvious that WWW builders should provide sophisticated navigational and authoring tools, and that Web authors should apply techniques developed for maintaining context and orientation in non-linear presentations. Yet a quick survey of WWW applications presents a sobering reality. Web servers and browsers provide only rudimentary support for hypertext functionality. Authors must represent all types of interrelationships and construct all advanced hypertext functionality (e.g., guided tours) from scratch using one simple anchor type and single-step forward browsing [5]. As a result, authors of individual WWW pages have little support to enhance their information presentations with the suite of features the concept of hypermedia provides, and few do [4].

For the past thirty years, the hypertext research community has advanced hypertext navigational functionality and studied how best to convey information when authoring hypertexts. Our goal in the project we describe here was to demonstrate one feature for helping people understand links. We define the concept of hypermedia as the science of relationships (i.e., the interrelationships among objects or pieces of information) and how people can access information using these relationships. Links represent relationships to readers. The vast majority of WWW authors rely on the text of the link's anchor to provide 100% of the semantic information about the destination and purpose of the link. Yet, following a link often takes the reader out of the current context, transporting him or her to a new document or a different *chunk* of the current one. By providing semantic link labels together with a lot of other information about the link's purpose and its destination (besides its URL), readers can evaluate whether to follow a link without having to select it. In other words we provide the reader with *meta-information* about the relationships within the WWW information corpus.

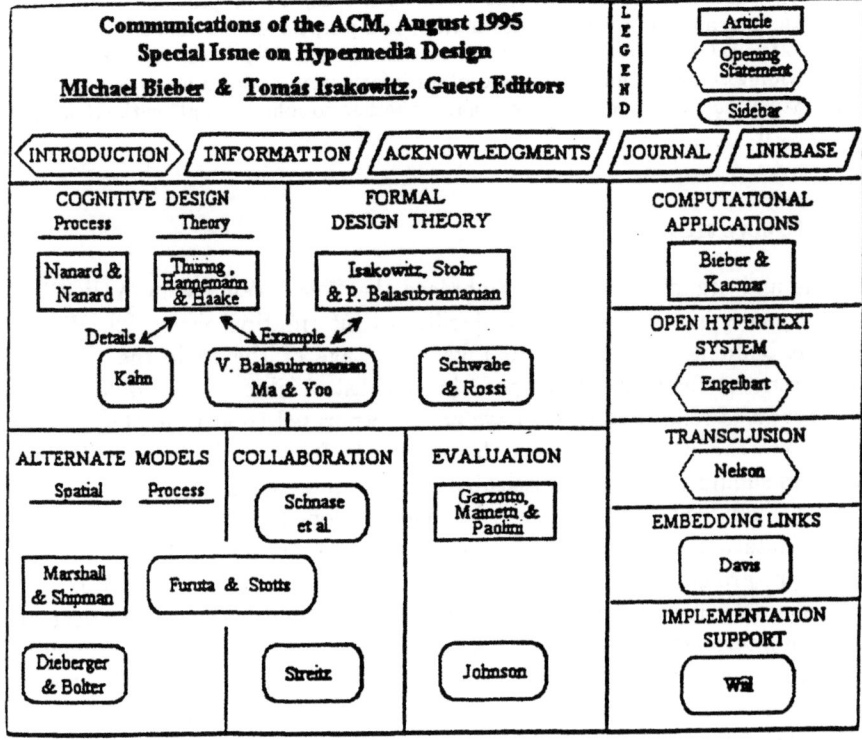

Fig. 1.1. Spatial overview of the *Communications of the ACM*, August 1995's WWW version

This chapter discusses the process, issues and lessons learned in designing and implementing the World Wide Web version of the August 1995 special issue of the *Communications of the ACM* on hypermedia design. The printed journal version contains an introduction, two opening statements (about two pages each), ten sidebars (up to a page in length), and six 5000-word papers, two of which have inserts of up to 1000 words. Figure 1.1 gives a spatial overview [7, 12] of the special issue's electronic version.

We were inspired to present hypertext *through* hypertext by the electronic versions of the July 1988 special issue of the *Communications of the ACM* [14, 17, 19] and by Nielsen's Hypertext'87 Trip Report (of which [13] provides a printed description). While each of these collections is highly enjoyable and a great contribution in its own right, students using them in our hypermedia course have identified shortcomings concerning disorientation [13, 15] and link specificity [11], which we tried to overcome in our design. We employ semantic link labels as a weapon against each, allowing readers to see information about a link's purpose and destination before choosing it. Figures 1.2 and 1.3 provide examples of anchors with semantic link labels.

Thus we had several goals for producing an electronic version of the August 1995 special issue on Hypermedia Design. First, we believe that experiencing papers about hypertext design within a hypertext environment helps readers understand the concepts better. Second, we believed the paper links such as "(see XYZ's paper in this issue for more details)" typically used by authors—especially within a tight corpus such as a special issue—are often vague and rarely point to exact positions within the destination paper. On-line cross-reference links would better reinforce the special issue's cohesion. Third, we believe that many authors are not using the hypertext features of the WWW to their full advantage [5]. To demonstrate some of the ideas and functionality the *concept* of hypertext could provide the WWW community, we wanted an environment for experimenting with semantic link labeling on the World-Wide Web.

In what follows we shall describe the process undertaken to develop the issue's semantic links, present some of the technical details in generating the WWW pages incorporating these and cover additional issues, which others undertaking similar projects may wish to consider.

2. Semantic Link Design

We originally did not think of putting the special issue on-line. Authors wrote their papers and sidebars strictly for the printed journal. Only while drafts were out for review did we consider producing an electronic version to supplement the issue. The timing thus required the journal authors to retrofit all semantic links (including those existing in the printed journal) on an existing corpus. We asked the authors to revisit theirs and the other journal papers to craft semantic labels for five types of links:

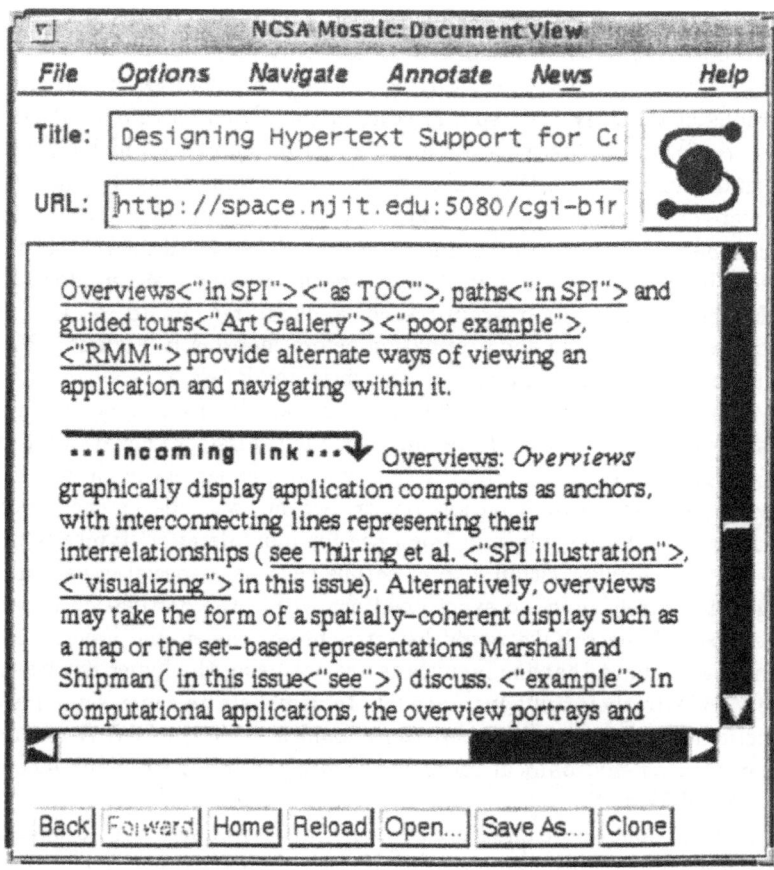

Fig. 1.2. A page from the electronic version of the *Communications of the ACM*, August 1995 special issue. The anchor labels have been customized for the reader to include a short semantic label in angle brackets to supplement the anchor's regular text. An arrival icon marks the destination of the last link the user followed (in arriving at this document).

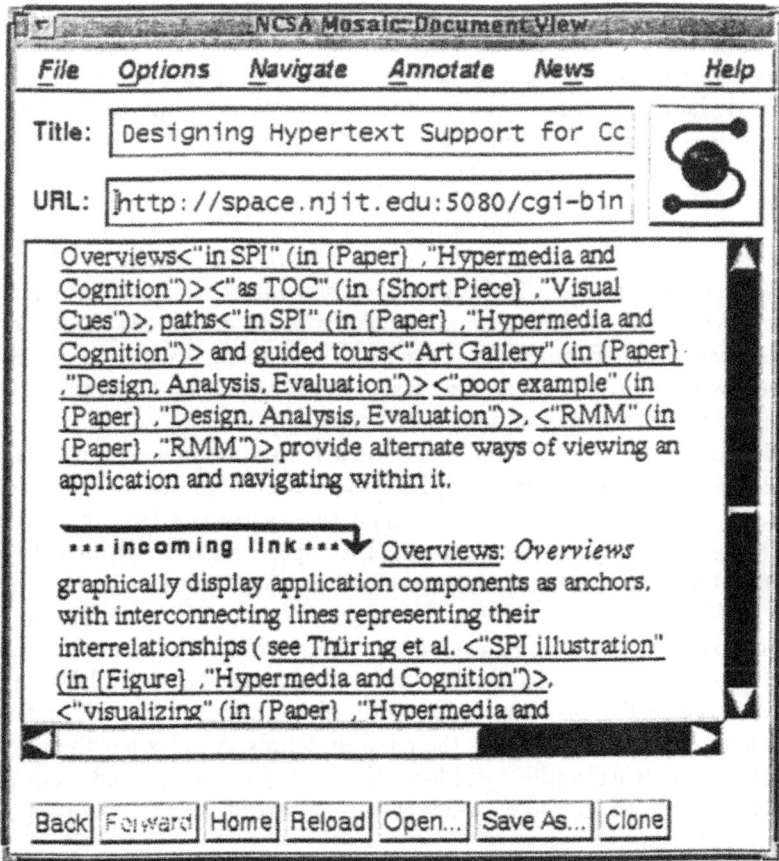

Fig. 1.3. Figure 1.2's page from the electronic version of the *Communications of the ACM*, August 1995 special issue. Here the anchor labels have been customized for the reader to include a short semantic label as well as the destination's type and a portion of its title, in order to supplement the anchor's regular text.

- internal links to passages within one paper,
- links to or from passages in other papers or sidebars, and
- links to citations, footnotes and figures within papers.

Reviewing these links revealed several problems. We do not intend these as criticisms of the special issue authors. Instead these reflect a lack of experience on our part and, in hindsight, a lack of full planning. While we thought our instructions were clear, authors did not follow them entirely. Perhaps our largest error was not providing examples of both expressive and inappropriate semantic labels for each of the five link types. We hope that our experience helps others considering similar projects.

The following are among the problems we encountered.

- It surprised us how few hypertext researchers could switch to a *hypertext mindset* (function cognitively under a hypertext paradigm) and provide useful semantic labels. For example, we saw many "related discussion" labels, which give readers minimal specific information. We also found several instances where an author used the same label (e.g., "complex objects") for links with multiple destinations which neither adequately described every destination nor clearly differentiated them.
- This lack of a *hypertext mindset* seems also to have hindered authors from adding link labels to anything but text. Almost no one added labels to footnotes, figures or citations. Because the figures and footnotes are usually visible on paper without turning the page, these relationships often are clear. On-line, readers must traverse a link to access them, and on many WWW browsers they replace the departure text, taking the reader temporarily out of the immediate context. Citations in the paper version lead to the reference section at the end of the paper. Semantic labels might assist the reader in determining both whether to jump to the reference section and physically locate the cited materials. Also, as per the previous bullet item, when authors did label these, they often specified "footnote," "figure" or "citation" as the semantic label instead of describing its content or relationship.
- Similarly, authors often did not specify destinations at the granularity WWW browsers allow. For example, when the printed version stated "see XYZ's article or sidebar for further details" authors sometimes created a link to the top of that piece, instead of specifying an exact paragraph or sentence. We even found links to a section or subsection sometimes not specific enough to capture the specific point authors appeared to want to express.

Besides short semantic labels, we decided to include other meta-information about a link (e.g., a long or more descriptive semantic label) and about the destination node (e.g., its title, document type and author). Figure 3 hints at the clutter that could result when displaying all this meta-information (we did this project in the days before browsers supporting frames). We decided to let readers specify how much meta-information to display. The following section describes some of our implementation details.

3. Semantic Labels: Technical Details

HTML departure anchors have the following format:

<A HREF = "*destination-document-URL#arrival-anchor-internal-label* "
parameter[1] = "value[1] " ... **parameter[n]** = "value[n] ">
display text to highlight, which the user selects to activate the anchor
</A>

The corresponding arrival anchor within *destination-document-URL* has the following format:

<A NAME = "*arrival-anchor-internal-label* ">**</A>**

When the reader chooses an HTML departure anchor, the WWW browser displays the document at the *destination-document-URL*. If the departure anchor specifies an *arrival-anchor-internal-label* (which is optional), the browser automatically scrolls to the line in the destination document containing it. Parameters are optional and completely under the author's control. When the user selects an anchor, the browser automatically passes all its parameters to the destination WWW server. That server processes them if it has a program to do so (in its "cgi-bin" directory), else it ignores them and displays the destination document in the normal manner.

We take advantage of the standard HTML anchor format, and use the following departure anchor parameters to store *meta-information* about each link. We process these parameters (along with reader preferences) to generate customized HTML for the destination page, which our server then returns to the reader's browser for display. Figures 1.2 and 1.3 show the same page customized for different readers.

<A HREF = "*destination-document-URL*
#arrival-anchor-internal-label "
short = "*short-semantic-label* "
long = "*long-semantic-label* "
type = "*link-type* "
document = "*destination-document-code* "
section = "*destination-document-subsection-number* ">
anchor text
</A>

We distinguish nine different *link-types*: citation, footnote, figure, to article text, to the text of a short contribution, to an article insert, to author contact information at the end of a contribution or URL of an author's home page, to the external URL for an author's home institution, and to miscellaneous external URLs. Traversing a link often takes the reader out of the current context, transporting him or her to a new document or a different chunk of the current one. To help the reader decide whether to traverse a link, we can provide a lot of meta-information. Our anchor format, utilizing the parameters described above, allows us to generate many different views of departure anchors. We could include the link type by name or icon, the destination document's title, the section within the destination (by name for semantic information, or by position [9]—"section i out of n"—so the reader knows whether it is toward the top (indicating introductory material), in the middle (main content) or toward the end (concluding discussion)), a concise semantic label, or a longer, more descriptive semantic label. Alternatively we could just rely on the WWW browser's default highlighting of the anchor text or display an icon indicating that a link exists.

The reader can set his or her preferred anchor display format through a preference form, and can change this at any time. We maintain reader preferences across sessions in a file at our server.

To achieve this customization, we generate all document displays dynamically through a program in our WWW server's "cgi-bin" directory.

4. Additional Issues

Besides semantic link labels, we encountered many issues and faced several decisions in designing and implementing this corpus. Some of these include:

- Our first concern was getting all authors to agree to allow others to add links to their works (e.g., the second half of bidirectional links returning out of their paper.) We decided that each author should have veto power over every link embedded in his or her work.
- Perhaps because we approached this project with a "WWW mindset" (knowing we would implement it on the WWW), we did not anticipate the several cases of empty link anchors, i.e., encompassing no content from the document. In this case the semantic label solely describes the link's purpose. This arose with links to related concepts for which it was hard to specify an exact span within the document content to associate as the anchor. This occurred, for example, with related discussions for an entire paragraph or section. Empty link anchors also arose with *n-ary* and multiple adjacent links. N-ary links have multiple destinations for a single anchor, e.g., several examples, or a set of supportive and contrasting destinations for the same source. Multiple adjacent links are actually separate links for separate, possibly overlapping, source items. Systems such

as Hypertext on Hypertext [17], Intermedia [18], Max [1, 6, 10] and Microcosm [8] implement these by listing all possible endpoints in a dialog box (sometimes technically in a separate node). The reader then chooses which to traverse. We decided against this for two reasons. First, it would add an additional step for readers. Second, in all these other systems the link dialog does not obscure the main document. HTML provides no direct support for such a solution; one has to manually place the links in a separate HTML document and place a link to it in the original document. Thus, in most WWW browsers, the link dialog document would replace the main document, possibly disorienting the reader [15].

– The larger the corpus, the less likely all authors would be able to read and make links between his or her paper and all other ones. Large corpora would require more time for developing links or perhaps be on-going. Like Trigg's vision of an on-line scientific community [16], this most likely would require someone to coordinate and maintain it.

5. The Next Step: Further Enhancing Information Comprehension

We approached the electronic version of the CACM special issue with the fundamental objective of providing link context through useful semantic link labels. Yet, to show the World Wide Web community the full measure of functionality that hypertext *as a concept* provides, we could include much more. We treat hypertext as a full paradigm for considering information access and comprehension [2, 3]. We could include document *chunking*, make indexes such as a table of contents optional, implement trails or guided tours through the special issue's corpus, or even develop a full annotation system to gather and present reader comments. Each is feasible within today's WWW browsers with a bit of creativity and programming. Thus, for us semantic labels constitutes just a first step. We hope to address the rest of this functionality in future work.

Readers can access the electronic version of the August 1995 special issue of the *Communications of the ACM* on hypermedia design through the World Wide Web URL http://www.acm.org/siglink/.

Acknowledgement. We wish to thank P. Balasubramanian of Boston University and Murray Turoff of the New Jersey Institute of Technology (NJIT) for valuable discussions concerning the conceptual nature of the links in the CACM special issue. Special thanks, too, to the authors who took the time to craft these links. Rong-Shyan Chen and Chao-Min Chiu at Rutgers University encoded the parameterized link anchors for the electronic version. Leon Jololian, Jay Seo, Brian White, and Zhijian Zhu of NJIT, and especially V. Balasubramanian of E-Papyrus Inc. provided valuable technical assistance on this project. Shaji Abraham and Praveen

Ramanathan at NJIT have moved mountains in producing version 2 of the system, which takes advantage of frames. We gratefully acknowledge funding for this project by the New Jersey Center for Multimedia Research, the New Jersey Institute of Technology under Grant 990967, by the National Center for Transportation and Industrial Productivity under Grant 990905, grants from the Sloan Foundation and the AT&T Foundation, and the NASA JOVE faculty fellowship program.

References

1. M. Bieber. Automating hypermedia for decision support. *Hypermedia*, 4(2):83–110, 1992.
2. M. Bieber, T. Isakowitz, and J. Oliver. An analysis framework for information comprehension and access management. In *Proceedings of Twenty-Eighth Annual Hawaii International Conference on System Sciences, Vol. IV*, pages 604–613, Maui, Jan. 1995.
3. Michael Bieber and Charles Kacmar. Designing hypertext support for computational applications. *Communications of the ACM*, 38(8):99–107, 1995.
4. Michael Bieber and Fabio Vitali. Toward hypermedia support on the world wide web. *IEEE Computer*, 30(1), 1997.
5. Michael Bieber, Fabio Vitali, Helen Ashman, V. Balasubramanian, and Harri Oinas-Kukkonen. Fourth generation hypermedia: Some missing links for the world wide web. *International Journal of Human-Computer Studies*, 1997 (forthcoming).
6. M.P. Bieber and S.O. Kimbrough. On generalizing the concept of hypertext. *Management Information System Quarterly*, 16(1):77–93, 1992.
7. Andreas Dieberger and Jay Bolter. On the design of hyper'spaces'. *Communications of the ACM*, 38(8):98, 1995.
8. A.M. Fountain, W. Hall, I. Heath, and H.C. Davis. MICROCOSM: An Open Model for Hypertext With Dynamic Linking. In A. Rizk, N. Streitz, and J. André, editors, *HYPERTEXT: CONCEPTS, SYSTEMS AND APPLICATIONS, Proceedings of European Conference on Hypertext (ECHT'90)*, pages 298–311. Cambridge University Press, Versailles, France, Nov. 1990.
9. Mark E. Frisse, Steve B. Cousins, and Scott Hassan. WALT: A research environment for medical hypertext. In *Hypertext '91 Proceedings*, pages 389–394, San Antonio, December 1991. ACM.
10. S.O. Kimbrough, C. Pritchett, M. Bieber, and H. Bhargava. The Coast Guard's KSS project. *Interfaces*, 20(6):5–16, 1990.
11. George P. Landow. Hypertext in literary education, critisism, and scholarship. *Computers and the Humanities*, 23:173–198, July 1988.
12. Catherine Marshall and Frank Shipman III. Spatial hypertext: Designing for change. *Communications of the ACM*, 38(8):88–97, 1995.
13. Jakob Nielsen. The art of navigating through hypertext. *Communications of the ACM*, 33(3):296–310, March 1990.
14. Ben Shneiderman, editor. *Hypertext on Hypertext (electronic Hyperties version for the IBM PC)*. ACM Press, New York, NY, 1988.
15. Manfred Thuering, Joerg Hannemann, and Joerg Haake. Hypermedia and cognition: Designing for comprehension. *Communications of the ACM*, 38(8):57–69, 1995.
16. Randall H. Trigg. A network based approach to text handling for the online scientific community, 1983. University Microfilms #8429934.

17. Nicole Yankelovich, editor. *Hypertext on Hypertext (electronic HyperCard version for the Macintosh)*. ACM Press, New York, NY, 1988.
18. Nicole Yankelovich, Bernard J. Haan, Norman K. Meyrowitz, and Steven M. Drucker. Intermedia: The concept and the construction of a seamless information environment. *IEEE Computer*, pages 81–96, January 1988.
19. Elise Yoder and Rob Akcsyn, editors. *Hypertext on Hypertext (electronic KMS versions for the Apollo and Sun)*. ACM Press, New York, NY, 1988.

Efficient Techniques for Adaptive Hypermedia

Peter Brusilovsky

Human Computer Interaction Institute
School of Computer Science
Carnegie Mellon University
Pittsburgh, PA 15213 USA
E-mail: plb+@andrew.cmu.edu

Abstract. Adaptive hypermedia is a new direction of research within the area of adaptive and user model-based interfaces. Adaptive hypermedia (AH) systems build a model of the individual user and apply it for adaptation to that user, for example, to adapt the content of a hypermedia page to the user's knowledge and goals, or to suggest the most relevant links to follow. AH systems are now used in several application areas where the hyperspace is reasonably large and where a hypermedia application is expected to be used by users with different goals, knowledge and backgrounds. This chapter provides a brief survey of existing adaptive hypermedia techniques. Special attention is paid to the techniques implemented in the World Wide Web and to techniques which have been approved by an experimental study and shown to be effective. Among few others approved techniques we describe adaptive annotation techniques developed by our group at the Moscow State University.

1   Introduction

The use of adaptive hypermedia (AH) systems is one way to increase the functionality of hypermedia. AH systems can be useful in any situation when the system is expected to be used by people with different goals and knowledge and where the hyperspace is reasonably big. Users with different goals, knowledge, and backgrounds may be interested in different pieces of information presented on a hypermedia page and may use different links for navigation. AH tries to use knowledge about a particular user, represented in the user model, to adapt the information and links being presented to that user. Adaptation can also protect the user from being lost in hyperspace. Knowing user goals and knowledge, AH systems can support users in their navigation by limiting the browsing space, suggesting the most relevant links to follow, or providing adaptive comments to visible links.

The goal of this chapter is to present the ideas of adaptive hypermedia to a general hypermedia and WWW-oriented audience and to show some ways to implement AH systems. The main content of the chapter is a selective survey of adaptive hypermedia techniques (a complete review of AH techniques can be found in (Brusilovsky, 1996)). In selecting the techniques to present, we gave first priority to "efficient" techniques (i.e., to the techniques which have been validated by experiment), second priority to the techniques which were implemented in World Wide Web (WWW) context, and third priority to the techniques similar to the techniques of the two above groups. The survey itself is presented in the Section 3. Before presenting the survey, in Section 2, we discuss the issue "what can be adapted in adaptive hypermedia". From this point of view, we provide a simple classification of existing adaptive hypermedia techniques distinguishing two major ways to adapt hypermedia (adaptive presentation and adaptive navigation support) and five adaptive hypermedia technologies. After the survey, in Section 4, we review briefly the most important reported experiments with adaptive hypermedia. These experiments provide guidelines for the designers of new AH systems showing what adaptive hypermedia *can* and what *cannot* do. A reasonable part of Sections 3 and 4 is devoted to several adaptive hypermedia techniques designed by our group in the Moscow State University. In conclusion we summarize main arguments of the chapter.

2   What Can be Adapted in Adaptive Hypermedia

At some level of generalization, hypermedia consist of a set of nodes or "pages" connected by links. Each page contains some local information and a number of links to related pages. These links can appear within the content of a page, in a separate menu, or on a separate local map. Hypermedia systems can also include an index and a global map which provide links to all accessible pages. What can be adapted in adaptive hypermedia are the content of regular pages (content-level adaptation) and the links from regular pages, index pages, and maps (link-level adaptation). As a rule, content-level adaptation is used to solve the problem of hypermedia systems which are used by different classes of users, while link-level adaptation is used to provide navigation support and prevent users from getting lost in hyperspace. We distinguish content-level and link-level adaptation as two different ways of hypermedia adaptation and call the former *adaptive presentation* and the latter *adaptive navigation support*.

2.1   Adaptive Presentation

The idea of various adaptive presentation techniques is to adapt the content of a page accessed by a particular user to current knowledge, goals, and other characteristics of the user. For example, a qualified user can be provided with more detailed and deep information while a novice can receive additional explanations. Existing adaptive presentation techniques deals with text adaptation. Text adaptatioin implies that different users in different time may get different texts as a content of the same page. We group all these techniques into one technology which we call adaptive text presentation technology. Currently, this technology is the most studied technology of hypermedia adaptation. Most part of the early works on adaptive hypermedia was centered around adaptive text presentation (Beaumont, 1994; Boyle and Encarnacion, 1994; Brusilovsky, 1992; de Rosis et al., 1993; Fischer et al., 1990). This direction of research was influenced by the research on adaptive explanation and adaptive presentation in intelligent systems (Moore and Swartout, 1989; Paris, 1988). As we will show in the following sections, a number of different techniques for adaptive text presentation have been developed.

2.2   Adaptive Navigation Support

The idea of adaptive navigation support techniques is to help users to find their paths in hyperspace by adapting link presentation to the goals, knowledge, and other characteristics of an individual user. Though this area of research is new, a number of interesting techniques have been already suggested and implemented. These techniques can be classified in several groups according to the way they adapt presentation of links. We consider these groups of techniques as different technologies for adapting link presentation. The most popular technologies are *direct guidance*, *sorting*, *hiding*, and *annotation*.

Direct guidance is the most simple technology of adaptive navigation support. Direct guidance can be applied in any system which can decide what is the next "best" node for the user to visit according user's goal and other parameters represented in the user model. To provide direct guidance, the system can outline visually the link to the "best" node as it is done in Web Watcher (Armstrong et al., 1995), or present an additional dynamic link (usually called "next") which is connected to the "best" node as in ISIS-Tutor (Brusilovsky and Pesin, 1994), SHIVA (Zeiliger, 1993), HyperTutor (Pérez et al., 1995), and Land Use Tutor (Kushniruk and Wang, 1994). The former way is clearer; the latter is more flexible, because it can be used to recommend the node that is not connected directly to the current one (and not represented on the current page). A problem of direct guidance is that it provides no support for the users who would not like to follow the system's suggestions. Direct guidance is useful but it should be used together with a "more supportive" technology.

The idea of *adaptive ordering* technology is to sort all the links of a particular page according to the user model and to some user-valuable criteria: the closer to the top, the more relevant the link is. Adaptive ordering has a limited applicability: it can be used with non-contextual links, but it can hardly be used for indexes and content pages (which usually have a stable order of links), and can never be used with contextual links and maps. Another problem with adaptive ordering is that this technology makes the order of links non-stable: it may change each time the user enters the page. Recent research shows that the stable order of options in menus is important for novices (Debevc et al., 1994; Kaptelinin, 1993). However, this technology shows to be useful for information retrieval (IR) applications (Armstrong et al., 1995; Kaplan et al., 1993; Mathé and Chen, 1996). As we will see in Section 4, experimental research (Kaplan et al., 1993) showed that adaptive ordering can significantly reduce navigation time in IR applications where each page can have many non-contextual links. A related application area where adaptive ordering can be used is on-line documentation systems (Hohl et al., 1996).

Hiding is currently the most commonly used technology for adaptive navigation support. The idea of navigation support by hiding is to restrict the navigation space by hiding links to irrelevant pages. A page can be considered as not relevant for several reasons: for example, if it is not related to the user's current goal (Brusilovsky and Pesin, 1994; Höök et al., 1996; Vassileva, 1996) or if it presents materials which the user is not yet prepared to understand (Brusilovsky and Pesin, 1994; Gonschorek and Herzog, 1995; Pérez et al., 1995). Hiding protects users from the complexity of the unrestricted hyperspace and reduce their cognitive overload. Hiding has a wide applicability: it can be used with all kinds of non-contextual, index, and map links by hiding buttons or menu items (Brusilovsky and Pesin, 1994), and with contextual links by replacing clickable "hot words" to normal text (Gonschorek and Herzog, 1995; Pérez et al., 1995). Hiding is also more transparent to the user and looks more "stable" than adaptive ordering (links are usually added incrementally, but not removed or reordered). Hiding has, however, another problem: as noted by some psychologists, hiding can provoke formation of incorrect mental models of the hyperspace.

The idea of *adaptive annotation* technology is to augment the links with some form of comments which can tell the user more about the current state of the nodes behind the annotated links. These annotations can be provided in textual form (Zhao et al., 1993) or in the form of visual cues using, for example, different icons (Brusilovsky et al., 1996a; de La Passardiere and Dufresne, 1992), colors (Brusilovsky and Pesin, 1994; Brusilovsky and Zyryanov, 1993), font sizes (Hohl et al., 1996), or font types (Brusilovsky et al., 1996a). Link annotation is known to be an effective way of navigation support in hypermedia (Zhao et al., 1993). The typical kind of annotation considered in traditional hypermedia is static (user independent) annotation. Adaptive navigation support can be provided by dynamic user model-driven annotation. Adaptive annotation in its simplest history-based form (outlining the links to previously visited nodes) has been applied in some hypermedia systems including several World-Wide Web browsers. Even this simplest form of adaptive annotation which can distinguish only two states of links (links to visited/not visited nodes) appears to be quite useful. Current adaptive hypermedia systems (Brusilovsky and Pesin, 1994; Brusilovsky et al., 1996a) can distinguish and annotate differently up to six states on the basis of the user model.

Annotation seems to be a good way of adaptive navigation support. Annotation can be naturally used with all possible forms of links. This technique supports stable order of links and avoids problems with incorrect mental maps. Annotation is generally a more powerful technology than hiding: hiding can distinguish only two states for the related nodes - relevant and non relevant - while annotation, as mentioned above, can distinguish up to six states (for example, Hypadapter (Hohl et al., 1996) uses annotations to show several levels of relevancy). Annotations do not restrict cognitive overload as much as hiding does, but hiding technology can be quite well simulated by the annotation technology using a kind of "dimming" instead of hiding for "not relevant" links. Dimming can decrease cognitive overload in some extent (the user can learn to ignore dimmed links). Dimmed links are still visible though (and traversable, if required) which prevents the user from forming wrong mental maps.

Direct guidance, sorting, hiding, and annotation are the primary technologies for adaptive navigation support. As we will see in the following sections, most existing adaptation techniques use exactly one of these ways to provide adaptive navigation support. However, these technologies are not mutually exclusive and can be used in combinations. For example, ISIS-Tutor (Brusilovsky and Pesin, 1994) uses direct guidance, hiding, and annotation; Hypadapter (Hohl et al., 1996) uses sorting, hiding, and annotation. In particular, the direct guidance technology can be naturally used in combination with any of the other three technologies.

3 Adaptive Hypermedia Techniques

3.1 Adaptive Presentation Techniques

A simple, but effective technique for content adaptation is the "conditional text" technique which is used in ITEM/IP (Brusilovsky, 1992), Lisp-Critic (Fischer et al., 1990), and C-book (Kay and Kummerfeld, 1994). With this technique, all information about a concept is divided into several chunks of texts. Each chunk is associated with a condition on the level of user knowledge represented in the user model. When presenting the information about the concept the system presents only the chunks where the condition is true. This technique is a low-level technique (it requires some "programming" work from the author to set all the required conditions) but it is also very flexible. By choosing appropriate conditions on the knowledge level of the current concept and related concepts represented in the user model the author can implement different methods of adaptation. A simple example is hiding chunks that contain irrelevant explanations if the user's knowledge of the current concept is good enough, or turning on a chunk with comparative explanations if the corresponding related concept is already known. This conditional text technique can be easily applied in the WWW context. The work of Kay and Kummerfeld (1994) presents several ideas which can be used to implement this technique in a WWW-based system.

A higher level technique which can also turn off and on different parts of the content according to the user knowledge level is suggested in MetaDoc (Boyle and Encarnacion, 1994) and developed further in KN-AHS (Kobsa et al., 1994). This technique is based on *stretchtext* which is a special kind of hypertext. In a regular hypertext, a result of clicking on a hot word is moving to another page with related text. In stretchtext this related text can simply replace the activated hot word (or a phrase including the hot word), thereby extending the text of the current page. If required, this extended or "uncollapsed" text may be collapsed back to a hot word. Each node in MetaDoc is a stretchtext page which may contain many "uncollapsable" hot words. The idea of adaptive stretchtext presentation in MetaDoc is to present a requested page with all stretchtext extensions that are non-relevant to the user being collapsed, and all extensions relevant to the user being uncollapsed. To achieve this result an author can declare some uncollapsable textual information contained in a node as an additional explanation of a particular concept, or as a low level detail of a particular concept. Optionally, the user of MetaDoc with good knowledge of a concept will always find additional explanations of this concept hidden (collapsed) and all low level details uncollapsed. On the contrary, the user with poor knowledge of a concept will always find additional explanations of this concept visible and all low level details collapsed. The user with medium level knowledge will see both kinds of information. An important feature of the adaptive stretchtext technique is that it lets both the user and the system adapt the content of a particular page, taking into account both the knowledge and the preferences of the user. After its initial presentation, the stretchtext page can be further adapted by the user who can uncollapse and collapse appropriate explanations and details according to his or her preferences. The system updates the user model according to the preferences demonstrated by the user to ensure that the user will always see the preferred combination of collapsed and uncollapsed parts. For example, if the user has collapsed additional explanations of a particular concept, the system will always show additional explanations of this concept collapsed until the user changes the preferences.

The most powerful of the all content adaptation techniques is the frame-based technique implemented in Hypadapter (Hohl et al., 1996), and EPIAIM (de Rosis et al., 1993). With this technique all the information about a particular concept is represented in the form of a frame. Slots of a frame can contain several different explanations of the concept, links to other frames, examples, etc. Special presentation rules are used to decide which slots should be presented to a particular user and in which order. More exactly, in EPIAIM these rules are used to select one of existing presentation schemes (each scheme is an ordered subset of slots) and the scheme is used to present the concept. In Hypadapter, the rules are used to calculate the "presentation priority" for each slot. Then a subset of slots with high priority are presented in order of decreasing priority. In their conditional parts, these rules can refer not only to the user knowledge of a concept being presented, but also to any feature represented in the user model. In particular, both systems which use this technique take into account the background of the user.

A good example of implementation of the frame-based technique on WWW is PEBA-II system[1] (Milosavljevic et al., 1996). This system uses frame-based

---

knowledge representation and natural language generation techniques to generate descriptive and comparative information about different animals. This information is adapted to the user level of expertize (current version of PEBA-II is rather adaptable then adaptive: users have to select their level of expertize themselves).

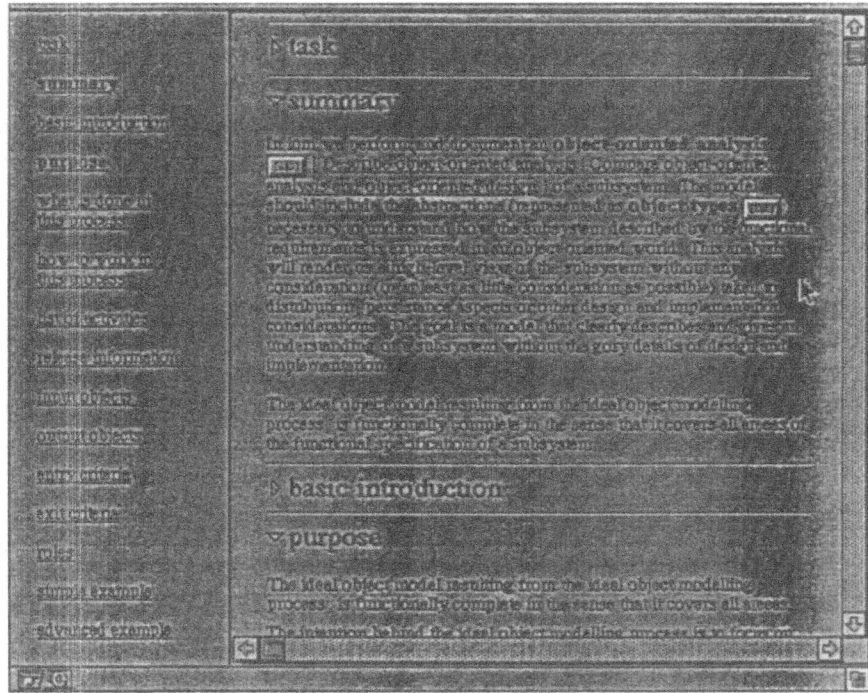

Fig. 1. Adaptive presentation with WWW interface in PUSH

A technique developed recently in the PUSH project (Höök et al., 1996) can be considered to be a combination of stretchtext and frame-based adaptation. A hypermedia page in this on-line information system provides a complete description of a particular object structured as an ordered sequence of typed information entities. Each type of object in PUSH has its own assortments of information entity types which are used to describe an object of that type. This technique is similar to the frame-based model (objects may be considered as frames and information entities as slots). The difference is that each information entity in PUSH is a reasonably large portion of hypertext. The complete description of an object is usually itself large, and takes several pages of information. To protect users from information overflow and to help them to find a required piece of information, the system uses hiding: it presents only those types of information about the current object which are relevant to the current goal of the user (the goal can be set by the user or deduced by the system). At the same time, to keep the adaptation transparent, the system maintains the stable presentation order of the information and never hides non-relevant entities completely: the titles of hidden non-relevant entities are always shown. If the user is not satisfied with the system's decision to show or to hide a particular entity, he or she can collapse or uncollapse the content of the information entity by clicking on an icon near its title. The resulting interface looks similar to MetaDoc stretchtext interface: non-relevant pieces of material are not presented to the user, showing only a keyword (in MetaDoc) or the title (in PUSH), but the user can override the adaptation by opening and closing any desired piece of information.

Figure 1 shows an example from the PUSH system of implementing stretchtext-like adaptive presentation technique in WWW context. Generally speaking, a stretchtext-based technique is not the easiest one to implement on WWW. However, present developments in WWW area, such as Java[2] technology open the way to stretchtext-based adaptive presentation techniques on WWW (Espinoza and Höök, 1996)

3.2 Adaptive Navigation Support Techniques

One of the most frequently cited techniques for adaptive sorting of links was implemented in HYPERFLEX (Kaplan et al., 1993), which can be considered to be an on-line information system or IR hypermedia system. HYPERFLEX provides the user with navigation support by displaying an ordered list of nodes related to the current node. The links are ordered according to their relevance to the current node (the most relevant appearing first). In addition, HYPERFLEX maintains a list of possible search goals. If the user selects one of these search goals, sorting takes into account the relevance of the displayed links to the selected goal. New goals can be created by users themselves. The main component of the user model in HYPERFLEX is a relevance matrix which stores relevance values between each pair of documents and from each goal to each document. This matrix reflects mainly user preferences for the link order: in HYPERFLEX a user can move the links to tell the system directly his or her preferences on the relative order of links (i.e., which relevant links and in which order he or she would like to see when viewing a particular document or when pursing a particular goal). These preferences are processed by the system to update the user model. Therefore the preferences selected in one context can influence adaptation in another context.

An example of an adaptive navigation support technique based on hiding is the rule-based technique implemented in educational hypermedia systems HyperTutor (Pérez et al., 1995) and SYPROS (Gonschorek and Herzog, 1995). Both systems use special sets of pedagogical rules to decide which concepts and nodes should be visible at the given moment and which should not. These rules take into account the type of the concept and its links to other concepts and the current state of user knowledge

---

[2]http://java.sun.com/

reflected in the user model. If the system decides not to make a node visible, then all contextual links to this node are changed from hot words to normal text. The rule-based hiding technique is very flexible. By manipulating the text with hiding rules it is possible to implement several navigation support methods based on hiding, such as hiding nodes the user is not yet ready to learn, or hiding nodes which belong to future lessons.

A very different hiding technique is suggested in Hynecosum (Vassileva, 1996). This system supports hierarchies of tasks for users of different categories. Each hyperspace node in the system is indexed by the elementary (terminal) tasks which require access to this node. Thus, for each terminal task the system can compile the associated list of nodes relevant to this task. By definition, a list of relevant nodes for more high level tasks includes all the nodes relevant at least to one of its subtasks. Using this knowledge Hynecosum can provide local orientation support by hiding. In Hynecosum the user directly tells the system which task he or she is currently performing by selecting one of the tasks from a personal hierarchy. After that, the system shows the user only the nodes which are relevant to the current task. It makes the set of visible nodes manageable.

An example of annotation-based adaptive navigation support technique can be provided by our systems ISIS-Tutor (Brusilovsky and Pesin, 1994) and ITEM/PG (Brusilovsky and Zyryanov, 1993). The backbone of the hyperspace in these systems is formed by a conceptual network which represents the pedagogical structure of the subject being taught. Each concept of the conceptual network is represented by a node of the hyperspace. Concept nodes of the network are connected by different kinds of relationships such as "is-a", "part-of", and "prerequisite". Another kind of nodes in the hyperspace are learning units (such as presentation units, problems, and examples). Each learning unit is connected to all concept nodes which are required to work with this unit. The weighted overlay student model represents separately the level of the student's knowledge of each of the concepts. Using this student model and prerequisite links, the systems can distinguish four educational states for each node represented by a hypermedia page: not-ready-to-be-learned (i.e., has unlearned prerequisites), ready-to-be-learned, in-work (learning started), and learned (student has solved the required number of problems for the concept). Our idea is that concepts with different educational states have different meanings for the student and making educational states visible will help the student in hyperspace navigation. To make educational states visible, links to the concepts with different educational states are annotated differently using different colors and some special characters (more details about annotations used in the current version of ISIS-Tutor are given in Section 4.3).

The same framework was used in ISIS-Tutor to implement an adaptive navigation support technique based on the learning goal. In this system, the teacher can set for each student a sequence of learning goals. A goal is a set of concept nodes of the network which must be learned. Concepts which belong to the same goal are expected to be learned together and then mastered by solving a number of problems before a student moves to the next goal. ISIS-Tutor uses two methods to adapt to the learning goal: first, to attract the student's attention, it can outline links to the concepts belonging to the current goal; second (as an option), to decrease the student's cognitive load, it can hide concepts which belong to future learning goals.

Annotation is a very suitable technique for implementing adaptive navigation support on WWW. An example of adaptive annotation on WWW is provided by a tutoring system ELM-ART[3] (Brusilovsky et al., 1996a) and an authoring system InterBook[4] (Brusilovsky et al., 1996b). These systems use the same technique as ISIS-Tutor for knowledge-based and learning goal-based annotation of links. Different are the visual cues which are used by ELM-ART and InterBook: rather then changing the color of the hot words themselves (as was done in ISIS-Tutor and ITEM/PG), these systems change the color of icons and the typeface of the font (for users without color monitors). In particular, for the links to unvisited nodes ELM-ART uses the traffic light metaphor: links to not-ready-to-be-learned nodes are annotated by a red ball icon and italic font, links to ready-to-be-learned nodes belonging to the current goal are annotated by a green ball icon and boldface font, and links to ready-to-be-learned nodes not belonging to the current goal are annotated by a yellow ball icon and normal font (Figure 2). ELM-ART and InterBook implement adaptive annotation of links using Common Gateway Interface[5], Common Lisp Hypermedia Server CL-HTTP[6] (Mallery, 1994) and on-the-fly page generation.

Currently, all major adaptive navigation support technologies are implemented on WWW. ELM-ART and InterBook (Brusilovsky et al., 1996a; Brusilovsky et al., 1996b) provide an example of annotation-based and sorting-based adaptive navigation support. WebWatcher (Armstrong et al., 1995) implements direct guidance technology in information-retrieval context (WebWatcher is not completely adaptive yet: the adaptation is currently based on a group user model rather then on individual user model). Some ideas how to implement hiding-based adaptive navigation support in WWW context can be found in (Lai et al., 1995). The system described there has all the required knowledge to implement hiding of links to not-ready-to-be-learned pages, but rather then hide such links, the system modifies their behavior. If a page behind a link is not-ready-to-be-learned (i.e., it has prerequisite pages not visited by the user), the link drives the user not to the requested page, but to the list of pages which must be learned before viewing the requested page.

---

[3]http://www.psychologie.uni-trier.de:8000/elmart
[4]http://www.contrib.andrew.cmu.edu/~plb/InterBook.html
[5]http://hoohoo.ncsa.uiuc.edu/cgi/
[6]http://www.ai.mit.edu/projects/iiip/doc/cl-http/home-page.html

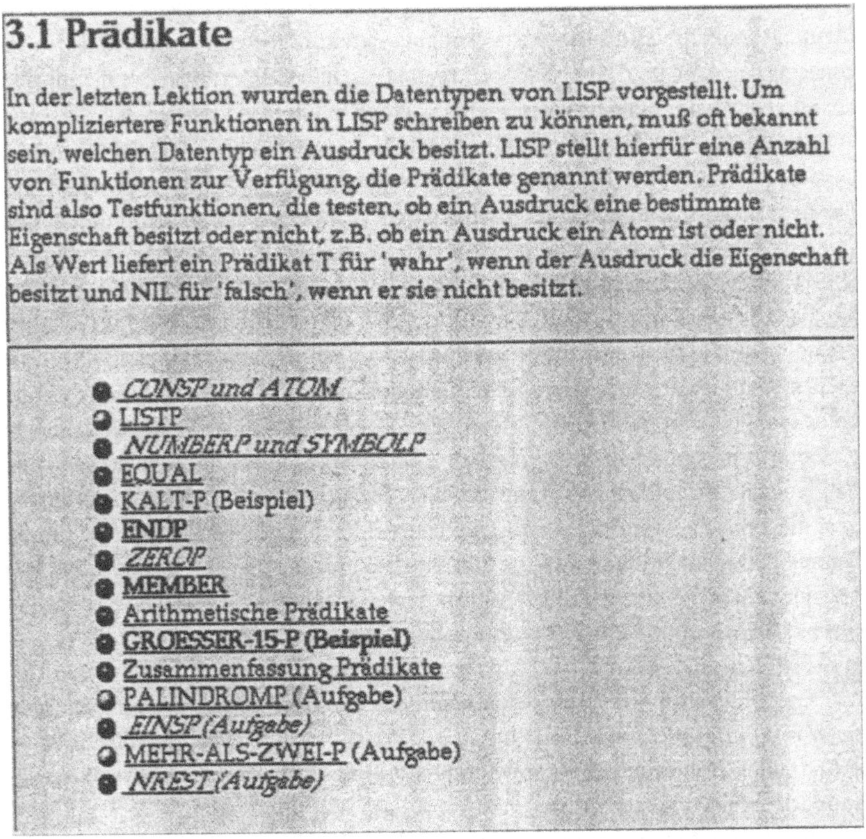

3.1 Prädikate

In der letzten Lektion wurden die Datentypen von LISP vorgestellt. Um kompliziertere Funktionen in LISP schreiben zu können, muß oft bekannt sein, welchen Datentyp ein Ausdruck besitzt. LISP stellt hierfür eine Anzahl von Funktionen zur Verfügung, die Prädikate genannt werden. Prädikate sind also Testfunktionen, die testen, ob ein Ausdruck eine bestimmte Eigenschaft besitzt oder nicht, z.B. ob ein Ausdruck ein Atom ist oder nicht. Als Wert liefert ein Prädikat T für 'wahr', wenn der Ausdruck die Eigenschaft besitzt und NIL für 'falsch', wenn er sie nicht besitzt.

- *CONSP und ATOM*
- LISTP
- *NUMBERP und SYMBOLP*
- EQUAL
- KALT-P (Beispiel)
- ENDP
- *ZEROP*
- MEMBER
- Arithmetische Prädikate
- GROESSER-15-P (Beispiel)
- Zusammenfassung Prädikate
- PALINDROMP (Aufgabe)
- *EINSP (Aufgabe)*
- MEHR-ALS-ZWEI-P (Aufgabe)
- *NREST (Aufgabe)*

Fig. 2. Example of adaptive annotation of links using WWW interface in ELM-ART.

The metaphor is traffic lights. Red (italic typeface) means not ready to be learned, green (bold) means ready and recommended (belongs to the learning goal), yellow means ready but not recommended.

4   Evaluation of Adaptive Hypermedia Techniques

The luck of experimental investigation of adaptive hypermedia is currently a weak point of this research direction. Very few reported AH techniques have been validated by a special study (Boyle and Encarnacion, 1994; Brusilovsky and Pesin, 1995; Clibbon, 1995; Höök, in press; Kaplan et al., 1993). In this section we review briefly the most important reported studies.

4.1   Evaluation of an Adaptive Presentation Technique

The most comprehensive evaluation of adaptive presentation in hypermedia was performed by Boyle and Encarnacion (1994) with their system MetaDoc. The goal of the experiment was to compare three kinds of hypertext: normal hypertext, stretchtext (i.e., hypertext extended with stretchtext functionality), and adaptive stretchtext in the context of on-line information access. Two kinds of tasks were used to compare these kinds of hypertext: reading comprehension tasks and navigation tasks. The systems compared were the original MetaDoc with all functionality and two "disabled" versions of MetaDoc: the stretchtext version which had all stretchtext functionality, but no user modeling and adaptation and the hypertext-only version which had no stretchtext functionality at all.

The subjects (computer science students) were randomly assigned to one of the three systems forming three groups: the hypertext group, the stretchtext group and the MetaDoc group. The subjects had some time to learn their systems and to browse the actual document. Then each subject received a booklet with five search and navigation questions and eight reading comprehension questions. The subject was allowed three minutes to find the answer to the search and navigation questions and then five minutes for the reading comprehension questions. For each question the subject was allowed three tries in finding the correct answer. For the search and navigation questions, the subject simply pointed out the location of the answer. For reading comprehension questions, the answer was provided orally.

The main results of the experiment are shown in the Table 1. Analysis of Variance (ANOVA) was the primary statistical test used. For all shown parameters the effect was significant at the 1 percent level. On a paired test a significant difference for reading comprehension time was found between stretchtext and MetaDoc groups. For the reading comprehension correctness and the search time a significant difference was found between hypertext and both other groups, though no significant difference was found between stretchtext and MetaDoc. For the three other parameters related with navigation: search correctness, number of visited nodes (including repetitions), and number of operations, no significant difference was found.

Table 1. Significant results of MetaDoc evaluation

	Hypertext		Stretchtext		MetaDoc	
	Expert	Novice	Expert	Novice	Expert	Novice
Reading comp. time (sec.)	1780	1930	1250	1780	810	1420
Reading comp. correct	5	3	6.5	7	7	7
Mean search time (sec.)	755	725	645	530	555	575

Thus, the experiment has shown that stretchtext-based content adaptation is an efficient adaptation technique which can increase user performance by improving reading comprehension. With this technique, reading comprehension time decreases significantly, without loss in understanding. In fact, understanding even increases, but this effect is possibly provided by the stretchtext technology itself rather then by the adaptation technique. At the same time, content adaptation does not affect user navigation. For all navigation-related parameters including time and number of visited nodes there was no significant difference between adaptive and non-adaptive versions of MetaDoc.

4.2   Evaluation of an Adaptive Navigation Support Technique: Sorting

The first evaluation of adaptive navigation support by sorting was performed by Kaplan et al. (1993) with their system HYPERFLEX. They performed two pilot studies. In the first small study (with four subjects) they examined the usefulness of goal-directed search in the hypertext. The subjects were asked questions relating to information stored in the hypertext. Each user answered ten questions. For five of these questions there existed relevant goals among the system supported goals. That is, the user could select this goal as the current goal and use the adaptively sorted list of links to related nodes as a navigation support. For five other questions no relevant goals were provided. In the version of HYPERFLEX used in this experiment the users were not able to create their own goals. The results of the experiment shown in Table 2, demonstrate that goal-based adaptive sorting seriously decrease search time and the number of searched topics, while the correctness of answers even increased slightly.

Table 2. First pilot study with HYPERFLEX

	Search time	# Topics	% correct
With relevant goal	462 sec.	8.8	83%
No relevant goal	716 sec	12.2	75%

The goal of the second pilot study was to compare the efficiency of two main methods of adaptation in HYPERFLEX: current-node-based adaptation (the user selects the current node of interest and the system orders the relevant links according their relevancy to the current node) and "current goal" based adaptation (the user selects the current goal and the system orders the relevant links according their relevancy to the current goal). Three versions of HYPERFLEX were used in experiment: the version with node-based adaptation only, the version with goal-based adaptation only, and a fully functional system with both kinds of adaptation available. Eighteen subjects participated in the study (six subjects for each version). Each subject was asked to perform four search tasks. Dependent measures were the time to complete each task and the number of topics (nodes) searched for each task. Since all the subjects completed the task successfully, "% correct" was not a relevant measure.

The results shown in Table 3 demonstrate that both methods of adaptation are efficacious, because the users of the fully functional system showed better performance then either of the two other groups.

Table 3. Second pilot study with HYPERFLEX

	Search time	# Topics	Time / topic
With current goal	387 sec.	8.6	45 sec.
With current node	356 sec.	6.8	52 sec.
Fully functional	345 sec	9.0	38 sec.

While the results of both studies should be interpreted with caution due to the small sample size (the original paper contains no data about significance of the results), they show that sorting-based adaptive navigation support can improve user performance in information search tasks.

4.3   Evaluation of Adaptive Navigation Support Techniques: Hiding and Annotation

The first evaluation of adaptive navigation support by hiding and annotation was performed by our group in the Moscow State University. The goal of our study was to check the efficiency of these two adaptation technologies and, in particular, to compare these technologies in an educational context. As a base system, we used for the experiment our ISIS-Tutor system (Brusilovsky and Pesin, 1994) which was briefly described above.

The current version of ISIS-Tutor uses adaptive annotation as a primary technique for adaptive navigation support. As an optional mode of work, ISIS-Tutor also implements adaptive hiding of links. The idea of hiding in ISIS-Tutor is to reduce the cognitive load by hiding from students all links to nodes which they are "not expected to learn". There are two kinds of hidden nodes in ISIS-Tutor: not-ready-to-be-learned nodes and ready-to-be-learned nodes that are outside the current educational goal. In normal annotation mode, the links to these nodes are not specially annotated. In hiding mode, these links are hidden. Note that hiding mode in ISIS-Tutor is more advanced then typical hiding. It is a combination of hiding and annotation, because learned, in-work and ready-to-be-learned nodes are still annotated as in normal annotation mode.

In our experiment, we used three versions of ISIS-Tutor: a non-adaptive version "A" which provided neither annotation nor hiding; a normal version "B" with adaptive annotation; and a version "C" that worked in hiding mode. In adaptive versions of ISIS-Tutor links to not-ready-to-be-learned nodes were not specially colored, ready-to-be-learned were colored red, both in-work and learned were colored green, and learned concepts was additionally marked with a "+" sign (we used special signs to avoid using too many colors). Links to nodes which are within the current educational goal were marked with a "-" sign. Links to not-ready-to-be-learned nodes and nodes outside the current educational goal were not specially annotated in version B and hidden in version C. The summary of different annotations applied in these three versions is shown in the table 4.

Table 4. Summary of annotations applied in three versions of ISIS-Tutor. NA means no annotation.

	A. Non-adaptive	B. Adaptive annotation	C. Adaptive hiding
Outside educational goal	NA	NA	hidden
Within educational goal	NA	mark "-"	mark "-"
Well-learned	NA	mark "+"	mark "+"
Known	NA	green color	green color
Ready-to-be-learned	NA	red color	red color
Not-ready-to-be-learned	NA	NA	hidden

Twenty-six subjects (first year computer science students of the Moscow State University) took part in the experiment. They were briefly introduced to ISIS-Tutor and then had up to 45 minutes to work with the system. The same educational goal (ten concepts and ten test problems) was given to each student. To complete the course, each user had to solve all ten problems. The subjects were divided randomly into three groups. Group A worked with version A (non-adaptive version). Group B worked with version B (adaptive annotation). Group C worked with version C (adaptive annotation and hiding). All actions of students working with the system were recorded and then analyzed to compare various aspects of user performance. The most important dependent variables were the time required to complete the course and the overall number of navigation steps. According to the results of the experiment with HYPERFLEX, we expected that both the time and the number of steps would decrease for adaptive versions.

Table 5. Results of the experiment with ISIS-Tutor

Group	Number of steps	Concept repetitions	Task repetitions
A. Non-adaptive	81.33	11.17	6.17
B. Adaptive annotation	65.20	5.00	0.80
C. Adaptive annotation and hiding	58.20	4.80	0.40

Though not all the results of the experiment are processed by now, we can already report the results concerning our main hypothesis. These results are shown in the table 5 (all data are average numbers for each group). As we can see, the overall number of navigation steps, the number of unforced repetitions of previously studied concepts, and the number of task repetitions (i.e., trials to solve previoulsy visited task) are much less for both versions with adaptive navigation support. For the overall number of navigation steps and the number of task repetitions the difference was significant (we have used ANOVA to check the significance). On a paired test the significant difference for all three variables was found between non-adaptive group and joint adaptive group (B+C), but no significant difference was found between the two adaptive groups.

The results of the experiment with ISIS-Tutor show that both applied adaptive navigation support techniques - hiding and annotation - are efficient adaptation techniques. These techniques can improve user performance in hypermedia by significantly reducing navigation difficulty. Adaptive annotation and hiding in an educational context can reduce user's floundering in the hyperspace and make learning with hypermedia more goal-oriented. With these kinds of adaptive navigation support, the user can achieve the same result using a smaller number of navigation steps and visits to hypernodes. It is interesting to compare our results with the results of Kaplan et al. (1993), presented in Section 4.2. We have seen that adaptive presentation in hypermedia can reduce the time for learning the material and improve the comprehension of it, but cannot reduce the number of nodes visited in the process of learning. At the same time, adaptive annotation of links can hardly improve the quality of learning, but can reduce the number of visited nodes thus further reducing the learning time. These techniques look complimentary and can be used together for further improvement of the effectiveness of learning with hypermedia.

Conclusion

Adaptive hypermedia is a new direction of research at the crossroads of hypermedia, adaptive systems and intelligent systems. It is a promising and fast developing direction: more and more groups are starting work on adaptive hypermedia problems, more and more techniques are being developed. A weak point of current research on adaptive hypermedia is the luck of experimental investigation of AH efficiency. Very few reported AH techniques have been validated by empirical study, and only two of these studies reported significant results. However, the results of the reported studies are quite promising. It was found that adaptive presentation can significantly improve user comprehension of hypertext material, while adaptive navigation support techniques can significantly decrease user search and navigation efforts. Both group of techniques can decrease the time required to complete a task of the user. These groups of techniques can compliment each other and provide even better effect when used together.

Recently, adaptive hypermedia as a direction of research has received special attention in the WWW context We argue that adaptive hypermedia is one of the ways to increase the functionality of WWW. It can be demonstrated by several systems which implement adaptive hypermedia techniques in WWW context. We hope that the research works presented in this chapter can be used as a source of ideas for researchers interested in making local and networked hypermedia systems more efficient and functional.

Acknowledgments

Part of this work was supported by an Alexander von Humboldt-Stiftung Fellowship to the author.

References

Armstrong, R. et al. (1995) WebWatcher: A learning apprentice for the World Wide Web. *Proceedings of AAAI Spring Symposium on Information Gathering from Distributed, Heterogeneous Environments*. Stanford, CA, March 27-29, 1995, http://www.isi.edu/sims/knoblock/sss95/mitchell.ps.

Beaumont, I. (1994) User modeling in the interactive anatomy tutoring system ANATOM-TUTOR. *User Modeling and User-Adapted Interaction* 4 (1), 21-45.

Boyle, C. and Encarnacion, A. O. (1994) MetaDoc: an adaptive hypertext reading system. *User Modeling and User-Adapted Interaction* 4 (1), 1-19.

Brusilovsky, P. (1996) Methods and techniques of adaptive hypermedia. *User Modeling and User-Adapted Interaction* 6 (2-3), 87-129.

Brusilovsky, P. and Pesin, L. (1994) ISIS-Tutor: An adaptive hypertext learning environment. *Proceedings of JCKBSE'94, Japanese-CIS Symposium on knowledge-based software engineering*. Edited by H. Ueno and V. Stefanuk. Pereslavl-Zalesski, Russia, May 10-13, 1994, pp. 83-87.

Brusilovsky, P. and Pesin, L. (1995) Visual annotation of links in adaptive hypermedia. *Proceedings of CHI'95 (Conference Companion)*. Edited by I. Katz et al. Denver, May 7-11, 1995, pp. 222-223.

Brusilovsky, P. et al. (1996a) ELM-ART: An intelligent tutoring system on World Wide Web. In *Intelligent Tutoring Systems, Proceedings of Third International Conference on Intelligent Tutoring Systems, ITS-96*, Lecture Notes in Computer Science, Vol. 1086, C. Frasson et al. (eds), Springer Verlag, Berlin. pp. 261-269.

Brusilovsky, P. et al. (1996b) A tool for developing adaptive electronic textbooks on WWW. *Proceedings of WebNet'97, World Conference of the Web Society*. San Francisco, CA, October 15-19, 1996, http://www.contrib.andrew.cmu.edu/~plb/WebNet96.html.

Brusilovsky, P. and Zyryanov, M. (1993) Intelligent tutor, environment and manual for physical geography. *Proceedings of Seventh International PEG Conference.* Edinburgh, Edinburgh, 2-4 July, 1993, pp. 63-73.

Brusilovsky, P. L. (1992) Intelligent Tutor, Environment and Manual for Introductory Programming. *Educational and Training Technology International* **29** (1), 26-34.

Clibbon, K. (1995) Conceptually adapted hypertext for learning. *Proceedings of CHI'95 (Conference Companion).* Edited by I. Katz et al. Denver, May 7-11, 1995, pp. 224-225.

de La Passardiere, B. and Dufresne, A. (1992) Adaptive navigational tools for educational hypermedia. In *Computer Assisted Learning, Proceedings of ICCAL'92, 4-th International Conference on Computers and Learning,* I. Tomek (ed) Springer-Verlag, Berlin. pp. 555-567.

de Rosis, F. et al. (1993) User tailored hypermedia explanations. *Proceedings of INTERCHI'93 (Adjunct proceedings).* Amsterdam, 24-29 April 1993, pp. 169-170.

Debevc, M. et al. (1994) Adaptive bar implementation and ergonomics. *Informatica : Journal of Computing and Informatics* **18**, 357-366.

Espinoza, F. and Höök, K. (1996) An interactive WWW interface to an adaptive information system. *Proceedings of Workshop "User Modelling for Information Filtering on the World Wide Web" at the Fifth International Conference on User Modeling.* , http://www.sics.se/~kia/espinoza_hook.html.

Fischer, G. et al. (1990) Minimalist explanations in knowledge-based systems. *Proceedings of 23-th Annual Hawaii International Conference on System Sciences.* Kailua-Kona, HI, January 2-5, 1990, pp. 309-317.

Gonschorek, M. and Herzog, C. (1995) Using hypertext for an adaptive helpsystem in an intelligent tutoring system. *Proceedings of AI-ED'95, 7th World Conference on Artificial Intelligence in Education.* Edited by J. Greer. Washington, DC, 16-19 August 1995, pp. 274-281.

Hohl, H. et al. (1996) Hypadapter: An adaptive hypertext system for exploratory learning and programming. *User Modeling and User-Adapted Interaction* **6** (2-3), 131-156.

Höök, K. (in press) Evaluating the usefulness of an adaptive hypermedia system. *Proceedings of 1997 International Conference on Intelligent User Interfaces.* Orlando, Florida, January 6-9 1997.

Höök, K. et al. (1996) A glass box approach to adaptive hypermedia. *User Modeling and User-Adapted Interaction* **6** (2-3), 157-184.

Kaplan, C. et al. (1993) Adaptive hypertext navigation based on user goals and context. *User Modeling and User-Adapted Interaction* **3** (3), 193-220.

Kaptelinin, V. (1993) Item recognition in menu selection: The effect of practice. *Proceedings of INTERCHI'93 (Adjunct Proceedings).* Amsterdam, 24-29 April 1993, pp. 183-184.

Kay, J. and Kummerfeld, R. J. (1994) An individualised course for the C programming language. *Proceedings of Second International WWW Conference.* Chicago, IL, 17-20

October,
http://www.ncsa.uiuc.edu/SDG/IT94/Proceedings/Educ/kummerfeld/kummerfeld.html.

Kobsa, A. et al. (1994) KN-AHS: An adaptive hypertext klient of the user modeling system BGP-MS. *Proceedings of Fourth International Conference on User Modeling.* Hyannis, MA, 15-19 August 1994, pp. 31-36.

Kushniruk, A. and Wang, H. (1994) A hypermedia-based educational system with knowledge-based guidance. *Proceedings of ED-MEDIA'94 - World conference on educational multimedia and hypermedia.* Edited by T.Ottman and I.Tomek. Vancouver, Canada, June 25-30, 1994, pp. 335-340.

Lai, M.-C. et al. (1995) Toward a new educational environment. *Proceedings of 4th International World Wide Web Conference.* , Boston, USA, December 11-14, 1995, http://www.w3.org/pub/Conferences/WWW4/Papers/238/.

Mallery, J. C. (1994) A Common LISP hypermedia server. *Proceedings of the First International Conference on the World-Wide Web.* , May 25, 1994.

Mathé, N. and Chen, J. (1996) User-centered indexing for adaptive information access. *User Modeling and User-Adapted Interaction* 6 (2-3), 225-261.

Milosavljevic, M. et al. (1996) Text Generation in a Dynamic Hypertex Environment. *Proceedings of Nineteenth Australasian Computer Science Conference (ACSC'96).* Melbourne, Australia, 31 January - 2 February 1996, pp. 417-426, http://www.mri.mq.edu.au/~mariam/papers/acsc/.

Moore, J. D. and Swartout, W. R. (1989) Pointing: A way toward explanation dialogue. *Proceedings of Eight National Conference on Artificial Intelligence.* , pp. 457-464.

Paris, C. L. (1988) Tailoring object description to a user's level of expertise. *Computational Linguistics* 14 (3), 64-78.

Pérez, T. et al. (1995) An adaptive hypermedia system. *Proceedings of AI-ED'95, 7th World Conference on Artificial Intelligence in Education.* Edited by J. Greer. Washington, DC, 16-19 August 1995, pp. 351-358.

Vassileva, J. (1996) A task-centered approach for user modeling in a hypermedia office documentation system. *User Modeling and User-Adapted Interaction* 6 (2-3), 185-224.

Zeiliger, R. (1993) Adaptive testing: contribution of the SHIVA model. In *Item banking: Interactive testing and self-assessment,* NATO ASI Serie F, Vol. 112, D. Leclercq and J. Bruno (eds), Springer-Verlag, Berlin. pp. 54-65.

Zhao, Z. et al. (1993) Visualization of semantic relations in hypertext systems. *Proceedings of ED-MEDIA'93, World conference on educational multimedia and hypermedia.* Edited by T.Ottman and I.Tomek. Orlando, FL, pp. 556-564.

Exploring Annotated 3D Environments on the World Wide Web

Enrico Gobbetti[1,2] and Russell Turner[1]

[1] Computer Science and Electrical Engineering Department, UMBC, Baltimore MD 21250, USA
[2] CESDIS, NASA Goddard Space Flight Center, Greenbelt MD, USA

Summary. The long-term goal of combining virtual reality and the Internet is to create networked multi-user simulations of virtual environments. The Virtual Reality Modeling Language (VRML) represents a limited but significant step towards this goal by creating a standard data file format for representing 3D scene information, together with hyperlinks for associating it with other types of Web documents. The recent adoption of the VRML-2.0 standard, which extends VRML-1.0 to add behaviors, will bring this goal closer, but much work remains to be done. This chapter gives a brief summary of VRML and then describes two significant projects currently under development based on i3D, a high-performance VRML browser developed by one of the authors. The first of these, currently being used at the European Laboratory for Particle Physics (CERN), uses an annotated virtual environment to visualize and walk through the physical design of the new Lepton-Hadron Collider (LHC) before it is built. The second project, "Virtual Sardinia", allows the user to tour a 3D terrain visualization of the island and access historic and tourist information through hyperlinks.

1. Introduction

The World Wide Web (WWW) has rapidly become one of the fundamental structures of the Internet. By imposing a universal organization on the variety of formats in which data resides around the world and allowing each piece to be viewed as a uniquely addressable data source, it has allowed the entire Internet to be treated as a single structured document [12, 4]. This unified distributed database, which can be universally accessed using a single software Web browser application, takes the form of an enormous hypermedia document, combining text, images, sound and video into a seamless, hyperlinked user interface.

While the multimedia user interface style of the Web manages to incorporate all the standard forms of electronic mass-media, it has until recently been conspicuously lacking in one of the most important new modes of human-computer interaction. Paralleling the meteoric and highly-publicized rise of the Internet in recent years has been the development of "virtual reality" (VR): the most advanced type of user interface in which all human sensory input is synthesized by the computer to create an illusion of immersion in a virtual world [5]. While technical obstacles remain which limit the quality of the fully immersive experience, advances in 3D graphics display and input technology have now made possible a higher quality and more practical – if rather limited – form of "desktop" VR in which the user simply views an interactive 3D image rendered on a traditional color monitor. This configuration can then be augmented to various degrees of immersion by adding stereo viewing glasses, head tracking devices, 3D mouse input, localized sound and head-mounted displays. Even the most limited forms of virtual reality open up immense possibilities for us to change the way we interact with the computer. Virtual reality is more than a buzz-word. As a long-term goal, it represents the ultimate man-machine interface, as well as the most general-purpose medium of human expression.

1.1 Adding 3D Contents to the Web

It is therefore no surprise that a union between Virtual Reality and the Internet should be proposed. Given their respective enormous potentials and their complementary nature, VR and the Internet seem to be a natural match. A marriage between them presents tantalizing possibilities: cyberspace becomes a virtual 3D information space in which remote participants may immerse themselves. The World Wide Web is transformed into a world-wide virtual museum where every home page becomes a home room. Inside these rooms every door or picture on the wall is a potential "portal" or 3D hyperlink to another room in the museum, or to a piece of information in some other form. Inherently three-dimensional tasks, such as architectural or engineering walkthroughs, can be enhanced by adding traditional WWW-style information in the form of annotations. Novel ways of representing complex data sets, whether it be three-dimensional scientific visualizations, multi-dimensional financial data, or non-numerical textual information, allow the Web browser to become a data visualizer. By making queries to remote sites, which return custom 3D data on-the-fly, the Web browser becomes a graphical front-end for large distributed databases.

Perhaps the most significant product of the Internet/VR union may be the development of virtual environments with distributed interactive behaviors. Most virtual environment applications to date have been static scenes in which user interaction is limited to viewpoint motion, pointing and selecting. Our own real-world environment, however, is dynamic. It contains objects with intrinsic behavior which interact with each other and with us humans when we manipulate them. Most importantly, it contains other humans, with whom we interact in a social context. All of these can be simulated in a virtual world. Behavior algorithms, based on physical laws or other rules, can be added to objects. Remote users, represented in some virtual form (sometimes known as an "avatar") can be present in the virtual space, allowing multiple users to interact with each other in a form of graphical "multi-user-dungeon" (MUD). Virtual reality has the potential to change the World Wide Web, currently a static and solitary universe, into a dynamic and social one.

All of these ideas were very much in the minds of the participants at the first birds-of-a-feather meeting at the 1994 Geneva World Wide Web conference at which was launched the project to create a Virtual Reality Markup Language. VRML, which later became "Virtual Reality Modeling Language" was intended to become a standard data format for writing networked virtual environment simulations on the Web. During the intense e-mail discussions in the following months, it became obvious that a truly general-purpose language for representing arbitrary environments was not a practical short-term goal. In fact no such language truly existed, even in an experimental form. Since the ultimate goal of VR is to create a virtual world with the same richness and complexity as the real world, such a general-purpose language must attempt to model many of the complexities of real-world objects, including not only their form and visual properties, but also their intrinsic behavior and dynamic relationships to other objects. Most importantly, such a language must be able to encode the manner in which both remote and local users interact with the virtual objects, and provide a protocol by which multiple distributed users may synchronize their local environments so as to give the impression of coexisting in the same virtual environment.

1.2 VRML-1.0

Given the extremely ambitious nature of the task, and keeping with the technical spirit of the World Wide Web, it therefore seemed more practical to take an incremental approach to creating a VRML standard. While no general-purpose virtual environment data format existed, 3D graphical file formats such as the GKS-3D and PHIGS metafile formats did exist and were well-understood. A first version of a VRML standard file format was therefore proposed which can be thought of as something analogous to an image file format. Rather than 2D pixel information, however, it instead contains the actual 3D geometric data of the objects comprising the virtual world. In addition, surface material information specifies the colors and other reflective properties of the various objects, lighting information describes the position and orientation of lights in the scene, and viewing information determines from what vantage point and angle it is initially viewed by the user.

Selecting a hyperlink to such a VRML file loads the 3D data into the local machine and allows it to be viewed in three dimensions using whatever 3D viewing techniques the local browser software and workstation hardware allow. Like an HTML document, the VRML document can be structured so that portions of it may be associated with hyperlinks to other Web URLs, while other portions may be "inline" references to other VRML files. VRML is also hierarchical, so that complex 3D scenes can be built up from combinations of object components and assemblies. This allows a single virtual space to contain a combination of objects located at distributed sites, as well as "hot" objects which are analogous to text or multimedia hyperlinks in an HTTP document. Interactively selecting a hot object hyperlinked to another VRML file will cause the user to be "teleported" to the associated 3D space.

Selecting a hot link to a more traditional HTML document would invoke a standard document browser to view it.

Most importantly, rather than the ultimate design goal of a true "networked interactive simulation" standard, the first version of the proposed VRML standard describes an essentially static world. There are no behaviors, no interaction techniques and there is no support for multiple users. Given the fast-paced development of the Web, it seemed that the highest priority should be to make a minimal level of VR functionality available to everyone to allow a basic standard of interoperability. This would prevent a potentially debilitating plethora of competing standards and buy time for people to explore the less well-understood problem of adding behavior extensions to the initial standard.

The desire for quick results also dictated that the initially somewhat idealistic plan to build up a VRML standard from scratch be abandoned in favor of modifying an existing standard. While several standards were proposed, including ones based on OOGL [13], Labyrinth [15], CDF [21], and MSDL [16], a consensus rapidly developed around using a simplified version of the Open-Inventor file format. OpenInventor [19], a general-purpose object-oriented 3D graphics toolkit developed by Silicon Graphics, is well-poised to become the industry standard 3D graphics toolkit, and SGI proposed a VRML-1.0 standard based on a simplified version of its ASCII file format.

In fact, this VRML-1.0 standard, which was announced at the 1995 WWW conference in Darmstadt, added only two new constructs to the Open-Inventor standard: a WWWAnchor statement, which allows a piece of geometry to be associated with a URL as a hyperlink, and the WWWInline statement, which indicates the URL of a VRML document to be loaded into the currently-viewed scene. This relationship between VRML-1.0 and the commercial OpenInventor product has made it very easy to develop VRML-based software by using the OpenInventor toolkit and has helped SGI to position itself as a leading supplier of VRML-based products. It has also raised some important questions about who controls the future course of the VRML standardization effort, and whether or not the original dream of a true virtual reality modeling language has resulted in little more than just another industry-standard 3D graphics file format.

1.3 VRML-1.0 Applications

Even if it is is far from truly being a "virtual-reality modeling language", VRML-1.0 is enjoying a big success. The possibility of making available annotated 3D environments on the World Wide Web opens the road to the creation of a new class of World Wide Web applications. The relatively low cost of modern 3D graphics platforms makes it possible for a large community of users to benefit from this evolution. Although the static nature of VRML-1.0 limits user's interaction with 3D environments to real-time navigation and hyperlink selections, these operations are still sufficient for a large number of applications. In scientific visualization, CAD, and virtual environment applications, virtual camera motion specification is often the most important form of three-dimensional interaction[23, 6, 9]. The visual cues provided by interactive 3D viewing with continuous viewpoint control can offer invaluable help in understanding the represented data. If images are rendered smoothly and quickly enough, an illusion of real-time exploration of a virtual environment can be achieved as the simulated observer moves through the model[6]. For example, in architectural CAD applications, this gives both the architect and the client the ability to naturally walk through virtual buildings and inspect them from any angle, allowing the architect to explore complex spaces and the client to provide feedback early in the design process[6, 1]; for scientific visualization, large multi-dimensional data sets can be inspected and better understood by walking through their 3D projections[22].

The effectiveness of interactive 3D viewers for communicating information about 3D environments can be dramatically enhanced by attaching multimedia annotations to the environment's models. This is one of the major advantage that VRML browsers have over simple 3D viewers. By allowing users to interactively recall and view the attached information by selecting objects of interest during navigation, a VRML browser becomes a natural front-end for querying information about 3D models. Since the latest graphics workstations have become true digital media platforms that combine sound generation, interactive 3D graphics and movie playback capabilities, annotations can refer to text, still images, animations or even other 3D models. In the architectural CAD example, the virtual building representation could be augmented in this way by linking to its various components the original drawings showing engineering details of the structure, photographs of the real site, and so on. The interactive 3D model can therefore be used for data management purposes during the design phase, and information about the building can be presented to the client with maximum efficiency.

2. VRML-1.0 Browsers

A number of VRML 1.0 browsers that offer interactive viewing and hyperlink selection capabilities have been developed so far. These include Webspace [25], WebOOGL [26], and WebView [27].

Most of these systems are limited to mouse-based interaction and are not able to ensure constant high frame rates when dealing with large datasets, thus limiting their appropriateness for large scale projects. To provide an overview of current VRML browsers' advanced capabilities, we describe in the following sections a Web browser, developed by one of the authors, called i3D. i3D is [3], the only VRML browser to date that incorporates the 3D input and high-performance rendering capabilities of high end VR system with the data retrieval abilities of standard browsers. It is implemented on

top of X11/OpenGL and runs on Silicon Graphics and DEC Alpha workstations. Using a 3D device, the user can explore its three-dimensional data and
request access to other documents. When retrieving and displaying media
documents, i3D handles the three-dimensional data directly and collaborates
with NCSA Mosaic or Netscape for other types of media. Stereo-glasses are
used to provide binocular perception of the 3D world.

Executable versions of i3d for supported platforms are made publicly
available at the address `http://www-venus.cern.ch/i3d/`.

2.1 Application Overview

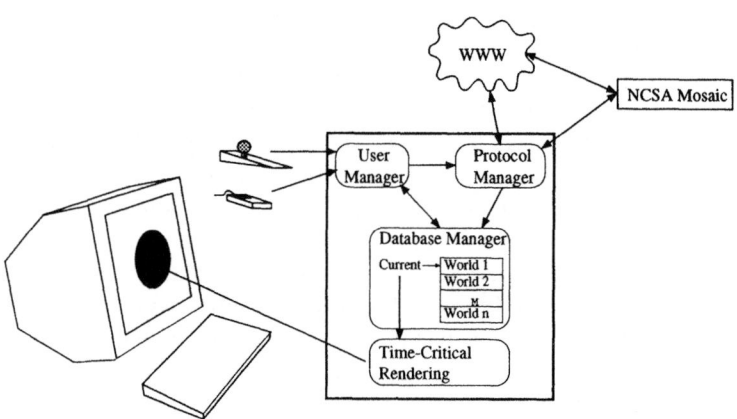

Fig. 2.1. Application overview

As shown in Figure 2.1, i3D is composed of the following units: the user manager, the protocol manager, the database manager, and the rendering manager. The user manager is responsible for sensing and analyzing the user's
movements and actions in order to recompute the new viewpoint position
and orientation, to trigger retrieval of media documents by the protocol manager, and to navigate among the stack of worlds that is maintained by the
database manager. The protocol manager is responsible for the retrieval of
media documents from the World Wide Web. Three-dimensional scenes are
loaded locally and transmitted to the database manager, while requests for
other types of media documents are delegated to a WWW browser (NCSA
Mosaic or Netscape) for retrieval and display by the most adequate viewer
application. The database manager maintains the state of the 3D scenes in
order to provide the necessary geometrical information and visual attributes
for the user and rendering managers to perform their tasks. The database
manager also maintains a stack of all the scenes that have been visited to
reach the current world and provides fast switching between worlds upon the

user manager's request. The rendering manager is responsible for the generation of the visual representation of the current scene at a high and constant frame rate (e.g. 10 frames per second).

2.2 User Interaction

i3D's device configuration uses a Spaceball and a mouse as input devices. The Spaceball is used for the continuous specification of the camera's position and orientation using an eye-in-hand metaphor[24], while the mouse is used to select objects and access multimedia documents through hyperlinks. Both user's hands can therefore be employed simultaneously to input information. Keyboard commands are used to control various visibility flags and rendering modes. The ability to continuously specify complex camera motions in an intuitive way together with high visual feedback rates provides an accurate simulation of motion parallax, one of the most important depth cues when dealing with large environments[1].

Fig. 2.2. i3D's device configuration.

While navigating inside a three-dimensional scene, the user can request additional information by accessing Web documents associated with the geometrical data. Since these hyperlinked geometrical figures are drawn with a blue silhouette, they can be visually identified easily. Selecting an annotated geometry by clicking on its visual representation with the mouse triggers the associated Web document's retrieval and display. Object selection is implemented using ray-tracing. For three-dimensional scenes, i3D maintains a stack of active worlds. Using keyboard commands, the previous or next world in the stack can be made current, thus providing a means to quickly navigate among active worlds.

2.3 World Model

i3D's database manager stores the representation of three-dimensional scenes as a collection of 3D objects, including light sources and cameras. This collection of objects is obtained by flattening the hierarchical input VRML file. From the resulting set of objects representing the virtual world, the database manager then builds an octree spatial subdivision to enable rapid spatial queries. For example, to select objects using the mouse, a ray is traced from the viewpoint through the current mouse position until it intersects an object in the scene.

2.4 Rendering

The task of the i3D's rendering manager is to display a visual representation of the current world at high and constant frame rates. During navigation, the rendering manager is activated at regular intervals by the main i3D event loop and is requested to refresh the screen while adhering to the user-specified timing constraint. At each activation, the rendering manager renders a single frame by executing a sequence of operations. These operations are:

2.4.1 Visibility determination. First, the database is traversed and the objects visible from the observer's viewpoint are identified. This task is accelerated by first hierarchically determining the visibility of portions of the scene through a traversal of the spatial subdivision maintained by the database manager;

2.4.2 Display list construction. Each of the objects identified in the previous step is then compiled into a graphical description by stripping off its appearance attributes and compiling them into a device-dependent sequence of commands (in the current version of i3D, OpenGL display lists are used for storing the compiled versions of graphical objects). During this conversion, geometries are optimized to reduce their rendering time (in particular, structured triangular meshes are generated from the triangle lists stored in the database). To avoid recreating compiled versions at each frame, as it is done in systems like Performer[17], i3D caches the graphical descriptions generated for each database object and reuses them until they become invalid. The validity of a description is checked by using a time-stamping scheme: the database manager maintains for each of the attributes of the model a time-stamp that is updated every time the attribute is modified, and graphical descriptions are time-stamped by the rendering manager with the time-stamp of the most recently modified attribute requested by the graphical description.

2.4.3 Level of detail selection. To reduce the number of polygons rendered in each frame, so as to be able to meet the constant-time rendering requirements, the rendering manager traverses the generated display list and selects the level of detail at which each of object will be represented. Level of detail selection is based on the importance of each object for the current frame (which is determined by computing an approximation of its size projected on the screen) and on feedback regarding the time required to render previous frames. The feedback algorithm is similar to that presented in[17];

2.4.4 Display list optimization. Once the levels of details are selected, the system has all the information required to render the frame. To exploit coherence, the display list is sorted to optimize the rendering speed. In particular, objects sharing the same texture and/or material are grouped together. In other visual simulation systems, this task is left to the scene designer, who must encode this information together with the scene description[17, 7, 19];

2.4.5 Display list rendering. The sorted display list is finally traversed and rendered by executing each of the compiled command sequences. Rendering statistics for the current frame are updated and stored so as to be used when determining the level-of-detail selection for the next frame.

3. VRML-1.0 Application Examples

During the last year, a number of projects that exploit VRML-1.0 capabilities have started to be developed. CERN VENUS and Virtual Sardinia are two of the larger such projects. These two projects, described in the following sections, use i3D as a VRML browser because of its suitability for dealing with complex scenes.

3.1 The CERN VENUS Project

The European Laboratory for Particle Physics (CERN) is currently involved in designing its next generation particle accelerator, namely the Large Hadron Collider (LHC). In any project of this scale, the design phase is probably the most delicate one, as this is when some critical choices are made which might dramatically affect the final results, timing and costs. The ability to visualize the model in depth is essential to a good understanding of the interrelationships between the parts. An iterative design optimization process can remarkably improve solutions to space management and ergonomic issues. However, with the visual capability of present CAD tools, it takes a fair amount of time and imagination to isolate eventual design faults. A pilot project named VENUS (Virtual Environment Navigation in the Underground Sites) was started at CERN in January 1994. Its mandate is to produce a detailed virtual prototype of the LHC premises and allow navigation and access to engineering data in the form of flythroughs by natural interaction. The i3D system is being actively used for the exploration of the virtual prototype. Figure 3.1 shows a snapshot of a typical i3D session.

Fig. 3.1. Exploring CERN Alice.

The VENUS virtual prototype is extracted entirely from the original EU-CLID CAD database. As soon as engineers add new drawings, these are extracted and converted to an internal i3D format in two steps: first, EUCLID data is converted to Wavefront OBJ format. Then, the resulting Wavefront objects are converted to the i3D format and assembled into a scene. Some minor manual treatment is necessary at this point, in order to compensate for the lack of some features (e.g. color and textures) in the EUCLID-to-Wavefront converter utility supplied by Matra-Datavision. Hypertext annotations that refer to various sources of information are then added by associating URLs with relevant 3D objects. A further step is necessary to optimize the geometry for interactive navigation. The entire process is fairly automatic and does not require a major effort, since the data conversion and optimization are handled by software utilities.

When dealing with geometries, the way objects are constructed or exported from the modeling tool or CAD system may influence the visual representation of the objects or the rendering performance. A typical problem is the direction of surface normals not being specified, or defined only per face (rather than per vertex), resulting in a flat shading rendering of the object.

Another typical problem is that often multiple topologically separated models are merged inside a single geometry file, hence preventing efficient culling of non-visible objects when rendering. Filtering tools are provided to help world designers to work around these problems by smoothing normal vectors and splitting geometries. Additionally, another filter can be used to define levels of detail by creating oriented bounding-box geometries around small objects.

The entire conversion process should be completely automated in the near future, and triggered from the EUCLID side upon any significant changes to the geometry. In this way the virtual prototype will always reflect the latest state of the design. i3D is made available to all CERN users, allowing any CERN user with a Silicon Graphics workstation to connect to the CERN server, fly through the latest models of the detectors, and inspect all hyperlinked annotation information attached to the three-dimensional model. A subset of all the information available to CERN designers is made publicly available on the Internet at the address http://www-venus.cern.ch/.

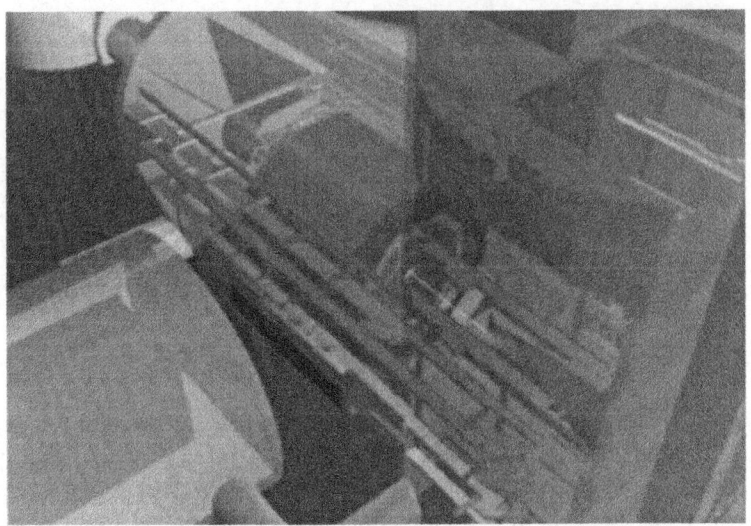

Fig. 3.2. CERN Alice pit viewed using i3d

3.2 The Virtual Sardinia Project

The Virtual Sardinia project [8] under development at the Center for Advanced Studies, Research, and Development in Sardinia (CRS4) aims at collecting a large amount of heterogeneous data concerning the island of Sardinia and representing it in such a way that a casual user can easily navigate through it in a virtual trip. All these data are interconnected in a Web-browsable hypermedia style, both in 2D and 3D, ranging from geographic and archaeological data to historical and tourist information.

Using i3D, users can explore a 3D model of the island, built from digital terrain model data textured with satellite images. 3D markers representing hyperlinks are positioned on the surface of the terrain to indicate sites of interest. Using the mouse to interactively select of one of these markers during navigation triggers the loading of a descriptive Web document, while the selection of any other location on the terrain triggers the request to view a high-resolution version of the area surrounding the selected point.

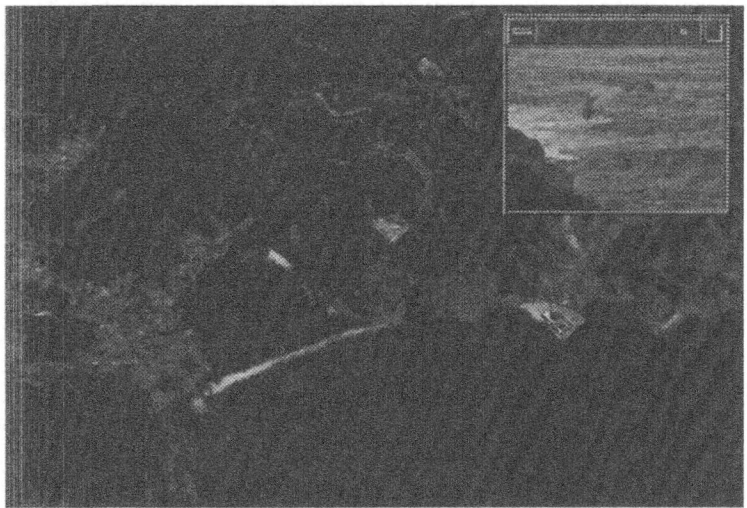

Fig. 3.3. Sight-seeing in Virtual Sardinia

The possibilities of i3D are exploited to allow the exploration of detailed terrain models on a range of machines. To produce a VRML description of the terrain, the original terrain data (a regular grid) is subdivided into subregions that can be drawn and culled independently, and each subregion is described at various levels of detail by transforming the original regular grid into simpler irregular triangular meshes through a decimation process that iteratively groups nearly coplanar polygons and simplifies them. Different tolerances for planarity checks are used to produce the various levels of detail. To avoid cracking problems, small tolerances are used at the borders of the subregions. In addition to the optimization of the geometric model, images that are to be used as textures are clipped and rescaled so as to have them fit into texture memory. All these optimizations are done automatically by a tool that takes as input the original digital terrain model, the satellite images and a list of descriptions of geographical location that have to be marked and associated to a hyperlink. Thanks to hierarchical culling and on-the-fly level of detail selection, the resulting model can be explored at interactive speed (more than 10 frames per second) on a Silicon Graphics Onyx RE2. The Virtual Sardinia project shows that, with appropriate preprocessing tools, it is possible to use VRML even for applications that usually require real-time visualizations of detailed terrain representations.

World Wide Web users may access the Virtual Sardinia project at the address http://www.crs4.it/PRJ/VIRTSARD/.

Fig. 3.4. Collaboration between i3d and Netscape during a Virtual Sardinia Session

4. Conclusions

The marriage of virtual reality and the Internet can be viewed from both an evolutionary and a revolutionary perspective. As a revolution, it presents us with no less than the possibility of giving cyberspace a tangible 3D form. The Internet could becomes a distributed virtual space in which we can move around, explore information, manipulate dynamic objects and tools and inter-act with other users in a social context. As an evolution, it is little more than a 3D data format standard for the Web. Just as a hyperlink may represent a piece of text or a 2D image, it may also point to a piece of 3D geometric information. To understand the vision behind extending World Wide Web browsers to support virtual reality, and its current state of development, it is important to examine the Internet/virtual reality union from both these perspectives.

While virtual reality promises us limitless possibilities for the man-machine interface, the Internet is delivering on the promise of limitless access to information. Most VR applications are information poor, requiring tremendous amounts of data to flesh out their virtual environments with enough detail to satisfy the user's desire for visual complexity. The Internet, on the contrary, is information rich, usually presenting the user with too much information in too disorganized a way to be useful. While textual (or verbal) communication is certainly the most general-purpose means of delivering data to the human brain, visual communication has the highest bandwidth. Adding three-dimensional information, with highly interactive multi-modal user interfaces that make use of sound, tactile and haptic display, has the potential to make the greatest use of the human brain's sensory and motor processing capabilities to create the highest possible bandwidth of man-machine interface.

Despite its name, VRML-1.0 is not a truly "Virtual Reality Modeling Language", at least no more than GKS-3D and PHIGS are. It is limited to providing a standard way for describing static 3D scenes composed of objects that can be annotated with hyperlinks. The challenge of virtual reality, creating synthetic worlds that "look real, act real, sound real, feel real" [20] is only partially addressed. While VRML-1.0 offers some support for describing worlds that "look real", these worlds have little possibility to "act real", as all VRML-1.0 objects have only one possible behavior: asking the browser to fetch associated documents when selected.

In the past year, several competing VRML extensions have been proposed [18] [10] which start to focus on this problem by providing low-level mechanisms to specify animated and interactive behaviors in VRML worlds. Despite the recent adoption of one of these, SGI's Moving Worlds proposal, as the official VRML-2.0 standard, the problem of describing animated and interactive behaviors remains a long term research topic, which people in computer graphics, computer simulation, knowledge engineering and other disciplines have been studying for years, and it is unlikely that a high-level standard for appropriately describing these behaviors will emerge anytime soon.

Despite all its limitations from the "revolutionary" perspective, VRML-1.0 is very successful in allowing the use of 3D graphics as an effective medium to share information on the Web. Much as the availability of graphics library standards such as PHIGS, GKS-3D and OpenGL allow the creation of portable 3D graphics applications, the availability of a standard file format for describing annotated 3D scenes allow a larger distribution of 3D graphics documents. An entire new class of hypermedia applications has been enabled by the standardization of this technology.

Acknowledgement. i3D was designed and developed by Enrico Gobbetti at the Center for Advanced Studies, Research, and Development in Sardinia (CRS4), Cagliari, Italy, with help from Jean-Francis Balaguer. The work is now continued by Jean-Francis Balaguer at CERN, Geneva, Switzerland. The Virtual Sardinia processing tools were developed by Enrico Gobbetti and Andrea Leone at CRS4. Research and development for i3D and Virtual Sardinia have been carried out at CRS4 with the financial support of the Sardinia Regional Authorities.

References

1. F. P. Brooks Jr and P. Frederick: Walkthrough - A Dynamic Graphics System for Simulating Virtual Buildings, Proc. ACM SIGGRAPH Workshop on Interactive 3D Graphics (1986): 9–22.
2. J.-F. Balaguer and E. Gobbetti: A New Dimension to HyperMedia. http://www.crs4.it/ 3diadm/ (1995).
3. J.-F. Balaguer and E. Gobbetti: i3D: A High-Speed 3D Web Browser. Proc. ACM Symposium on VRML (1995).
4. T. J. Berners-Lee, R. Cailliau, J.-F. Groff, and B. Pollermann: World Wide Web: The Information Universe. Electronic Networking: Research, Applications, and Policy 2(1) (1992): 52–58.
5. S. Bryson, R. Pausch, W. Robinett W, and A. van Dam: Implementing Virtual Reality. ACM SIGGRAPH Course Notes 43 (1993).
6. T. A. Funkhouser and C. H. Séquin, Adaptive Display Algorithms for Interactive Frame Rates During Visualization of Complex Virtual Environments. Proc. ACM SIGGRAPH (1994): 247–254.
7. S. Ghee and J. Naughton-Green, Programming Virtual Worlds. ACM SIGGRAPH Tutorial Notes on Programming Virtual Worlds (1994): 6.1–6.58.
8. E. Gobbetti, A. Leone, A. Marini: Virtual Sardinia: a hypermedia fly-through with real data. Proc. International Workshop on Soft Computing in Remote Sensing Data Analysis, Milan (1995).
9. J. D. Mackinlay, S. Card, and G. Robertson: Rapid Controlled Movement Through a Virtual 3D Workspace. Proc. ACM SIGGRAPH (1990): 171-176.
10. Microsoft Corporation: ActiveVRML White Paper. http://www.microsoft.com/intdev/avr/avwhite.htm (1995).
11. T. Munzner: An Experiment in Three-Dimensional Distributed Hypermedia. The Geometry Center, University of Minnesota (1995).
12. M. Pesce, P. Kennard, A. Parisi: Cyberspace. Proc. First International World Wide Web Conference (1994).
13. M. Phillips, S. Levy, and T. Munzner: Geomview User Manual. The Geometry Center, University of Minnesota (1994).
14. A. Parisi, M. Pesce: Virtual Reality Markup Language (VRML). http://www.wired.com/vrml/ (1994).
15. A. Parisi, M. Pesce: Virtual Reality Markup Language (VRML) Working Specification. http://vrml.wired.com/vrml/ (1994).
16. M. Preston, N. Gatenby, W. T. Hewitt: The Manchester Scene Description Language (MSDL) Version 1.01. http://info.mcc.ac.uk/CGU/MSDL/MSDL-intro.html (1994).
17. J. Rohlf and J. Helman: Performer: A High Performance Multiprocessing Toolkit for Real-Time 3D Graphics. Proc. SIGGRAPH (1994): 381–395.

18. Silicon Graphics Inc.:   The Moving Worlds Proposal for VRML 2.0. http://webspace.sgi.com/moving-worlds/ (1996).
19. P. S. Strauss and R. Carey: An Object-Oriented 3D Graphics Toolkit. Proc. SIGGRAPH (1992): 341–347.
20. I. Sutherland: The Ultimate Display. Proc. IFIP 2 (1965): 506-508.
21. C.   Tollander: Cyberspace   Description   Format   (CDF). http://vrml.wired.com/proposals/cdf/cdf.html (1994).
22. C. Upson, T. Fulhauber, D. Kamins, D. Laidlaw, D. Schlegel, J. Vroom, R. Gurwitz, and A. van Dam A: The Application Visualization System: A Computational Environment for Scientific Visualization, IEEE Computer Graphics and Applications 9(4) (1989): 30–42.
23. V. Watson: A Breakthrough for Experiencing and Understanding Simulated · Physics, ACM SIGGRAPH Course Notes on State of the Art in Data Visualization (1989): IV.26–IV.32.
24. C. Ware, and B. Osborne, Exploration and Virtual Camera Control in Virtual Three Dimensional Environments, Proc. ACM SIGGRAPH Workshop on Interactive 3D Graphics (1990): 175-183.
25. Webspace... because the World is not Flat! http://www.webspace.com/
26. WebOOGL: Integrating   3D   graphics   and   the   Web. http://www.geom.umn.edu/software/weboogl/
27. SDSC   WebView   -   A   VRML   Internet   Browser. http://www.sdsc.edu/EnablingTech/Visualization/vrml/webview.html

User Models for Customized Hypertext

Judy Kay and Bob Kummerfeld

Department of Computer Science, University of Sydney

Summary. PT, the personalised text system enables authors to create hypertext customised to match the individual user's preferences, interests, current goals, background and other attributes. This chapter describes the motivation for such a system in terms of its use in tutoring systems that generate a hypertext layout dynamically, based on a user model. The customisation is driven by two essential elements: a meta-hypertext which is an augmented-html document and a user model that tracks relevant information about the user. This chapter describes the ways that we have constructed these elements and explains how this has been driven by a commitment to user control. We also describe some fundamental elements of the design and implementation of such a system. One of the challenges of managing PT's meta-hypertext documents derives from the increased complexity of author's task. We describe our approach to this problem.

1. Introduction

Hypertext systems such as the World Wide Web hold great promise as a vehicle for delivering self-paced instructional material. Hypertext systems enable the learner to select their path through the hyperspace and their own speed.

In this chapter, we describe work that provides customised hyperspaces, offering a variety of learning and presentation options without increasing the complexity of the learner's hyperspace. This augments the choice of path through the space with the creation of different pages and links between them.

We come to this work in two roles: as authors who would like to be able to reach a range of different audiences; and as researchers exploring the possibilities for customisation of hypertext.

The PTproject uses a conventional book about C [13] as its base. The goal is that a future version of this book be used in conjunction with a hypertext version of much the same material.

In writing a book, one is charged with making many compromises: a fixed written text can only have one form and that must be chosen to approximate the expected needs and preferences of a target audience. If the authors achieve this, their book can at least meet the needs of one target audience.

The audience we selected for our book was people who have learnt one programming language. Indeed, the students who are half way through the second year of our own computer science major programme were the first target group. Our stereotypical model of this audience represents the users as competent Pascal programmers, who know some computer architecture and have a good grounding in many aspects of programming and computer science. Further, we assume they want to become highly competent programmers.

Our book appears to have matched the requirements of such an audience quite well: it has had very positive reviews and good levels of acceptance from readers who match this audience expectation closely. However, there are many levels at which it has failed to satisfy some readers. A brief discussion of these highlights the types of adaptation we are trying to offer in the hypertext edition and from this we will indicate the areas in which a user model and adaptation are useful for achieving effective communication.

2. Motivation for generating diverse forms of a text

There is considerable evidence that different people learn best in different ways. This means that one person who wants to learn some aspect of C will learn well when the information is represented in one way where another person would find that same information confusing and a barrier to their learning. This means that it is unlikely that a single presentation would be helpful for all learners. Some of the differences between learners can easily be accommodated in current hypertext systems while others cannot.

The section explains our motivation for PTin terms of the several dimensions of customisation that we have explored. Then we discuss the limitations of conventional hypertext for supporting these.

2.1 Customisation based on background knowledge

Perhaps the most significance difference between learners is the preknowledge that they bring to a new learning task. In the case of users learning C, knowledge of other programming languages constitutes the major difference to their learning various elements of C.

Learners will find it easy to understand aspects of C involving concepts they already understand well. Even so, they will benefit from explanations cast using familiar terms for concepts. For example, some Pascal programmers use var-parameter and non-var-parameter for the terms call-by-reference and call-by-value. The former terms are very useful for such readers and totally irrelevant to people not coming from Pascal.

On the other hand, some language aspects will pose problems precisely because of the learner's background knowledge. In this case, the best presentation of material would carefully identify the bases for their likely misconceptions about C and provide information to help develop the new concepts. In general, it would seem helpful to draw attention to similarities between a known language and C and then to build on relevant existing knowledge while highlighting important differences between known languages and C.

It may also be helpful to give some readers consolidation of new ideas, perhaps with a series of examples each reinforcing the same concept. This treatment may be irrelevant and tedious for a user with a different background.

In writing our conventional book, we had to compromise and make assumptions about reader's backgrounds. Even then, we had to decide which concepts were so important they should be treated in spite of the likelihood that many readers knew them.

In PT we can deal with this quite differently. We ask the reader to do a 'concept inventory' [23] a short dialogue to build an initial model of their background knowledge, especially the most important conceptual foundations. Then, users who claim to have a solid understanding of the underlying concepts will have those relegated to a glossary where others see them explained in the main text. So, for example, a user who is comfortable with the terms call-by-value and call-by-reference is told about C parameters using these terms. By contrast, the reader who is unfamiliar with the terms will see text that introduces the terms and the concepts they describe.

Glossary words are initially highlighted in the hypertext to show they are accessible in a glossary. So the reader can check out their meanings if they wish. Once the reader has successfully progressed through relevant stages of the book, even these terms no longer appear highlighted. We do not wish to distract the reader with clearly irrelevant links to a glossary. This applies regardless of whether the reader decides to move arbitrarily through the hypertext. For example they may start with material that appears in Chapter 1 of the conventional text and then move to Chapter 7, something that the hypertext medium invites. With PT, such a C-novice will see glossary links for the concepts assessed as unknown in their user model.

There is also much merit in customisation of the glossary items. Readers may consult a glossary at various stages of their learning and a single explanation is unlikely to be helpful for the novice without being tedious for the more advanced reader. There may even be cases where the glossary should tell the reader that they are really not ready to understand this concept because they need to understand various other concepts first.

Note that the term 'successfully progressed' has a precise meaning in our system. The hypermedia system not only includes the text of the book. It also has exercises for the reader to do as they read. If the reader can give good answers to the exercises, they are regarded as have 'successfully progressed'.

Interaction with the reader involves more than simple traversal of a hyperspace. The user is asked to do a task and submit their answer. Our system can do various forms of analysis on these. This is used to update the user model.

2.2 Customisation based language level and writing style

Our original book was terse and the writing and explanation style tended to be rather abstract. We chose this as matching the style of the standard documentation for C and its support tools, seeing it as likely to match many readers preferences and appropriate for others to become comfortable with.

However, we would have liked to offer more choice, especially in the *Getting started* material. Several researchers have noted the benefits of different language level for different users. For example, Paris [20] customised the presentation of text and noted the very different presentations used to explain the same concepts to children and adults.

We are also very conscious of the different needs of many readers for whom English is a second language: they are often confused by humour and may have difficulty with sophisticated or subtle language use.

It is common to use humour to make texts more pleasant to read. This is fine for users who understand it. Humour can only be effective if it is understood. It also can be irritating to individuals who happen to dislike the author's sense of humour. It should be a simple matter to cut the humour for those who do not want it.

The same applies for tangential but potentially interesting material. Some readers delight in learning the history and motivation for design decisions within C while others do not care. Conventional hypertext can deal with this by making such material linked but it often involves a short sentence or two and we note that the individual reader is likely to be consistent in their like/dislike of such material. The reader who dislikes it does not benefit from the distraction of the extra links while the interested reader has the tedium of having to select these links repeatedly.

2.3 Customisation of examples and exercises

An even more serious area of compromise in a conventional hypertext is in the choice of examples to present concepts and to test them. These are a central part of the learning of a programming language.

For example, we know that some people like mathematical examples and others loathe them. Equally, some of our readers are excited by examples that are related to systems programming, even (or especially) if these introduce new ideas, while some readers find these confusing and irrelevant.

Some people like tiny focused examples while others prefer longer complete programs that they can actually play with to explore the ideas. Similarly, a single task that is used to explain a series of concepts suits some readers while others prefer separate, unrelated examples.

It is easy to provide additional examples, of various sorts, that illustrate an element of the language. These can be indicated by a link that the user can select. So, for example, the user who likes a mathematical example could use the link offering that, while a user who prefers a text-based example would select the button for that. A problem with this is that the user who likes mathematical examples will, most likely, need to select that link every time they meet a concept. It would be more convenient if they could tell the system that they would always prefer to be presented with a mathematical example by default.

2.4 Customisation by level of abstraction

An important aspect of technical writing is its level of abstraction. Some users like the terseness that can be achieved using abstract presentation. Unix manual entries and BNF are good example of concise but abstract descriptions. Many readers, especially those who are new to an area prefer a new concept to be presented in concrete terms with examples driving the introduction of concepts, and careful explanation of each.

2.5 Summary of motivations for customisation beyond conventional hypertext

The common theme in the above is that we could use normal hypertext to offer the diversity that would enable a range of users to learn C from the same hypertext document. But the users would be faced with a greatly increased navigation problem, that would counter the benefits. Moreover, as they met each concept, they would be tediously selecting the same set of options, having to sort through the ones that they do not want to use.

Similarly, the glossary links can be usefully customised. Any coding such as that distinguishing glossary entries adds cognitive load and distracts the user from their central tasks. So, the coding of many glossary terms is a needless irritation for the user who does not need them.

2.6 Customisation based on varied teaching strategies

In our experiments with PT, we explored the use of various teaching strategies. The simplest is that of the initial book, a conventional textbook, with presentation of major ideas, examples to support them and exercises with answers in the back of the book. We knew that readers would benefit from attempting the exercises and in a hypertext we could make readers more likely to do them by requiring answers before allowing the reader to progress.

However, we also explored a very different role for exercises. We know that learning is more effective if the learner is actively involved in the learning task. So, one teaching strategy used the exercises as the basis for the teaching: rather than present important concepts directly, we presented them in a manner that should enable the reader to deduce things for themselves as far as possible. For example, if the reader is familiar with Pascal and we want to introduce a concept that is different in C and derives from principles the reader has met, we can ask the user to deduce the C concept. Ideally, they should be able to do this without direction, realizing which C concepts are relevant. If they fail to do so, we can offer a hint by stating the C principles that are the basis for the concept.

3. Customisation without duplication

If we want to support customisation of the types just described, we need to appreciate the potential and limitations of conventional hypertext. Essentially, we will argue that the primary benefit of user modeling for adapting hypertext is that it permits far greater customisation without additional complexity in the hyperspace the learner sees. Our system operates on a large *meta-hyperspace* of the full range of customisability. Yet each learner should see a quite manageable hyperspace.

Figure 3.1 shows the way a conventional hypertext system can allow for learner's preferences among three classes of examples. At the left (A) is the hypertext space that allows the learner the choice of three classes of examples: mathematical, text oriented and systems oriented. The dark nodes across the top introduce the concept being explained. All are substantially the same, with small differences to account for the different examples that each will use. The next row of nodes is for the actual example used. These nodes are lighter to indicate that they are quite different from each other. The next row of nodes is for the discussion of the examples. Here, too, there is much commonality in all three: in each case, the examples are being used to illustrate the same concept. Of course, there will also be considerable differences too because each text discusses the concept in terms of different examples. The rest of Figure 1A shows how each of the three possible paths continue to pass through nodes: darker nodes at the same level indicating texts that do the task described at the left with much in common and the lighter nodes showing text that is very different.

The major problem with this approach is that the author of the hypertext needs to manage several texts that are very similar. Any corrections may need to be made over each parallel text. From the learner's point of view, this approach partitions the hypertext, with the learner deciding at the top of the figure which partition they will follow.

The right hand part of the figure (B) shows an alternate approach that avoids the almost identical repetitive nodes in the hypertext. Here the common aspects of the explanation are separated from those that are specific to the example. Now all learners see the same *introduction* node and then they must select the node for the type of example they prefer. Similarly for the *discussion* and *wrapup*. Now the repetition is with the learner. If they prefer the mathematical examples, they must select the *"mathematical example"* node every time they want an example of the concept. This approach also forces identical text for the introduction, discussion and wrapup nodes: any

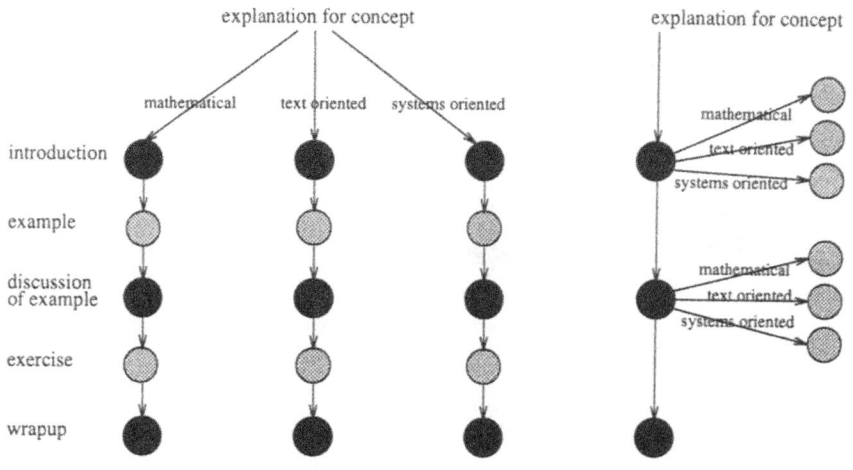

Fig. 3.1. Standard hypertext allowances for individual preferences.

of these that are specific to the examples must be in their nodes, potentially causing near-repetition.

The solution in Figure 1B poses another problem because the learner will only see the example and exercise if they detour from the main learning path. This has two undesirable effects. First, it imposes additional cognitive load on the reader who must now be mindful of the main path they are following (dark nodes in Figure 1B) and the side-trips to their chosen grey nodes. The second problem is that the reader may not bother to detour. This is especially important in the case of the exercises which enable the reader to practice what they are reading. Our own experience and some recent work [24] indicate that readers are reluctant to take such detours. In addition to these problems for the reader and the learning process, the two sets of grey nodes are now completely decoupled. So the user could easily explore the mathematical example for the example and then attempt the text-oriented exercise. The hypertext author then has an additional burden in ensuring that all such combinations make sense. The user has the extra cognitive load of remembering which class of examples they selected.

Figure 3.2 shows the way that our system deals with alternate explanations. The path at the left depicts the user's actual hyperspace. At the right is the meta-hyperspace from which it came. The dark nodes are the elements that are common to all the hyperspaces generated for different users. The lighter nodes hold the alternate examples.

There are two important differences between the hyperspace at the left of Figure 3.2 and those in Figure 3.1. Most obvious is that in Figure 3.2 the

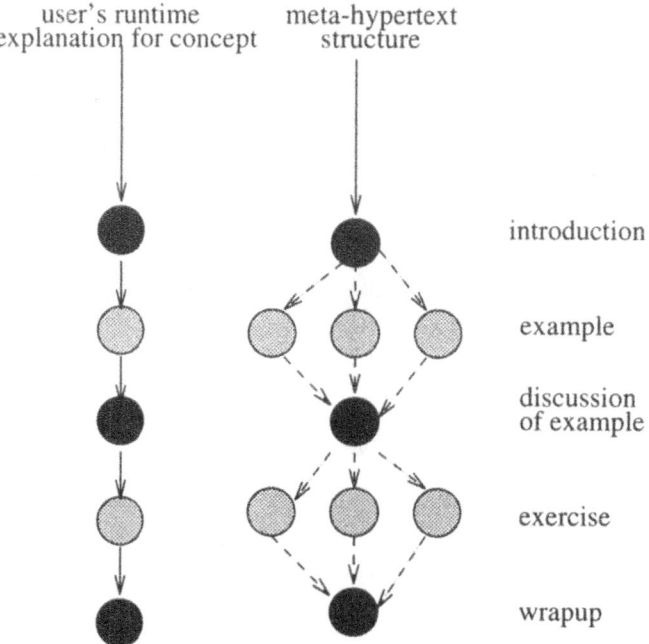

user's runtime
explanation for concept

meta-hypertext
structure

introduction

example

discussion
of example

exercise

wrapup

Fig. 3.2. Metahypertext structure and the learner's hypertext.

user no longer needs to decide which example type they will select because
this has been done by the system.

Less obvious is that we no longer have to limit customisation to the hypertext node level. Since we generate the hypertext, we can allow customisation
at arbitrarily detailed levels. For example, we can now add a few words relating to the particular example in the 'wrapup'.

We can also extend the customisation. The example of Figures 3.1 and
3.2 illustrates customising exclusively in terms of three classes of examples.
We can also provide customisation based on aspects such as those described
in Section 2.

4. User models to customise hypertext

A user or student model is information that enables the system to model
the learner. In teaching systems that attempt to customise their interaction
to match the individual, or where the system has been designed to match
models of learning, this 'user model' is critical. In our management of the
user model (often called a student model in literature on Intelligent Teaching
Systems), we distinguish three main levels:

– domain representation level;

– representations of important learner groups or *stereotypes* and
– the individual model of this learner, in terms of the above two as well as other sources of information about the user.

In a hypertext for teaching, it makes sense for the the user model to contain the learner's preknowledge, learning goals and preferences. The remainder of this section explains these in terms of the three levels of the user model.

4.1 Domain representation level

It makes sense to model only what can be used by the system to manage the interaction. For example, in the C-book, we can define a structure on some knowledge components of the domain as follows

```
parameter passing mechanisms
        call-by-value
        call-by-reference
        call-by-name
runtime structures
        stack
        heap
        static
```

where the indented concepts are refinements of their more general concept. The important thing about this structure is that it supports inferences. For example, if the user knows all the refinements of a concept, we can conclude the user knows the more general concept. The example above uses a domain structure similar to genetic graphs [9]. In general, one might apply arbitrary knowledge representation tools to support such domain level inferences.

4.2 Stereotype level

Stereotypes are a pervasive element in much user modelling work [21, 14]. The user model could usefully define several stereotypes over this domain. For example, it is common to define a model for the 'typical novice' and the 'typical expert' and possibly some other intermediate classes of users. Each of these would be intended to capture a useful set of assumptions about each class of users. So, for example, the 'typical novice' would be represented as knowing some things and not others and having preferences for particular styles of explanation, favouring the concrete over the abstract.

For the audience of our initial book, our stereotype would have shown the following values for the knowledge components above

User model component   Value
parameter passing mechanisms partly true

call-by-value	true
call-by-reference	true
call-by-name	not
runtime structures	slightly true
stack	partly true
heap	partly true
static	false

The author of a PTtext would normally envisage a small number of *types* of users, each with a corresponding stereotype. The important thing about such stereotypes is that they enable us to devise a few questions to ask users and from these to make many inferences that are treated as *statistically* true: we assume they are low grade default inferences to be used only until we have better information about the user.

4.3 Individual level

The third level of the user model is used to represent an individual. This models the user's membership of various stereotype groups as well as their individual differences from these.

An example might be

Type	User model component	Value
Knowledge	competent in Pascal	true
	understands run time structures	slightly true
	knows about functions	slightly true
	knows about function arguments	true
	understands call-by-value	true
	understands call-by-reference	true
	understands call-by-name	true
Preferences	abstract or concrete	abstract
	terse or more detailed	terse
	active or directed	active
	likes mathematical examples	true
	likes Unix system examples	true
	likes simple text-based example	false

The values listed at the right are derived from several sources: directly from the user in answer to questions, from data the systems collects as the user interacts with the system doing exercises and the like and inferred using domain and stereotype knowledge.

For example, if a user answers a question stating they are an expert Pascal programmer we can store that in the model plus the domain knowledge-based inferences that they know about the concepts, call-by-value and call-by-reference. Indeed, this type of inference enables the system to conclude that the expert Pascal programmer has a conceptual knowledge of the major common elements of Pascal and C.

The stereotype reasoning will be used for weaker inferences. For example, a learner who claims to be a Unix guru might be presumed to like 'abstract' and 'terse' descriptions since we believe this is common among those who cope well with Unix (and its documentation). Although this is plausible, it is merely a reasonable starting assumption that is true of many but not all users in this class.

4.4 Building the model

The user modelling toolkit provides various interfaces for interacting with the user. The initial interview is driven by a simple form-based interview program that is invoked by the web server. This is ci, the concept inventory interface, which takes a definition of a projection onto the user model and uses this to define the order of questions given to the user to collect a quick assessment of their relevant knowledge.

We plan to provide several other ways to collect useful modelling information. Essentially, these come from three sources: the learner's actions as they move through their hyperspace; analysis of the learner's performance on exercises; and by allowing the learner to volunteer additional information to improve the customisation.

One important class of indirect user modelling information can come from the learner's comparative assessment of different forms of customisation. This is particularly useful for establishing the language style that the learner prefers. For example, it is typically easy for a learner to read two versions of an explanation and say which they prefer. If we try to determine this in other ways, the learner may need to be familiar with what we mean by terms such as "abstract" and "concrete".

The tools for managing the user modelling come from our toolkit for user modelling [15, 7, 16] Essentially, they can use a range of sources to collect information. They also enable the learner to inspect the user model and to contribute information to it. The toolkit also offers tools to deal with problems of noise and non-monotonicity. The C *meta-hypertext* makes use of a simple reasoning mechanism based on endorsements [6].

5. Implementation

The customisation system developed in this project is based on a set of programs that is invoked by the web http server.

Web http servers allow a program to be executed in response to a user selecting a link. Parameters can be specified on the link and these are passed to the invoked program. The program is then expected to construct an HTML page with appropriate MIME headers and write it to standard output. The http server collects the HTML and returns it to the client browser. This facility, known as CGI or Common Gateway Interface, was originally designed to allow easy construction of gateways to databases and other services.

One program uses HTML *forms* to collect information from the user about their programming experience and learning style and another takes this information and tailors individual HTML pages of the course material according to their choices.

5.1 Authentication

In order to maintain a user model and use it to customise HTML pages, the current user must be identifiable and there must be some form of authentication. Our system uses the basic authentication system provided by http that requires a user to enter a user name and password before access to certain directories and files is allowed.

The current username is made available to the programs and is used when consulting the user modelling system for information about the user.

Before a user accesses the course for the first time, an account and password must be established as well as an initial user model or *stereotype*.

5.2 Concept Inventory

The ciprogram consults the user model using a particular *context* given as a parameter. In the case of the C language course this is simply "C" but the system has been used for other applications such as system for giving advice on movies and a system to construct a personalised radio programme.

Included in the context are questions that can be presented to the user to elicit the necessary information. The ciprogram constructs an HTML form with these questions and returns this to the http server.

When the user has filled in the form and clicked on the Finished button, the answers are returned using the HTTP *POST* method. The ciprogram analyses the answers and updates the user model appropriately. Only a modest number of questions are asked and the rest of the user model is derived from stereotypes.

5.3 Form of Course Pages

The course component pages are written in HTML but are augmented with a customisation language that describes how it should be customised for the current user. The PTprogram is configured to use another program to process the customisation language, so any suitable language could be used.

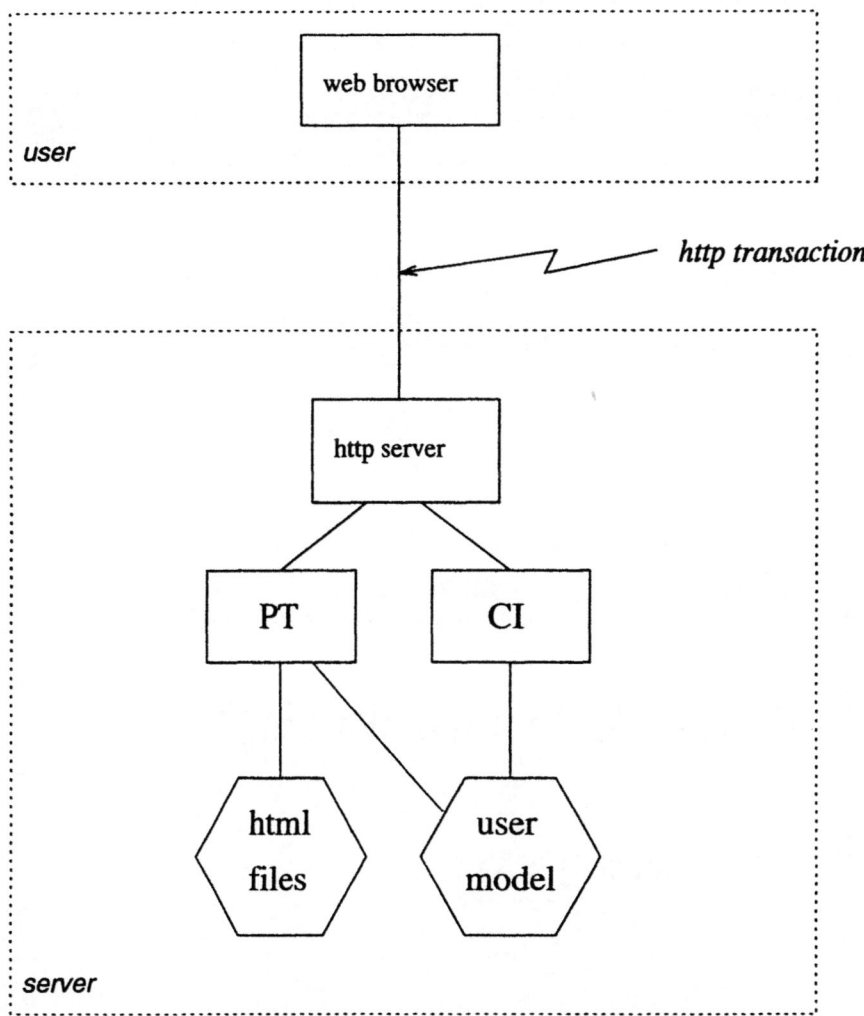

Fig. 5.1. Architecture of customisation system

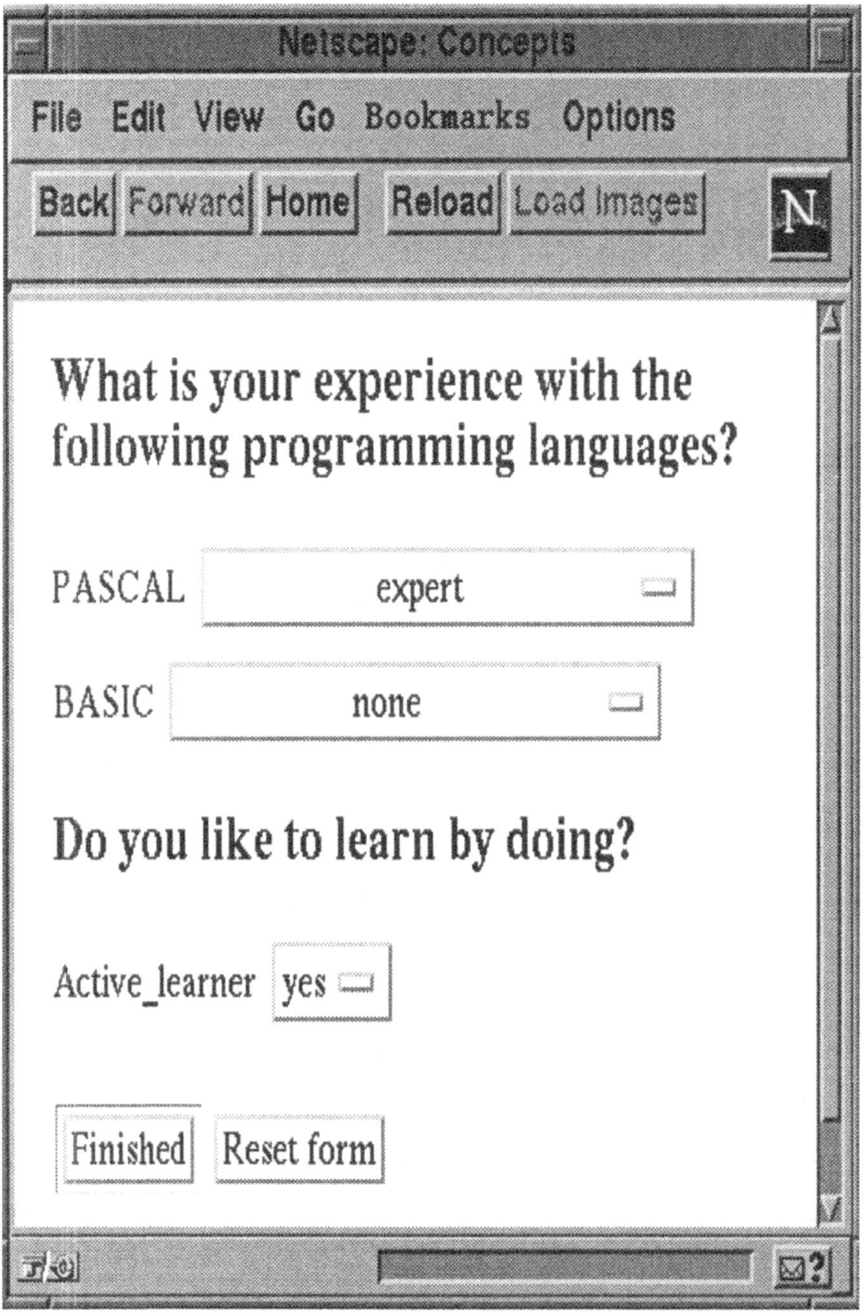

Fig. 5.2. An example concept inventory

For the C course we use the C preprocessor (cpp) since it is readily available and sufficiently powerful for this application.

5.4 Customisation

Apart from the process of gathering initial information about the user, all access to course pages is through the PTprogram.

PTis run by the web server and is passed the name of a page that is to presented to the user. The user model is then consulted using the 'c' context for the current user and the resulting information turned into a sequence of C preprocessor '#define' lines. PTthen invokes the customisation language processor (cpp in our case) and pipes into it the sequence of #define lines followed by the raw course page. The output of cpp is fed back to the http server as the HTML page to be returned to the user's web browser.

Here is a short example showing a fragment of a course page. The user has indicated that they are an expert Pascal programmer, have no knowledge of Basic and prefer an 'active learning' style of instruction.

The user clicks on the following anchor:

```
<A HREF=pt?C1/C1.2>
```

The raw course page includes the following:

```
<P>
A C program is a collection of functions.
One must be called <TT>main</TT> and this runs first.
#if PASCAL > 0   more than minimal Pascal knowledge?
As a Pascal programmer you should note that the line
<TT>main()</TT> does <I>not</I> have a semicolon at
the end of it.
#endif
```

PTadds a MIME header and, after consulting the user model, the following lines:

```
#define PASCAL 3
#define BASIC 0
#define Active-learner 1
```

This is then passed to the C preprocessor and the final text is:

```
other HTML text
<P>
A C program is a collection of functions.
One must be called <TT>main</TT> and this runs first.
As a Pascal programmer you should note that the line
<TT>main()</TT> does <I>not</I> have a semicolon at
the end of it.
other HTML text
```

The resulting page is shown in Figure 5.3.

As well as modifying the text shown to the user this customisation technique can be used to determine which path through the course is presented. This is done by presenting a link to one page in one situation and a different link or no link at all for another.

The technique can also be used to vary the appearance of pages and make it easier to move pages to other machines.

For example, at the end of most pages the user is presented with a *next* link and a right arrow icon. This may be represented as:

```
<HR>
#if (Active_learner > 0)&&(PASCAL > 0)
<A HREF=pt?C1/C1.1.1>
#else
<A HREF=pt?C1/C1.2>
#endif
<I>next</I>
<IMG ALIGN=bot src=RIGHTARROW>
</A>
<A HREF=http:pt?C1/C1.index>
<I>index</I>
<IMG ALIGN=bot src=UPARROW>
</A>
```

This indicates that if the user is an 'active learner' and has some Pascal experience they should move to page C1.1.1 when they select *next*, otherwise they move to C1.2.

The source for the right and up arrow icon data is also represented using a #define'ed symbol. This makes it easy to change the form and location of the arrow data.

6. Support for authoring

One of the problems with our current system is that it is even more complex for the author to manage than ordinary hypertext. This is a serious problem.

The system described above used the very simple approach of inserting pre-processor commands into the source for the hypertext documents. This is an additional burden to the hypertext author: writing in html is already a burden and the addition of another layer of customisation increases this in several ways. We have explored several approaches to improving this.

6.1 Customisation tags

First, and most natural in an html document, is to enhance the set of tags to define a customisation language. One example of this has been imple-

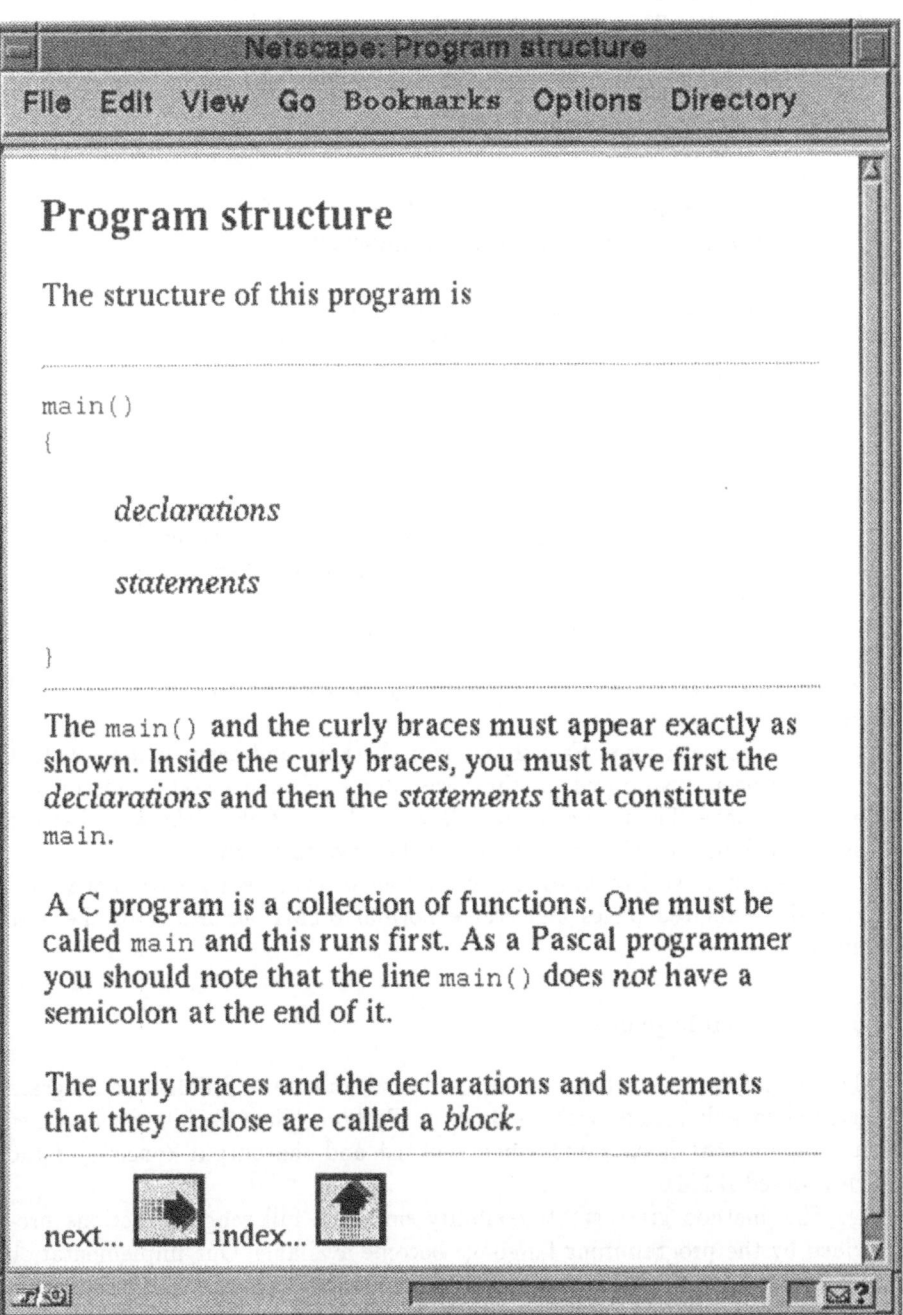

Fig. 5.3.

mented [11]. This has been used to create a customised set of documentation
for a text editor. This approach is still very close to the implementation we
have described but it offers some syntactic sugar for the author. We believe
this is important for the management of the authoring process. For example,
an excerpt of a customised text looks like this

```
<hr>
<h2>Moving the cursor in sam</h2>
<tailor attr="go_k" switch=on who="c">
  <p>
  Once you have selected a button with one click of
  button 1, the text you type goes where the cursor
  is. more text
<tailor attr="go_k" switch=off who="c">

<tailor attr="go_k" switch=on who="fn">
  <p>
  You may choose to go to a different position on the
  currently activated window, or make another window
  current. more text
<tailor attr="go_k" switch=off who="fn">
```

where both pieces of text are controlled by the user model component called
go_k.

This approach also offers some error checking and ensures that all text
that has been customised on the basis of a user model states this on the
hypertext page. The user can also follow a link to details of the way that the
user model affected the presentation of the page they saw.

This system still requires the web server to execute a program that will
read the enhanced pages and create normal HTML according to the user
model.

6.2 Executable pages

The second approach that we have used is to embed the HTML in a program
written in a language such as Java or Python. Then each page becomes
a program that is executed when selected and the output consists of the
customised HTML.

This method gives great flexibility since the full range of actions provided by the programming language become available. Our implementation
in Python provides a user model class with methods to consult various aspects of the model. In this system we have also experimented with embedding
Javascript statements in the resulting HTML to provide more interactive exercises.

While the executable page system gives the ultimate in flexibility in terms of the generation of the final customised pages, it does add yet more complexity to the task of the author.

6.3 Customisation interface

The final approach we have explored is to create a WYSIWYG editor to support authors in performing customisation [22]. Here the hypertext author has three active windows: one with the source text, one with a user model interface and the last able to display particular customisations. The author marks sections of the source text and selects the user model elements for the customisation.

6.4 Style sheets

The HTML language has been extended to include a *style sheet* facility [18]. This allows an author or user to specify default properties of text and layout to customise the presentation of web pages by browsers. The properties that can be customised including font style, size and colour. The style sheets are designed to *cascade*, allowing a user to over-ride properties set by an author or browser.

The initial version of the style sheet facility allows only properties of web page elements to be specified. However, it would seem a natural place for user modelling information and a mechanism to allow more general customisation of text apart from simple properties such as colour and size.

Future extensions to the style sheet facility may have a more general HTML customisation facility.

7. Related work

The distinctive character of PTcomes from the way it explores several classes of customisation for use of authors of WWW-based hypertext. There are many active projects in closely related areas. There are also clear links between this work the broader areas of various forms of adaptive hypertext, natural language generation and and intelligent teaching systems.

A comprehensive review of current work in the area of adaptive hypertext [4] distinguishes various levels of adaptation: the content of the page presented and the links. One of the earliest and best evaluated adaptive hypertext systems was for Unix manual entries presented in Stretchtext [8, 3] and there was a similar system [19] which made more sophisticated use of user modelling. These are limited to the customising the content of Unix manual entries, relatively small documents with the user's knowledge making various aspects more likely to be relevant and understandable. Other systems

explore various other issues like customising navigation by helping users identify nodes used by people with similar user models [2, 5]. Both presentation and navigation are adapted in a teaching system for a subset of Lisp [10]. That work also attends to concerns of learner control by making the user model accessible as does the intelligent help system of [12] where the user explicitly selects the stereotype to be used and then the system infers users plans from their actions.

There is also a strong relationship between research that aims to customise text and systems that generate natural language from an internal knowledge representation. In particular, both can benefit from effective user modelling and many of the systems described in [17] provide useful foundations for approaches to the user modelling for a system PT.

Finally, the current form of PT can be viewed as an intelligent system in the mould of the many where student (or user) modelling is central to the individualised instruction as described, for example in [1]. That the WWW implementation supports a rich set of possible interactions makes our hypertext more like a teaching system than any of the more typical hypertext books.

8. Issues for adaptive hypertext

We consider two critical aspects of adaptivity, and especially adaptive hypertext like PT. These are the problems of document instability that could disorient the user and the related problems of user control.

8.1 Document stability

One of the potential problems with our approach is that the learner could become disoriented and irritated if the revisited text were very different each time they come to it.

As present we have a number of strategies for dealing with this. None are enforced by the system: they require judgment and discipline on the part of the hypertext author. We need several strategies because the different classes of customisation can bring different problems.

Consider first the effects of different learner's backgrounds. Our current approach is that as learners progress through their learning of C, the material presented converges to the form of the printed text. This is intended for reference use by a reader who understands the underlying concepts but needs to check a detail or be reminded of some aspect of the language. Tutorial level material is still accessible, but deeper in the hyperspace.

Note that in our context, there are many details that readers would need to check on starting a new class of task. For example, this is common for the many library functions: a learner may never use certain groups of these for

long periods and then need to do a burst of work with them. They may forget details like the order of the arguments in a standard function. We consider that the learner then needs descriptions of these, with examples and notes about potential pitfalls and common errors. This type of information tends to have less customisation of its presentation level and very quickly converges to the reference form.

For customisations of example types, the learner would not expect instability. This means that we cannot apply a convergence approach. Effectively, this type of customisation has the effect of defining sets of parallel books. We deal with this by applying a somewhat different convergence principle: the printed version, hence the goal of the convergence, tends to have small highly focused examples compared with the teaching materials. The principle is that the learner actually understands the principles and is using this for reference so it is less critical to match their preferred example style.

Teaching style also has an interesting effect in the long term. For example, the active learner is provided with information in small steps, with the learner encouraged to guess or work out as much as possible. Once the learner has passed through such a sequence to complete the path to a concept, they are presented with direct information thereafter. It would be irritating to go through the other process repeatedly. At the same time, a learner may wish to retrace their footsteps. We consider that the best control for this is to ensure that the customised hypertext has information about the customisation and the user model elements that formed it. We also believe that the user must be able to control the user model and hence the customisation.

8.2 Learner Control

In all this the learner can control the customisation by altering their user model. If, for example, the model indicates the learner really knows a concept, like call-by-value, it will not make that a glossary button and explanations will be cast on this assumption. The learner can alter the user model and get alternate text.

The viewable (and adjustable) user model permits control at that level. If the learner wishes to explore the impact of their user model on hyperspace, they can do so by tinkering with the model and exploring the resultant hyperspace.

9. Conclusion

A *metahypertext* allows the essential elements of hypertext: pages, links between them and their semantic structure, to be dynamic. Our architecture uses WWW to deliver a metahypertext. It has three important aspects.

The first is the user model and the interaction that helps define it for each user. We have implemented a WWW-based interface to do concept inventories that seed the user model.

The second aspect is the use of rich interactions with the user as a part of the hypertext. This makes reading and traversing the hypertext far more active than is the case for conventional hypertext.

The third critical element of the architecture is the use of "on-the-fly" generation of html pages. This permits the generation of arbitrarily customised hypertext pages.

References

[1] *Student Modelling: The Key to Individualized Knowledge-based Instruction*, Springer-Verlag NATO ASI Series (1994).
[2] G. Boy, "On-line user model acquisition in hypertext documentation", *Proc. IJCAI Workshop Agent Modelling for Intelligent Interaction*, pp. 34-42, Sydney, Australia (1991).
[3] C Boyle and A O Encarnacion, "MetaDoc: an adaptive hypertext reading system," *User models and user adapted interaction* (In press).
[4] P Brusilovsky, "Adaptive hypertext: an attempt to analyze and generalise" in *Multimedia, Hypermedia and Virtual Reality Models, Systems and Applications*, ed. P Brusilovsky, P Kommers, and N Streitz, Springer (1996).
[5] Kaplan C, Fenwick J, and Chen J, "Adaptive hypertext navigation based on user goals and context," *User models and user adapted interaction*, 3, 2(1993).
[6] Paul R Cohen, *Heuristic reasoning about uncertainty: an artificial intelligence approach*, Morgan Kaufmann, Los Altos, California (1985).
[7] R Cook and J Kay, "The justified user model: a viewable, explained user model" in *UM94: User Modeling Conference*, pp. 145-150, Hyannis, Cape Cod, USA (1994). Also available as Technical Report 483 (ISBN 0 86758 9221).
[8] A Encarnacion and C Boyle, "A user model based hypertext documentation system", in *Proc IJCAI Workshop W.4: Agent Modeling for Intelligent Interaction*, ed. J Kay and A Quilici, pp. 43-66. IJCAI-91, Sydney, Australia (1990).
[9] I P Goldstein, "The genetic graph: a representation for the evolution of procedural knowledge" in *Intelligent tutoring systems*, ed. D Sleeman and J S Brown, Academic Press, New York (1982).
[10] H Hohl, H-D Bocker, and R Gunzenhauser, "Hypadapter: An Adaptive Hypertext System for Exploratory Learning and Programming," *User Modeling and User-Adapted Interaction*, 6, 2-3(1996).
[11] Andrew Hong, *A preprocessor for customising HTML documents: the Tailor customisation language*, Honours Thesis, Basser Dept of Computer Science, University of Sydney (1995).
[12] K Hook, J Karlgren, A Waern, N Dahlback, C G Jansson, K karlgren, and B Lemaire, "A glass box approach to adaptive hypermedia," *User Modeling and User-Adapted Interaction*, 6, 2-3, pp. 157-184 (1996).
[13] J Kay and R J Kummerfeld, *C in the UNIX Environment*, p. 340, Assison-Wesley (1989).

[14] J Kay, "Invited keynote address - Lies, damned lies and stereotypes: pragmatic approximations of users," *UM94 - 1994 User Modeling Conference*, pp. 175-184, Boston, USA (1994). Also available as Technical Report 482 (ISBN 0 86758 919 1).

[15] J Kay, "um: a user modelling toolkit," *Second Intl User Modelling Workshop*, p. 11, Hawaii (1990).

[16] J Kay, "The um toolkit for cooperative user modelling," *User Modeling and User-Adapted Interaction*, 4, 4, Kluwer (1995). And as SSRG Report 94/3/36.3.

[17] A Kobsa and W Wahlster, *User models in dialog systems*, Springer-Verlag, Berlin(1989).

[18] W H Lie and B Bos, *Cascading Style Sheets, level 1*, (Sept, 1996). http://www.w3.org/pub/WWW/TR/

[19] R Lithgo, *A hypertext user modelling Unix manual system*, Honours Thesis, Basser Dept of Computer Science, University of Sydney (1991).

[20] C L Paris, "The user of explicit user models in a generation system for tailoring answers to the user's level of expertise" in *User models in dialog systems*, ed. A Kobsa and W Wahlster, pp. 200-232, Springer-Verlag (1989).

[21] E Rich, "Users are individuals: individualizing user models," *Intl J of Man-Machine Studies*, 18, pp. 199-214 (1983).

[22] Brooke Smith, *CUSTOR*, Honours Thesis, Basser Dept of Computer Science, University of Sydney (1995).

[23] P Tamir, "What do learing theories and research have to say to practitioners in science education?", in *Research and Development in Higher Education*, ed. J Lublin, 7, pp. 162-166 (1984).

[24] D Tyerman, *Personal communications*, (1996).

Conceptual Analysis of Hypertext

Robert E. Kent[1]* and Christian Neuss[2]

[1] Washington State University, Pullman, WA 99164, USA
[2] Technische Hochschule Darmstadt, 64289 Darmstadt, Germany

Summary. In this chapter tools and techniques from the mathematical theory of formal concept analysis are applied to hypertext systems in general, and the World Wide Web in particular. Various processes for the conceptual structuring of hypertext are discussed: summarization, conceptual scaling, and the creation of conceptual links. Well-known interchange formats for summarizing networked information resources as resource meta-information are reviewed, and two new interchange formats originating from formal concept analysis are advocated. Also reviewed is conceptual scaling, which provides a principled approach to the faceted analysis techniques in library science classification. The important notion of conceptual linkage is introduced as a generalization of a hyperlink. The automatic hyperization of the content of legacy data is described, and the composite conceptual structuring with hypertext linkage is defined. For the conceptual empowerment of the Web user, a new technique called conceptual browsing is advocated. Conceptual browsing, which browses over conceptual links, is dual mode (both extensional and intensional) and dual scope (both global and local).

1. Conceptual Knowledge Systems

Using ideas from library science [2, 5], hypertext systems [8], and formal concept analysis [1, 3], tools are currently being developed [13, 18, 19] for the conceptual analysis of networked information resources in general, and the World Wide Web in particular. Networked information resources include (1) individual text files, (2) WAIS databases, and (3) starting points for hypertext webs.

Resources are best thought of, not as objects, but as formal concepts. We offer a concept-oriented approach for the description and organization of networked information resources, which will facilitate their subsequent discovery and access. This should not be thought of as yet another object-oriented approach. Although objects generate their own concepts, concepts are not only more general but also include intensional information. By identifying concepts with classes, this can be regarded as a class-oriented approach [17] — an approach advocated in early 1995 by Terry Winograd [16] in the IETF-URI working group discussion on library standards and URI, and supported by Ronald Daniel and Dirk Herr-Hoyman.

Formal concept analysis [1, 3] is a relatively new discipline arising out of the mathematical theory of lattices and the calculus of binary relations. It is closely related to the areas of knowledge representation in computer science and cognitive psychology. Formal concept analysis provides for the automatic

---

* This research was funded by a grant from Intel Corporation.

classification of both knowledge and documents via representation of a user's faculty for interpretation as encoded in conceptual scales. Such conceptual scales correspond to the facets of synthetic classification schemes, such as Ranganathan's Colon classification scheme, in library science.

Formal concept analysis uses objects, attributes and formal concepts as its basic constituents. Objects and attributes are connected through has-a incidence relationships, while formal concepts are connected through is-a subtype relationships. Incidence is the most primitive notion in formal concept analysis. A *formal context* represents incidence by collecting together all of the relevant has-a relationships. It is a triple $\langle G, M, I \rangle$ consisting of a set of objects G (Gegenstände, in German), a set of attributes M (Merkmale, in German), and a binary incidence relation $I \subseteq G \times M$, where gIm asserts that "object g has attribute m." In many contexts appropriate for Web resources, the objects are document-like objects and the attributes are properties of those document-like objects that are of interest to the Web user.

A *formal concept* is the central notion in formal concept analysis. A formal concept consists of a collection of entities or objects exhibiting one or more common characteristics, traits or attributes. Formal concepts are logically characterized by their extension and intension. The *extension* of a concept is the aggregate of entities or objects which it includes or denotes. The *intension* of a concept is the sum of its unique characteristics, traits or attributes, which, taken together, imply the intuitive concept signified by the formal concept. In this paper formal concepts are identified with the intuitive concept that they signify. The process of subordination of concepts and collocation of objects exhibits a natural order, proceeding top-down from the more generalized concepts with larger extension and smaller intension to the more specialized concepts with smaller extension and larger intension. This is-a relationship is a partial order called generalization-specialization. Concepts with this generalization-specialization ordering form a conceptual is-a hierarchy $\mathcal{L} = \mathcal{L}\langle G, M, I \rangle$ called a *concept lattice*. Formal concept analysis uses formal concepts as its central notion and uses concept lattices as an approach to knowledge representation [1]. The use of formal concepts as a conceptual structuring mechanism corresponds to the use of similarity clusters in information retrieval [8], although formal concepts are based more on logical implication rather than a nearness notion. However, see the discussion about conceptual linkage below.

The enriching notion of a *conceptual knowledge system* from formal concept analysis [4, 19] allows, not only the modeling of knowledge representation, but also the ability to do knowledge inferencing, knowledge acquisition, and knowledge communication. In a conceptual knowledge system there are three basic notions: objects, attributes, and conceptual views. These are connected through four basic relationships: an object has an attribute (incidence), an object belongs to a conceptual view (instantiation), an attribute abstracts from a conceptual view (abstraction), and a conceptual view is a subordinate to another conceptual view (subtype). These notions and relationships partition the frame of a conceptual knowledge system as in Table 1.1. In a conceptual knowledge system we distinguish between (1) anonymous concepts which are automatically and implicitly generated from the four basic relationships and represent a form of conceptual resource discovery, and (2) named and explicitly specified concepts which we call *conceptual views*. Compare the distinct, but closely related, notion of a Nebula-style view [19] in the Nebula file system.

Table 1.1. Conceptual Knowledge System Relationhips

	Views	Attributes
Views	subtype	abstraction
Objects	instantiation	incidence

Table 1.2 represents a conceptual knowledge system within the conceptual universe $\mathcal{D}$ of all documents in an information system and their properties (see Figure 2 in Bowman et al. [10]). In addition to a set of document-like objects and attributes, it contains the five conceptual views

{Object, Document, PostScript, Plan1, Plan2}.

The crosses in the table of basic relationships in Table 1.2 are partitioned into the four parts described in Table 1.1: subtype, in the upper left; abstraction, in the upper right; instantiation, in the lower left; and incidence, in the lower right. The bottom panel of Table 1.2 is the line diagram of the lattice of formal concepts, which represents the conceptual space for the document conceptual knowledge system.

The representational mechanism of conceptual knowledge systems serves as a firm foundation for the basic paradigms of internet resource discovery and wide area information management systems: organization-navigation and search-retrieval [19]. The use of conceptual knowledge systems is a natural outgrowth of the original formal concept analysis approach for structuring and organizing the networked information resources in the World Wide Web [13].

2. Resource Meta-information

Due to the rapid growth of the World Wide Web, resource discovery has become a serious problem. Because of its decentralized architecture, the user experiences the Web as a large information repository without an underlying structure. The process of "surfing" pages by repeatedly following hyperlinks

Table 1.2. Conceptual Knowledge System in the Document Universe

Views/Objects
1 Object
2 Document
3 PostScript
4 Plan1
5 Plan2
6 plan1.ps
7 plan2.ps
8 plan2.doc
9 notes0.txt
10 notes1.txt
11 notes2.txt

Basic Relationships									
	1	2	3	4	5	6	7	8	9
1	×								
2	×	×							
3	×	×	×					×	
4	×	×		×		×			
5	×	×			×		×		
6	×	×	×	×		×		×	
7	×	×	×		×		×	×	
8	×	×			×	×			
9	×	×		×		×			×
10	×	×			×	×			×
11	×	×			×	×			×

Views/Attributes
1 Object
2 Document
3 PostScript
4 Plan1
5 Plan2
6 project=plan1
7 project=plan2
8 format=postscript
9 format=text

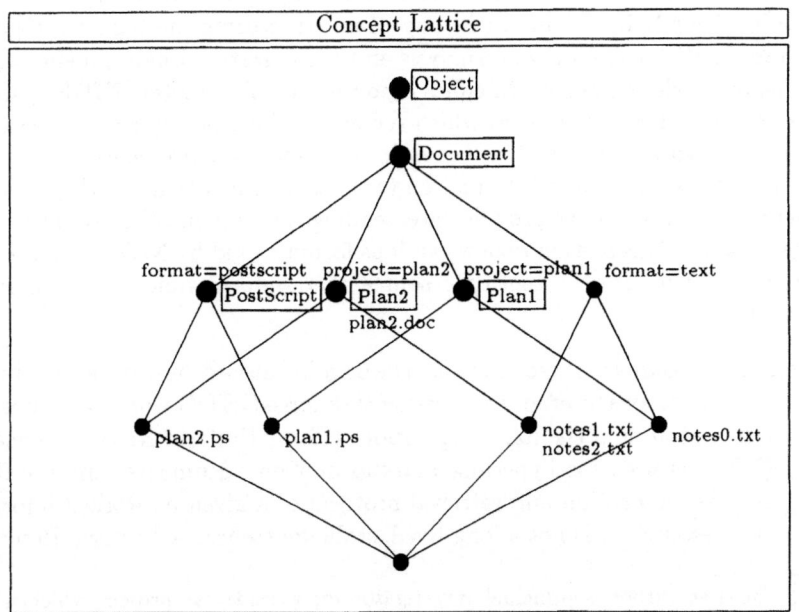

Concept Lattice

is the most popular use of the Web. It can however lead to the phenomenon of getting "lost in hyperspace."

From the very beginning of the World Wide Web, approaches have been made to organize information about networked information resources into catalogs and indexes. Index files were originally maintained manually. However, the rapid growth of the Web soon made necessary automatic methods for generating resource directories. Automatic tools called "robots", "Web wanderers" or "spiders" soon evolved. These are programs which automatically connect to a remote server and recursively retrieve documents. Since Web robots often put heavy loads on Web servers, they have been controversial, and are sometimes disliked by server maintainers.

Web robots are trailing-edge technologies. The main problem with robots is that they are not true Web wanderers — the retrieval program does not transfer itself from the index site to the provider site, but instead it transfers in the reverse direction over the network all the potentially indexable documents. Since document repositories may contain hundreds of megabytes, the bandwidth requirements are enormous. Exacerbating this problem is the fact that current indexing tools gather independently, without sharing information with other indexers.

A partial answer to these problems are Networked Information Discovery and Retrieval (NIDR) systems such as Harvest [14]. A more complete answer will involve NIDR systems with conceptual structuring mechanisms[13] such as the WAVE[1] system (Web Analysis and Visualization Environment) which is being developed using principles espoused in this chapter. NIDR systems are leading-edge technologies which reduce the load on information servers, reduce network traffic, and reduce index disk space requirements, principally by use of resource meta-information (also called metadata) — they extract meta-information at the provider site, sending this, and not the raw data, over the network. This section reviews various formats used by NIDR systems and library science for representing resource meta-information as bibliographic records [18].

Uniform Resource Characteristics: The ongoing discussions concerning metadata in various internet engineering task force (IETF) working groups are centered around the following notions [12]. A Uniform Resource Locator (URL) is used for hyperlink markup in Web documents. Since a URL specifies a location and retrieval protocol of a given networked information resource, it is not a long-lived, stable reference. A Uniform Resource

---

[1] The first author is principal investigator for a multiyear project which is developing and assessing the WAVE system. This project, entitled "Creating a WAVE," is funded by Intel Corporation. More information about the project can be obtained at the Web address

http://wave.eecs.wsu.edu/

Name (URN) is used to identify a resource. It is long-lived and persistent, and uniquely names a networked information resource. A Uniform Resource Locator is used to locate an instance of a resource identified by an URN. A Uniform Resource Idenifier (URI), which is either a URL or a URN, is the generic set of all names/addresses that refer to networked information resources. A Uniform Resource Characteristic (URC) is used to represent URNs with associated meta-information. URCs are analogous to the bibliographic records of library science. URCs encode meta-information about network resources in the form of attribute-value pairs.

IAFA Templates: The Internet anonymous ftp archives (IAFA) working group of the IETF has proposed a format for indexing information that can be used to describe various internet resources. The IAFA template specification [9] encodes pieces of meta-information. The IAFA templates are intended to be both human and machine readable. Archie servers support this format to provide information about items available for anonymous ftp. Work is currently underway for the construction of Uniform Resource Identifiers.

Harvest Summary Object Interchange Format: Harvest is a set of tools to gather, extract, and search relevant information across the internet [14]. It provides methods for distributed indexing, building topic specific indices, flexible search strategies, and replica systems. Harvest generates a content summary for each information object it gathers. These records are stored in a format called the Summary Object Interchange Format (SOIF). SOIF is based on a combination of the IAFA templates and BibTeX.

Bibliographic Records from Library Science: In order to compare URCs, IAFA templates, and Harvest SOIFs with bibliographic description in library science, listed here are some attributes, which are classified according to the eight areas of the international standards for bibliographic description (ISBD) [5]: title and statement of responsibility (title, author); edition (version); material (or type of publication) specific details; publication, distribution, etc.; physical description (content-type, content-length, size, cost, etc.); series (time-to-live); notes (abstract); and standard number and terms of availability (uniform resource name, uniform resource locator).

Table 2.1 lists two generic interchange formats which can be used to specify faceted information in conceptually scaled networked information resources [18]. Such faceted information can occur in various interfaces in a resource discovery system. From a mathematical viewpoint, these two representations are equivalent. Software exists for converting between the two forms.

The left side of Table 2.1 displays the Formal Context Interchange Format (FCIF). FCIF is oriented towards the formal contexts of formal concept analysis. FCIF represents order-theoretic formal contexts of networked information resources, consisting of two partially ordered sets, a poset of objects and a poset of single-valued attributes, and an order-preserving incidence matrix which represents the has-a relationship between objects and attributes. The right side of Table 2.1 displays the Concept Lattice Interchange Format (CLIF). CLIF is oriented towards the concept lattices of formal concept analysis. CLIF provides a storage-optimal representation of order-theoretic lattices of formal concepts for networked information resource meta-information, consisting of (the inverse relationships for) two generator monotonic functions, from the posets of objects and attributes to the lattice of formal concepts, and a successor matrix which represents the subtype relationship between formal concepts.

Table 2.1. Interchange Formats for Faceted Resource Meta-information

Formal Context Interchange Format	Concept Lattice Interchange Format
TYPE $\quad T$ OBJECT $\quad O_1 \ \{ \ O_{1,1} \ O_{1,2} \ \cdots \ O_{1,o_1} \ \}$ $\quad O_2 \ \{ \ O_{2,1} \ O_{2,2} \ \cdots \ O_{2,o_2} \ \}$ $\quad \cdots$ $\quad O_n \ \{ \ O_{n,1} \ O_{n,2} \ \cdots \ O_{n,o_n} \ \}$ ATTRIBUTE $\quad A_1 \ \{ \ A_{1,1} \ A_{1,2} \ \cdots \ A_{1,a_1} \ \}$ $\quad A_2 \ \{ \ A_{2,1} \ A_{2,2} \ \cdots \ A_{2,a_2} \ \}$ $\quad \cdots$ $\quad A_m \ \{ \ A_{m,1} \ A_{m,2} \ \cdots \ A_{m,a_m} \ \}$ INCIDENCE $\quad O_1 \ \{ \ A_{1,1} \ A_{1,2} \ \cdots \ A_{1,i_1} \ \}$ $\quad O_2 \ \{ \ A_{2,1} \ A_{2,2} \ \cdots \ A_{2,i_2} \ \}$ $\quad \cdots$ $\quad O_n \ \{ \ A_{n,1} \ A_{n,2} \ \cdots \ A_{n,i_n} \ \}$	TYPE $\quad T$ GENERATOR:OBJECT $\quad C_1 \ \{ \ O_{1,1} \ O_{1,2} \ \cdots \ O_{1,o_1} \ \}$ $\quad C_2 \ \{ \ O_{2,1} \ O_{2,2} \ \cdots \ O_{2,o_2} \ \}$ $\quad \cdots$ $\quad C_p \ \{ \ O_{p,1} \ O_{p,2} \ \cdots \ O_{p,o_p} \ \}$ GENERATOR:ATTRIBUTE $\quad C_1 \ \{ \ A_{1,1} \ A_{1,2} \ \cdots \ A_{1,a_1} \ \}$ $\quad C_2 \ \{ \ A_{2,1} \ A_{2,2} \ \cdots \ A_{2,a_2} \ \}$ $\quad \cdots$ $\quad C_p \ \{ \ A_{p,1} \ A_{p,2} \ \cdots \ A_{p,a_p} \ \}$ SUCCESSOR $\quad C_1 \ \{ \ C_{1,1} \ C_{1,2} \ \cdots \ C_{1,s_1} \ \}$ $\quad C_2 \ \{ \ C_{2,1} \ C_{2,2} \ \cdots \ C_{2,s_2} \ \}$ $\quad \cdots$ $\quad C_p \ \{ \ C_{p,1} \ C_{p,2} \ \cdots \ C_{p,s_p} \ \}$

- O_i and $O_{i,o}$ are object names (strings).
- A_i and $A_{j,a}$ are attributes *tag#value*, where # is =, $\leq$, etc.
- C_k and $C_{k,s}$ are indexes (natural numbers) of formal concepts.
- x_i and y_j are coordinates (natural numbers) of formal concept nodes.

FCIF and CLIF subsume both the URCs of the IETF and the SOIFs of Harvest. The FCIF and CLIF interchange formats are more general mechanisms than either URCs or SOIFs, and allow for the specification of more complex conceptually structured systems of resources. Actually, as Figure 3 points out, both FCIF and CLIF are better thought to occur after conceptual scaling, whereas both URC and SOIF specify "raw meta-information" which exists before conceptual scaling [3].

From the philosophical viewpoint of formal concept analysis, conceptual scaling is an act of interpretation. It maps raw uninterpreted data, such as occurs in URC or SOIF, into the end-user's conceptual scheme. URC and SOIF represent database entity relations, whereas FCIF represents has-a incidence relationships between objects and attributes and CLIF represents is-a subtype relationships between formal concepts. These attributes are simple structured queries of the form tag#value, where # is any relational operator $=$, $\leq$, etc. The equality operator defines nominal scaling which models the intuitive notions of "partition" or "separateness." The inequality operator either defines ordinal scaling [3] which models the notion of "ranking" or defines interordinal scaling which models the notion of "betweenness." Through conceptual scaling we can compare FCIF and CLIF with URC and SOIF.

Fig. 2.1. Conceptual Scaling with Various Interchange Formats

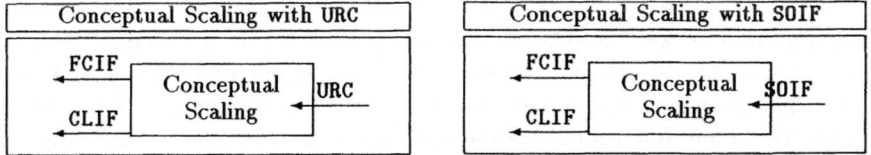

3. Conceptual Linkage

The structuring primitive for the World Wide Web is the hyperlink. The essence of a hyperlink is a (possibly typed) binary association between two objects [6]. The semantics of a hyperlink is that the two connected objects have something in common — a property or a semantic category [8]. By extending ideas from the field of formal concept analysis [1], in this chapter we offer a principled approach for elevating the notion of a hyperlink from objects to formal concepts (concepts). These new extended linkage structures, which preserve the idea that things are linked through shared attributes, are called *conceptual links*. The notion of conceptual links derived here can be compare to similar notions in hypertext systems [8], which are intuitive but not principled. The crisp notion of a conceptual link is represented here by the richer, graded notion of *conceptual linkage*. Conceptual linkage is a fuzzy relationship. It gives a measure of similarity and implication between concepts. Conceptual linkage can be reduced to conceptual links by a crispification operation. The crucial idea of conceptual linkage is derived from an extended theory of conceptual knowledge systems.

Conceptual linkage can be used as the structuring primitive for the conceptual organization of the knowledge implicit in the World Wide Web. There are important parallels between conceptual knowledge systems and hypertext systems. In particular, conceptual links are analogous to Web hyperlinks. Actually, this is more than an analogy, since objects (or their abstracted synoptic surrogates in the form of metadata objects) generate formal concepts. This impels us to make the following observations.

- *Networked resources are (formal) concepts.*
- *Conceptual linkage extends and enriches Web hyperlinks.*
- *Conceptual space customizes and makes coherent Web hyperspace.*

There are two modes for conceptual linkage: extensional and intensional. In the *extensional mode* of conceptual linkage, concepts are regarded as attributes and are represented by their extent. Any two concepts in extensional mode are linked by the objects which they share, the objects common to their extents. The more linking objects there are, the closer are those concepts and the stronger is the conceptual linkage. This closeness can be measured by the cardinality of the set of linking objects[2]. Dually, in the *intensional mode* of conceptual linkage, concepts are regarded as objects, are represented by their intent, are linked by the attributes which they share in their intents, and have closeness measured by the cardinality of the set of linking attributes. Since extensional and intensional notions are dual in lattices, here we only discuss the extensional notions.

The *extensional similarity* measure $\sigma_\bullet : \mathcal{L} \times \mathcal{L} \to \aleph = \{0, 1, \cdots\}$ is a measure of the similarity of any two concepts according to their common extent cardinality. It is the composite (meet) ∘ (extent) ∘ (cardinality), and is defined by the formulae

$$\sigma_\bullet(k_0, k_1) = \|\text{extent}\,(k_0 \wedge k_1)\| = \|\text{extent}(k_0) \cap \text{extent}(k_1)\|$$

for any two concepts k_0, k_1 in a concept lattice $\mathcal{L}$. The bounds on this measure are $0 \leq \sigma_\bullet(k_0, k_1) \leq \min\{\|\text{extent}(k_0)\|, \|\text{extent}(k_1)\|\}$. The extensional similarity between two concepts is a rough or fuzzy measure of their similarity. The closer the concepts, the larger the extensional similarity, up to a

---

[2] For any cardinality, we count only a kind of atomic concept called an irreducible concept: join irreducible for object concepts and meet irreducible for attribute concepts. In a concept lattice, an object (that is, an object concept) is *join irreducible* when it cannot be decomposed as the join of two other objects, and an attribute (attribute concept) is *meet irreducible* when it cannot be decomposed as the meet of two other attributes. For atomicity to be realizable, we assume that formal concept analysis optimization processes of purification and reduction have been carried out. Purification fuses objects which generate the same concept. With respect to this conceptual knowledge system, these objects are indiscernible and equivalent. Purification does the same for attributes. Reduction converts objects and attributes which are not irreducible into conceptual views.

maximum size of the extent cardinality of either. When this upper bound is reached, one concept is below the other in the concept lattice

$$k_0 \leq k_1 \quad \text{iff} \quad \|\text{extent}(k_0)\| = \sigma_\bullet(k_0, k_1).$$

The more dissimilar the concepts, the smaller the extensional similarity, with lower bound 0. When this bound is reached, the two concepts have nothing extensionally in common. For browsing over the conceptual space of a conceptual knowledge system, we take a state space approach where we regard concepts as conceptual states and browsing as state transition. Since extensional similarity is symmetric $\sigma_\bullet(k_0, k_1) = \sigma_\bullet(k_1, k_0)$, it does not accurately represent the notion of conceptual state and conceptual state transition, because it ignores the asymmetric nature of the current state: we are at state k_0, we are not at state k_1 (although we may want to transit there). The notion of "current state" is well represented by extensional linkage.

Extensional linkage $\lambda_\bullet : \mathcal{L} \times \mathcal{L} \to [0, 1]$, which ranges between 0 and 1, is a fuzzy measure of the implication between concepts. This asymmetric measure of linkage or implication, which is defined as the ratio of the sizes of extents

$$\lambda_\bullet(k_0, k_1) = \frac{\|\text{extent}\,(k_0 \wedge k_1)\|}{\|\text{extent}(k_0)\|} = \frac{\|\text{extent}(k_0) \cap \text{extent}(k_1)\|}{\|\text{extent}(k_0)\|} = \frac{\sigma_\bullet(k_0, k_1)}{\|\text{extent}(k_0)\|},$$

measures the implication "k_0 implies k_1". Extensional linkage can be informally interpreted as a measure of relevance: $\lambda_\bullet(k_0, -)$ measures the strength of connection, transitional strength, or relevance, from conceptual state k_0 to other conceptual states. Extensional linkage can be formally interpreted as the probability of k_1 conditioned on k_0; that is, the conditional probability $p(k_1|k_0)$. The maximum measure of linkage or implication represents a strict, full, or Boolean measure of linkage or implication "k_0 strictly implies k_1". This occurs at the concept lattice order

$$k_0 \leq k_1 \quad \text{iff} \quad \lambda_\bullet(k_0, k_1) = 1.$$

So, conceptual linkage subsumes the hierarchical linkage of the lattice order of concepts. Extensional linkage $\lambda_\bullet$ can be represented by a square matrix of real numbers in the interval $[0, 1]$, whose dimension is the cardinality of the set of formal concepts in the lattice of the conceptual knowledge system.

4. Conceptual Neighborhood

The lattice of concepts in a conceptual knowledge system is intuitively regarded as an environment or conceptual space. There are two dual senses or modes for the idea of a "local neighborhood" of a concept within its conceptual space. These two senses of neighborhood are closely bound up with the two modes of conceptual linkage. The *extensional neighborhood* $\mathcal{N}_\bullet(k)$ of a "seed" concept k regards the concept as an attribute: it fuses the intent of the concept as a collective attribute and distributes the extent downward over a local neighborhood lattice. Precisely defined, the conceptual knowledge system of the extensional neighborhood is the restriction of the global conceptual knowledge system to the extent of the concept — all objects not in the extent are ignored. In terms of conceptual structure, for any conceptual state k the local extensional neighborhood concept lattice $\mathcal{N}_\bullet(k)$ is the restriction of the global lattice $\mathcal{L}$ by means of the *meet restriction* operation $k \wedge (.)$. The meet restriction operation $k \wedge (.) : \mathcal{L} \to \mathcal{N}_\bullet(k)$ is right adjoint right inverse to a monotonic map $\mathcal{N}_\bullet(k) \to \mathcal{L}$ which embeds the extensional neighborhood lattice into the global lattice. This means that meet restriction is meet-preserving since it is right adjoint, and surjective since it is right inverse.

The size of the extensional neighborhood depends upon the universality or genericness of the seed concept. The extensional neighborhood of the top concept is very large, comprising the entire global conceptual knowledge system. The extensional neighborhood of the bottom concept is very small, having only one concept. Since the extent is usually much smaller than the entire set of objects of the global conceptual knowledge system, the concept neighborhood notion gives a drastic reduction in the size of the conceptual space. The collection of all attributes which label the "root" node (top concept) is the intent of the seed concept. At the opposite pole, any attribute which labels the bottom node is extensionally disjoint from the seed concept in the global lattice (except for any "solution objects" — objects which satisfy <u>all</u> properties). We can loosely regard the extensional neighborhood lattice line diagram to be a hierarchy labeled by the extent of k. These extensional objects are distributed over this local neighborhood lattice by means of "distinguishing attributes". By definition, these attributes are not in the intent of k. This observation forms the basis for local browsing in the extensional mode via intensional difference.

Between any two concepts k_0 and k_1 in a concept lattice $\mathcal{L}$ is the *intensional difference* $\partial^\bullet(k_0, k_1) = \text{intent}(k_1) \setminus \text{intent}(k_0)$, an asymmetric measure which records those attributes of k_1 that are not attributes of k_0. Elements in $\partial(k_0, k_1)$ are attributes which "distinguish" k_1 from k_0. The intensional difference $\partial^\bullet : \mathcal{L} \times \mathcal{L}^{\text{op}} \to \wp M = \langle \wp M, \supseteq, \cup, \emptyset \rangle$ is a generalized metric or distance function, which satisfies the zero law $\emptyset \supseteq \partial^\bullet(k, k)$ and the triangle law $\partial^\bullet(k_0, k_1) \cup \partial^\bullet(k_1, k_2) \supseteq \partial^\bullet(k_0, k_2)$. All lattice order information is contained in the intensional difference, since

$$k_1 \leq k_0 \quad \text{iff} \quad \partial^\bullet(k_0, k_1) = \emptyset.$$

The intensional difference is the basis for the idea of a dictionary definition. A word (thought of as an object concept) is defined by restricting or specializing a superordinate (more generic) concept by means of a collection of distinguishing properties: a concept k_1 is-a concept k_0 which satisfies all attributes m in the intensional difference $\partial^\bullet(k_0, k_1)$. For example, "a tree is a plant which is woody, perennial and has a main stem." Here "tree" is the concept being defined (definiendum), "plant" is the superordinate concept, and "woody", "perennial", and "main stem" are in the intensional difference. In the same fashion, in a concept lattice, we can then think of the collection of differentiating attributes as representing the difference between a defined concept and the superordinate concept.

The *intensional difference* measure $\delta^\bullet : \mathcal{L} \times \mathcal{L}^{\mathrm{op}} \to \aleph = \langle \aleph, \geq, +, 0 \rangle$ is also a generalized metric, which satisfies the zero law $0 \geq \delta^\bullet(k, k)$ and the triangle law $\delta^\bullet(k_0, k_1) + \delta^\bullet(k_1, k_2) \geq \delta^\bullet(k_0, k_2)$. It is a measure of the difference between any two concepts according to their intensional difference cardinality. The intensional difference measure is defined by the formulae

$$\delta^\bullet(k_0, k_1) = \|\partial^\bullet(k_0, k_1)\| = \|\mathrm{intent}(k_1) \setminus \mathrm{intent}(k_0)\|$$

for any two concepts k_0, k_1 in a concept lattice $\mathcal{L}$. Again, all lattice order information is contained in the intensional difference measure, since

$$k_1 \leq k_0 \quad \text{iff} \quad \delta^\bullet(k_0, k_1) = 0.$$

The minimum measure 0 occurs when concept k_1 is at or below concept k_0 in the main lattice. This occurs when no attribute distinguishes concept k_1 from concept k_0, although there might be an attribute which distinguishes concept k_0 from concept k_1. The intensional difference measure counts the number of distinct distinguishing attributes. It measures how distinguished k_1 is from k_0.

A *ranked order* $\langle \mathcal{X}, \rho \rangle$ consists of a partially ordered set $\mathcal{X} = \langle X, \leq \rangle$ and an monotonic map $\rho : \mathcal{X} \to \aleph = \{0, 1, \cdots\}$ to the natural numbers called a *ranking*. Ranked sets can be displayed by inverse image $\rho^{-1}(n) = \{x \in X \mid \rho(x) = n\}$, either directly $\left(\rho^{-1}(0), \rho^{-1}(1), \cdots, \rho^{-1}(\max) \right)$ or in reverse order $\left(\rho^{-1}(\max), \rho^{-1}(\max-1), \cdots, \rho^{-1}(0) \right)$. Ranked orders are used here as reduced representations for concept lattices. They are most useful for browsing via the local conceptual neighborhoods, in either the extensional mode where we browse over the views and attributes of the global lattice, or the intensional mode where we browse over the views and objects. Table 4.1 displays the extensional mode rankings for the conceptual view "Plan1". The upper panel displays the extensional similarity ranking at conceptual state "Plan1", a reduced representation for the global document conceptual space displayed in Table 1.2. Here concepts "Document" and "Object" have merged in the ranking with concept "Plan1", whereas the opposite ranking pole shows that concept "Plan2" is extensionally disjoint from concept "Plan1". This ranking displays all of the irreducible conceptual views and attribute concepts in the document universe $\mathcal{D}$. The lower panel displays the intensional difference ranking of concept "Plan1", a reduced representation for the local document neighborhood of "Plan1". This ranking displays only the extent of concept "Plan1".

Conceptual browsing is browsing over conceptual linkage. It is dual mode (both extensional and intensional) and dual scope (both global and local). Extensional and intensional mode are temporally disjoint, whereas global scope is antecedent to local scope both logically and temporally: choose a mode; first browse globally in that mode and then browse locally in the same

Table 4.1. Extensional Mode Rankings for the Conceptual View "Plan1"

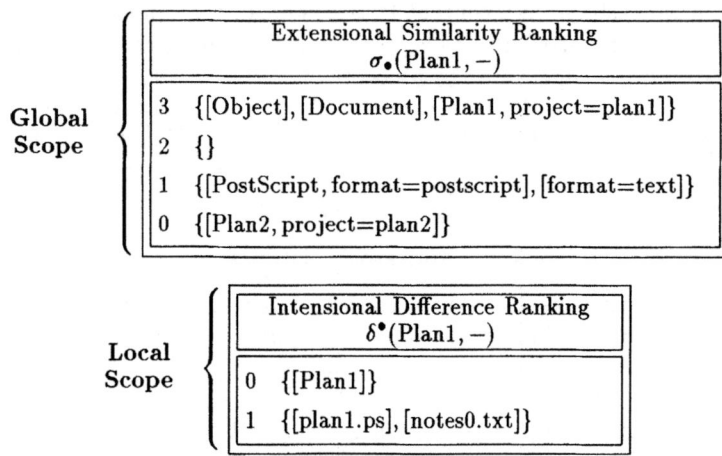

mode. Theoretically, conceptual browsing ranges over all concepts, with concepts being represented by internal indexes. Practically, conceptual browsing ranges only over named concepts: objects, attributes, and conceptual views. In extensional mode we browse over concepts by restriction to their extents. In intensional mode we do just the lattice dual — we browse over concepts by restriction to their intents. Browsing in the global scope means browsing over the global concept lattice, whereas browsing in a local scope means browsing over a local neighborhood concept lattice. Conceptual browsing is summarized in Table 4.2.

If a concept lattice is regarded as a form of database structure, then conceptual browsing can be used for database access, as in information retrieval [8]. In this approach conceptual linkage is used for processing queries. A query in intensional mode involves only the attributes of the formal context under consideration. By definition, an *intensional query* is a subset of attributes. It can be identified with a new temporary "goal query" object which has been added to the formal context. The goal query object is regarded as the current conceptual state for browsing in intensional mode. Then, intensional linkage ranking is a vector of similarity coefficients, each coefficient measuring the closeness of a concept to the goal query. Either conceptual views and objects can be display as a ranking, or those conceptual views and objects can be returned whose similarity coefficient is above a given threshold. By duality, an *extensional query* is a subset of objects. The query is identified with a new temporary "goal query" attribute, which is regarded to be the current conceptual state for browsing in extensional mode. The objects in the query are regarded as prototypes. Extensional queries correspond to a prototype representation for categories (formal concepts). Issuing an extensional query results in returning similarity measures between formal concepts and the collective prototype of the query's objects.

5. Conceptualization Processes

The intuitive idea behind hypertext is "semantic connection" [6]. Currently, hyperlink creation is done manually at document creation time [8]. There are two problems with this manual approach:

- The document creator (writer, publisher) may inadvertantly omit some important and meaningful semantic connections.
- Legacy data (pre-HTML documents) needs enormous manual effort to convert to hypertextual form.

Figure 5.1 gives a high-level description of processes involved in the conceptual organization and representation of the information in legacy databases. The interpretation process [15] is a composite of summarization followed by conceptual scaling [3, 13],

$$(\text{interpretation}) = (\text{summarization}) \circ (\text{conceptual scaling})$$

Summarization is the abstraction and construction of metadata objects from actual data. The gathering component of the Harvest system [14] is a good example of summarization. Conceptual scaling, also called relational data filtration, is a user-oriented process for customizing and building a faceted representation of information based upon user interest profiles, etc. Here a user may refer to either a single individual, a small group of individuals, or even a whole community. Conceptual scaling uses type-structured standing queries, known as conceptual scales [3], alerts, continuous queries, or SDI (selective dissemination of information) [2].

Fig. 5.1. Conceptual Interpretation and Database Hyperization

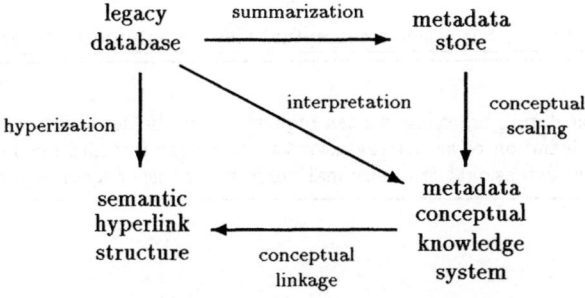

Table 4.2. The Process of Conceptual Neighborhood Browsing

Extensional Mode
Current Concept: k

Global Scope: Display the extensional similarity ranking

$$\sigma_\bullet(k, -) = \|\text{extent}(k) \cap \text{extent}(-)\|$$

for global lattice $\mathcal{L}$. Selection of a concept from this display to be
the next conceptual state will continue extensional mode browsing.

Local Scope: Display the intensional difference ranking

$$\delta^\bullet(k, -) = \text{intent}(-) \setminus \text{intent}(k)$$

for local lattice $\mathcal{N}_\bullet(k)$. Selection of a concept from this display to be
the next conceptual state will switch to intensional mode browsing.

In this mode k is either a conceptual view or an attribute concept.

Intensional Mode
Current Concept: k

Global Scope: Display the intensional similarity ranking

$$\sigma^\bullet(k, -) = \|\text{intent}(k) \cap \text{intent}(-)\|$$

for global lattice $\mathcal{L}$. Selection of a concept from this display to be
the next conceptual state will continue intensional mode browsing.

Local Scope: Display the extensional difference ranking

$$\delta_\bullet(k, -) = \text{extent}(-) \setminus \text{extent}(k)$$

for local lattice $\mathcal{N}^\bullet(k)$. Selection of a concept from this display to be
the next conceptual state will switch to extensional mode browsing.

In this mode k is either a conceptual view or an object concept.

At any time during browsing, we can request either the definition of a conceptual
view, the definition of an attribute, or the summary information for an object.
In either the extensional or intensional mode we can issue a corresponding query.

The hyperization process is a process of automatic web archiving. As such, it answers the concerns expressed above about manual web creation. Actually, hyperization could represent either the batch process of web archiving or the interactive process of web guidance during client browsing. Hyperization is a composite of interpretation followed by conceptual linkage, (hyperization) = (interpretation) ∘ (conceptual linkage). As depicted in Figure 5.1, conceptual linkage involves the automatic creation of *crisp* web hyperlink structure by a reduction process of crispification. There is, however, information loss in just the creation of crisp web hyperlinks. In this sense, it is better to remain at the higher level of the conceptual knowledge system, rather than reducing to web hyperlink structure. At the higher level of the conceptual knowledge system, conceptual linkage richly expresses conceptual structure and semantic content.

Figure 5.2 describes the equivalence between the hyperlink structure of the Web and its representation as a conceptual knowledge system. In the application of the conceptual knowledge system model to Web hyperlinkage, both objects and attributes are Web objects (HTML documents, images, etc.). There are two dual interpretations for hyperlink incidence: (cross-referential) one Web object has a second Web object as an attribute when the first points to the second; and (hierarchical, such as gopher-space) the opposite incidence [6, 8]. The equivalence in Figure 5.2 between web and conceptual knowledge system is mediated through the inverse passages of concept generation and incidence readout: (generation) ∘ (readout) ≡ (identity) and (readout) ∘ (generation) ≡ (identity). These inverse passages comprise the standard process diagram from formal concept analysis, here applied to the incidence relationships of Web hyperlinks. The process of concept generation results in a conceptual representation for Web hyperlinkage.

Fig. 5.2. Conceptual Structuring of Hypertext Incidence

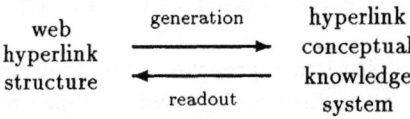

The information in the Web can be split into two distinct aspects: hyperlinkage and document content [6, 8]. Distinct processes applied to these two aspects generate distinct conceptual representatons. The semantic constraint between hyperlinkage and document content can be applied later during the process of conceptual scaling and data filtration. Substitution of the non-linked content of a web for the legacy database component in Figure 5.1 describes a process for the conceptual representation of Web content. In Figure 5.3 we describe an enriched process which combines the hyperlink conceptual representation of Figure 5.2 with the metadata conceptual representation of Figure 5.1. This enriched combining process uses a standard combinator from formal concept analysis called apposition. At the incidence matrix level of a conceptual knowledge system, apposition is a summing process, whereas at the concept lattice level it is a constrained producing process. The same comments that we made above about crisp conceptual linking are true here also: it is better to do conceptual linkage at the enriched conceptual knowledge system level — here there is a richer conceptual expression with no loss of information.

Fig. 5.3. Enriched Web Construction

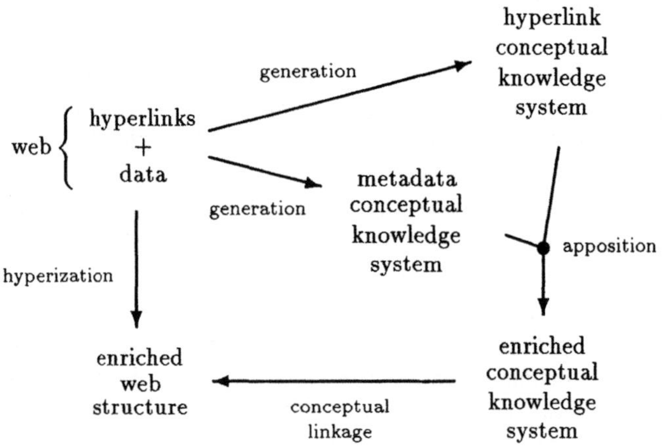

6. Summary, Implementation, and Future Work

This chapter has discussed two approaches for making use of automatic classification techniques: web archive construction and user navigational guidance (conceptual browsing). Automatic classification provides the foundation for the automatic generation of local web hypertextual structure based upon summarized and conceptually scaled information about objects. Manual specification of conceptual connectivity, such as for ordinary hyperlinks and conceptual views, can automatically be incorporated. Automatic classification also provides the foundation for guidance and analysis during user browsing and concept link traversal via the World Wide Web over any community's information space. In summary, formal concept analysis is a principled foundation for classification, organization, and indexing in NIDR systems. By using ideas from formal concept analysis, Web hyperlinks can be elaborated into Web conceptual links, and Web hyperspace can be coherently organized as Web conceptual space.

By the time of publication, many of the ideas discussed in this chapter will have been implemented in the NIDR system called WAVE which was mentioned above. These ideas include formal contexts, concept lattices, conceptual knowledge systems, conceptual optimization, conceptual linkage, and conceptual browsing. Development of the WAVE system will provide a preliminary answer to the research question: "What is the appropriate architecture for a digital library?" It will be demonstrated in the distributed context of the World Wide Web, by using both the technique of automatic classification and the notion of a conceptual knowledge system, that the WAVE system provides the kernel architecture for a digital library. A critical measure of success for the WAVE system will be the ability to *understand* a user's intentions. The understanding of intentions is a deep research question, and as Dennis Reinhardt has pointed out to the first author (private communication), machine understanding will not surpass human capability in this area during the course of this research. However, the WAVE system could augment human understanding with the ability to *express* a user's intentions. This sense of "understanding" a user's intentions will be a critical factor in the success of the WAVE system. Other measures, such as how customizable, how adaptable, or how flexible the system is for the user, are subordinate strategies which will aid the ability to express the user's intentions.

Both ongoing and future work can be discussed in terms of three processes for the conceptualization of networked information resources, as diagrammed in Figure 5.1: summarization, conceptual scaling, and conceptual linkage. The first process, summarization, has been implemented as the front component of a NIDR system, where meta-information is extracted. An important example of a summarization processor is the gatherer component of the Harvest system. The third process, conceptual linkage, is now being implemented as the first phase (funded) of the WAVE system development. This phase will replace the broker indexing component of the Harvest system, extending broker capabilities by adding dynamic and customizable knowledge organization techniques. In this phase the WAVE conceptual interface will be used for interactive information analysis and browsing guidance during exploratory search by client Web browsers over a community's information space. The second process, conceptual scaling, will be implemented next year as the second phase of WAVE system development. This phase will represent the process of faceted analysis which occurs in library science classification. It also corresponds to the design of user interest profiles in current awareness services [2].

References

1. Wille, R.: Restructuring Lattice Theory: An Approach Based on Hierarchies of Concepts. Ordered Sets, I. Rival (ed.), Reidel, Dordrecht-Boston (1982) 445–470
2. Rowley, J.: Organising Knowledge: An Introduction to Information Retrieval. Gower, Aldershot, Hants, England (1987)
3. Ganter, B., Wille, R.: Conceptual Scaling. Applications of Combinatorics and Graph Theory in the Biological and Social Sciences, Springer, New York (1989), F. Roberts (ed.), 139–167
4. Wille, R.: Concept Lattices and Conceptual Knowledge Systems. Computers and Mathematics with Applications, vol. 23, 493–522 (1992)
5. Wynar, B., Taylor, A.: Introduction to Cataloging and Classification, 8th ed. Libraries Unlimited, Englewood, Colorado (1992)
6. Berners-Lee, T., Cailliau R., Groff J., Pollerman, B.: World-Wide Web: The Information Universe. CERN, Geneva, Swizerland, (1992)
7. Kent, R.E.: Rough Concept Analysis. International Workshop on Rough Sets and Knowledge Discovery (RSKD'93), Banff, Alberta, Canada, October, 1993. Fundamenta Informaticae, vol. 27, 169–181 (August 1996)
8. Wilson, E.: Hypertext Libraries: The Automatic Production of Hypertext Documents. Research in Humanities Computing, S. Hockey and N. Ide (eds.), 232-246 (1994)
9. Deutsch, P., Emtage, A.: Publishing Information on the Internet with Anonymous FTP. Bunyip Information Systems Inc., (May 1994)
10. Bowman, M., Dharap, C., Baruah, M., Camargo, B., Potti, S.: A File System for Information Management. Proceedings of the Conference on Intelligent Information Management Systems, (June 1994)
11. Bowman, M., Danzig, P., Hardy, D., Manber, U., Schwartz, M.: Harvest: A Scalable, Customizable Discovery and Access System. technical report CU-CS-732-94, University of Colorado, (July 1994)
12. Mealling, M.: Encoding and Use of Uniform Resource Characteristics. Internet Engineering Task Force (IETF), Internet draft document draft-ietf-uri-urc-spec-00.txt, (July 1994)
13. Kent, R.E., Neuss, C.: Creating a 3D Web Analysis and Visualization Environment. Proceedings of the Second International World Wide Web Conference (WWWF'94), Mosaic and the Web, (October 1994) Computer Networks and ISDN Systems, vol. 28, 109–117 (1995) http://www.ncsa.uiuc.edu/SDG/IT94/Proceedings/Autools/kent/kent.html
14. Bowman, M., Danzig, P., Hardy, D., Manber, U., Schwartz, M.: The Harvest Information Discovery and Access System. Proceedings of the Second International World Wide Web Conference (WWWF'94), Mosaic and the Web, (October 1994)
15. Kent, R.E.: Enriched Interpretation. Proceedings of the Third International Workshop on Rough Sets and Soft Computing (RSSC'94), (November 1994)
16. Winograd, T.: Mail message in the URI Mail Archives. Discussion thread entitled "Library Standards and URIs," (January 1995) http://www.acl.lanl.gov/URI/archive/uri-95q1.messages/0023.html
17. Kent, R.E.: WHO I AM. Mail message in the Conference Discussion List Archive for the OCLC/NCSA Metadata Workshop: The Essential Elements of Network Object Description, (March 1995) http://union.ncsa.uiuc.edu/www/metadata-workshop/0009.html

18. Neuss, C., Kent, R.E.: Conceptual Analysis of Resource Meta-information. Proceedings of the Third International World Wide Web Conference (WWW'95), Computer Networks and ISDN Systems, vol. 27, 973–984 (April 1995) http://www.igd.fhg.de/www/www95/papers/94/www3.html

19. Kent, R.E., Bowman, M.: Digital Libraries, Conceptual Knowledge Systems, and the Nebula Interface. White paper, Transarc Corporation, Pittsburgh (April 1995)
    http://www.transarc.com/afs/transarc.com/public/trg/papers/techrep0495.ps

20. Kent, R.E., Neuss, C.: Web Conceptual Space. WebNet 96 - World Conference of the Web Society Proceedings, 255–260 (October 1996) http://wave.eecs.wsu.edu/WAVE/WebNet96.doc

Two–Level Models of Hypertext

James Mayfield

The Johns Hopkins University Applied Physics Laboratory
Johns Hopkins Road
Laurel MD 20723–6099 USA
James.Mayfield@jhuapl.edu

Summary. A two–level model of hypertext is one in which a set of texts is augmented with an ancillary structure that captures some aspect of the meaning of those texts. Links between texts are routed through the ancillary structure. This chapter surveys the wide range of two–level hypertext models that have been developed in the past few years. Declarative ancillary structures have included semantic nets, Petri nets, Bayesian nets, and clustering schemes. Procedural ancillary structures have been used to identify new links dynamically, and to create large sets of static links. Advantages of two–level models include greater link expressiveness, increased user control over the appearance and semantics of links, decreased hypertext construction costs, and improved robustness in the face of changing and ill–formed texts.

1. Introduction

Recent years have shown a significant increase in interest in models of hypertext that go beyond the explicit hard–wired links found in traditional hypertext models. In these new models, text is augmented with a secondary structure through which all links are routed. This chapter aims to give a broad introduction to these two–level models by examining the general properties of all such models, and by examining particular two–level models in detail.

In this Introduction, I place two–level models in historical perspective by describing the traditional conceptions underlying hypertext and pointing out problems that arise out of reliance on these traditional conceptions. In Section 2, I discuss hypertext models whose secondary structure is declarative in nature. Section 3 explores two–level models in which a process is initiated to traverse a hypertext link. I conclude with some observations on the applicability of two–level models to a variety of new directions in hypertext.

1.1 Traditional Hypertext

The hypertext literature is fraught with conflicting terminology, and even conflict about what does or does not constitute hypertext. While the distinction between hypertext, hypermedia, and multimedia systems has blurred in recent years, for the purposes of this chapter **hypertext** will refer to *text* that has been augmented with connections from one piece of text to another.

Such connections will be called **hyperlinks**, or **links** for short. The text connected by links is often divided into small pieces, which will be called **nodes** throughout this chapter. The origin (and on occasion the destination) of a link is often a small sequence of words in the source node called an **anchor**.

Hypertext usually implies a graphical user interface that allows point–and–click link traversal. This association between the user interface and the underlying hypertext structures is so strong that users often fail to distinguish between the two. For the purposes of this chapter though, I will ignore interface issues; the focus here is on the structures underlying hypertext. In particular, I will focus on the structure and properties of hyperlinks, because it is in links that the major impact of two–level architectures is seen.

The most obvious property of a link that might be influenced by a two–level architecture is its type. Many influential hypertext systems have provided link types. These range from systems that provide very few types (*e.g.* the World Wide Web [60], the KMS system [1] and the HDM paradigm [23]) to systems that provide a wide range of link types (*e.g.* the GIBIS [14] system and the TEXTNET system [55]). Systems with a small number of types often allow the source anchor to provide additional information about a link. For example, KMS has only two link types, but allows an anchor to express the semantics of the link to which it is attached. KMS also allows information about a link to be expressed in the mouse cursor that appears when the mouse is moved over an anchor.

1.2 Problems with Hypertext Links

A distinguishing feature of traditional hypertext systems is the static nature of their hyperlinks. Static links are *direct* connections from one node or anchor to another. Dynamic links on the other hand are computed each time an attempt is made to traverse them. DeRose calls these two types of links *extensional links* and *intensional links* respectively in his taxonomy of links [17]. Figure 1.1 depicts static links in this traditional model.

The static links found in most traditional hypertext systems suffer from a variety of problems. These include:

- *Stale links.* When a link points to a node that is subsequently moved or deleted, that link becomes stale; attempts to traverse it will fail. This is not much of a problem for traditional single–author, limited domain hypertexts, because the entire hypertext is typically static. However, as distributed hypertexts lacking clear authorship are developed, stale links are becoming a major problem (witness the number of dangling pointers in the typical WWW document).
- *Inexpressiveness.* Some conventional system lack link semantics. Even in systems that do provide typed links, if the number of link types is set *a priori*, then the information content that can be attached to a link is restricted to the defined set.

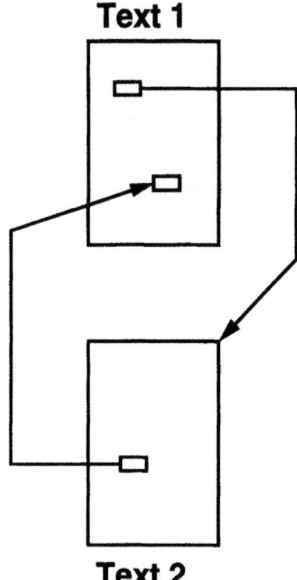

Fig. 1.1. In the traditional hypertext model, links are direct connections from one node or anchor to another.

- *Expensive construction.* Although hand–construction of links can provide high–quality connections between nodes (and is in fact for some an essential component of hypertext), it is nonetheless time–consuming and expensive.
- *Inflexibility.* In traditional hypertext, links are created once, and are thereafter fixed; they are unable to rearrange themselves to suit the needs of the moment.
- *Duplication.* The traditional approach leads to a proliferation of links that serve similar purposes. The semantic knowledge implicit in a particular link or link type cannot easily be reused or generalized.

Many of the two–level hypertext models described in this chapter were developed in response to one or more of these problems.

1.3 Two–Level Models of Hypertext

The main technique underlying two–level models of hypertext is borrowed from software engineering: an abstraction barrier is placed between the user's view of a link and the underlying representation of the link. The abstraction is accomplished by adding a layer of representation between the source of the link and its destination, as shown in Figure 1.2. This layer can be declarative (*e.g.* a semantic net) or procedural (*e.g.* a WAIS search). I will call this second layer an **ancillary** layer throughout the remainder of this chapter.

While I have made every attempt to present a comprehensive overview of two–level hypertext models in this chapter, I do not claim the coverage

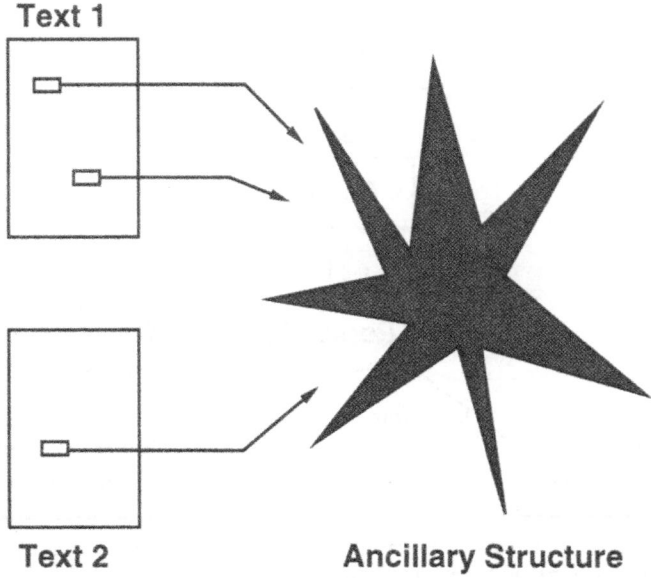

Fig. 1.2. In a two–level model of hypertext, text is augmented with an ancillary structure, through which links are routed.

presented here to be complete. The reason is that the range of systems that can be construed as 'hypertext systems' is large, and most of those systems can legitimately be placed under the two–level procedural model rubric. By this same reasoning, there is no hard and fast distinction between declarative and procedural two–level models; any so–called 'declarative model' must use some sort of process to traverse its ancillary data structure. The difference between the two types of model then is one of degree; in declarative two–level models the ancillary data structure is the focus of the model, while in procedural two–level models the process that resolves hypertext links is the focus.

2. Declarative Two–Level Models

A declarative two–level model of hypertext is one that augments a set of texts with a knowledge representation structure that captures some aspect of the meaning of the hypertext. A variety of ancillary structures have been used for this purpose; they are described in the following subsections.

2.1 Semantic Net–Based Models

A **semantic net** is a graph whose vertices correspond to concepts (*e.g.* "person" or "boomerang"), and whose edges correspond to relationships between

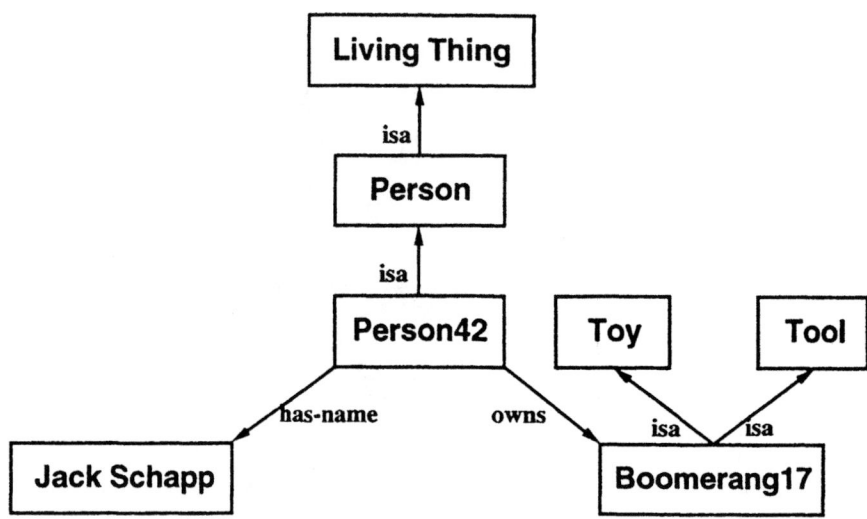

Fig. 2.1. A *semantic net* is a graph in which vertices denote concepts and edges denote relationships between those concepts.

those concepts (*e.g.* "owns"). Most semantic net formalisms support inheritance as well as a variety of other automatic inference processes. Semantic nets are used to represent knowledge about the world and to express the meaning of phrases and sentences of languages such as English. Semantic nets have been studied for over twenty–five years, and a wide variety of semantic net formalisms has consequently been developed [40, 47, 48, 49, 8, 59]. Figure 2.1 shows a small portion of a generic semantic net.

Many authors have noted the analogy between hypertext and semantic nets, suggesting that the techniques developed for semantic nets are also applicable to hypertext. The reason that this observation is so readily made is that both semantic nets and hypertext are at their core graphs. Rada [41] distinguishes two ways that a semantic net can be used in a hypertext:

> The semantic net of hypertext may be *independent* or *embedded*. In the 'independent' case the nodes and links are tagged with terms. The nodes or links point to text blocks, but the semantic net can be seen without necessarily seeing the text blocks. In the 'embedded' case a text block is at the end of a link. In traversing an embedded semantic net hypertext, the user has to visit a text block. [p. 127]

In Rada's terminology then, the semantic net of a two–level model is typically an *independent* net. Thus, two–level hypertext models based on semantic nets use their semantic net not as a view of the static hypertext graph, but rather as an addition to or replacement for that graph.

Large–Grained Models. One way to use a semantic net as an ancillary structure is to attach entire nodes to vertices or edges in the semantic net.

Rada and Wang [41, 58] for example describe how a semantic net can be used to classify portions of text in a document, making it easier to select relevant sub–documents for reuse in other documents. They build a semantic net representing the domain of discourse. Each paragraph of the hyperdocument is then placed on the edge of the semantic net that best expresses the meaning of that paragraph. New documents can be extracted from such a hypertext by performing a traversal (usually a depth–first traversal) of the semantic net. By choosing different starting vertices, and by eliminating undesired vertices and edges from consideration, the user can create documents for a wide range of purposes from a single hypertext.

Another good example of a hypertext system that uses a large–grained independent semantic net as its conceptual model is THOTH–II [13]. THOTH–II models a domain of discourse using a semantic net, then attaches each paragraph of text to a node in the semantic net. Thus, as with Rada and Wang's system, THOTH–II operates at a fairly coarse level of granularity. THOTH–II does allow links from semantic net nodes to particular fixed phrases in the text. These links are syntactic in nature though, because they connect a semantic net node to every location that matches a given string exactly.

Kheirbek [29] uses **Conceptual Graphs** [49] as ancillary structures to alleviate reader disorientation. A Conceptual Graph (CG) is a type of semantic net that has achieved considerable popularity in recent years. Instead of using individual vertices of the semantic net to represent concepts, this approach uses small discrete graphs called *Minimal Canonical Graphs* to represent the concepts of interest. Nodes or (more commonly) aggregates of nodes in the corpus are attached to the Minimal Canonical Graphs that represent their meaning. Under normal operation, the reader uses simple static links to navigate the hypertext. However, the reader also has the option to approach the hypertext through the semantic net if he or she becomes disoriented.

Fine–Grained Models. In contrast to the large–grained use of semantic nets in the above approaches in which entire nodes are associated with vertices or edges of the semantic net, the SNITCH system [32] uses a fine–grained semantic net. In SNITCH, individual words and phrases in a text are connected to semantic net vertices that capture their meaning. Each hypertext link in the SNITCH model comprises a connection from a text node to the semantic net, a path through the hierarchical and relation edges of the semantic net, and an edge from the semantic net back to another text node. Of course, not every such path represents a desirable hypertext link. Therefore, hypertext links are required to conform to particular path shapes. For example, any path that starts from a text anchor, follows a connection to the semantic net, follows an arbitrary number of SUBPART edges within the semantic net, and finally traverses another connection to return to a different anchor in the corpus will be a useful path. Hypertext links of that shape will represent connections to subparts of the objects described by their starting anchors.

Hu and Kirstein [27] also use a fine–grained semantic net as their ancillary structure. They focus on connectionist properties of the net to tailor the hypertext to individual users. Each semantic net vertex is assigned an activation level, while each edge is assigned a weight. Weights are then modified to reflect node popularity patterns as the system is used. Vertex activation levels are adjusted in response to the changing weights. When the user selects a link with several possible destinations, these activation levels are used to rank the alternatives.

2.2 Other Net–Based Models

Semantic nets are not the only useful net structure to be selected as the ancillary level of a two–level hypertext model; Petri nets and Bayesian nets have also been used in this capacity.

Petri Nets. A **Petri net** [39, 42] is a directed graph on which a process model has been defined. Figure 2.2 shows an example of a Petri net. Circular vertices, called **places**, are locations that may hold one or more **tokens**. Rectangular vertices are called **transitions**. When every place that has an edge to a particular transition contains a token, that transition is said to be **enabled**. When a transition is enabled, it can be **fired**; firing consists of removing one token from each place that has an edge to the transition, and placing a token in each place that has an edge from the transition. Execution of a Petri net is simply the repeated firing of transitions until no transition is enabled.

Stotts and Furuta [50, 20] show how a Petri net can be used for access control over the various paths through a hypertext. In their model, which is called TRELLIS, a Petri net is used to augment a hypertext with browsing semantics. For example, the hypertext author can use the Petri net to prevent the reader from accessing a particular node until all of its prerequisite nodes have been perused.

This basic Petri net mechanism can be used to provide a number of novel hypertext features. For example, TRELLIS' timing mechanism, which controls the duration of display of components of the hypertext, can be used to effect an apparent modification of a hypertext over time and for different readers [51]. This can be accomplished while leaving the underlying hypertext unchanged by manipulating the minimum and maximum duration of TRELLIS events. For example, a button in Trellis is simply an anchor that can be selected to traverse a hypertext link. The appearance of such a button is an event that can be controlled by Petri net transitions. By setting the maximum duration of a button appearance transition to zero, that button is effectively deleted from the reader's view of the hypertext.

Bayesian Nets. A **Bayesian net** [11] is a directed acyclic graph whose vertices represent random variables and whose edges represent (roughly) relationships between those variables for which known conditional probabilities

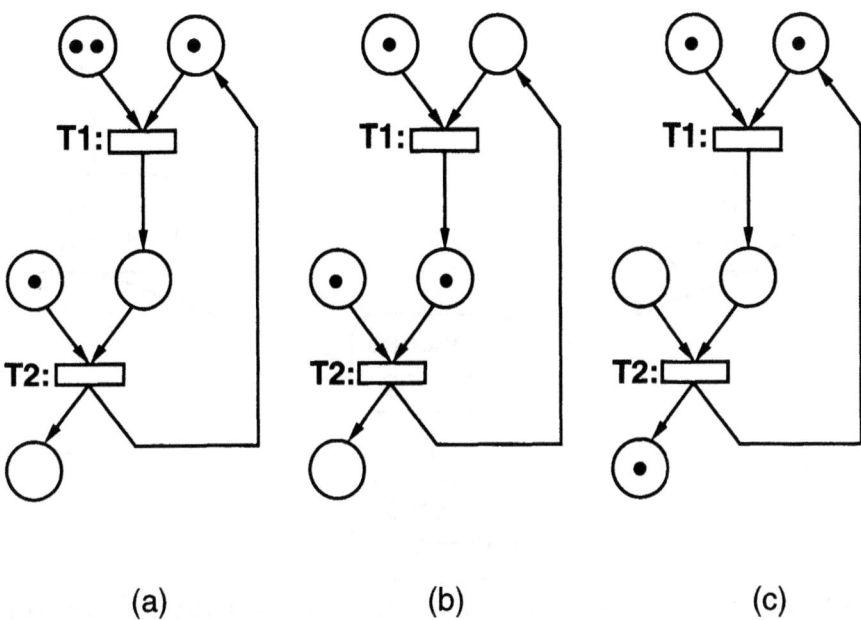

(a)   (b)   (c)

Fig. 2.2. In a *Petri net*, each *place* (represented by a circle) can hold zero or more *tokens* (represented by dots). A *transition* (represented by a rectangle) is enabled when every place that has an edge leading to that transition contains a token. In (a), transition T1 is enabled, while transition T2 is not. Any enabled transition can be *fired* by removing one token from each incoming place, and adding one token to each outgoing place. (b) shows the result after transition T1 has fired. Transition T2 is now enabled; (c) shows the result of its firing.

exist. Informally, the vertices can be thought of as states of the world, and the edges can be thought of as causality. For example, Figure 2.3 depicts a Bayesian net (without probabilities) that captures the relationships between the events of acorns falling from an oak tree, the branches of that oak tree moving, squirrels running on the branches, wind blowing, and the arrival of a storm front. A Bayesian net is used to determine the conditional probabilities of all of the variables (or states of the world) in the network, given that some of those variables (or states of the world) have been observed. To use a Bayesian net in this way, one must know the prior probability of each top–level node (squirrels running and storm coming in this example) as well as the conditional probability of each internal node for every combination of that node's predecessors. Given these probabilities, the Bayesian net in Figure 2.3 allows one to determine the probability that a storm front is nearing given the observation of a falling acorn.

Croft and Turtle [6] suggest the use of a Bayesian net for hypertext. In their model, a Bayesian net is used to associate index terms (*e.g.* words that might appear in hypertext nodes) with the concepts that those nodes might discuss. An edge from a vertex representing a concept to a vertex representing

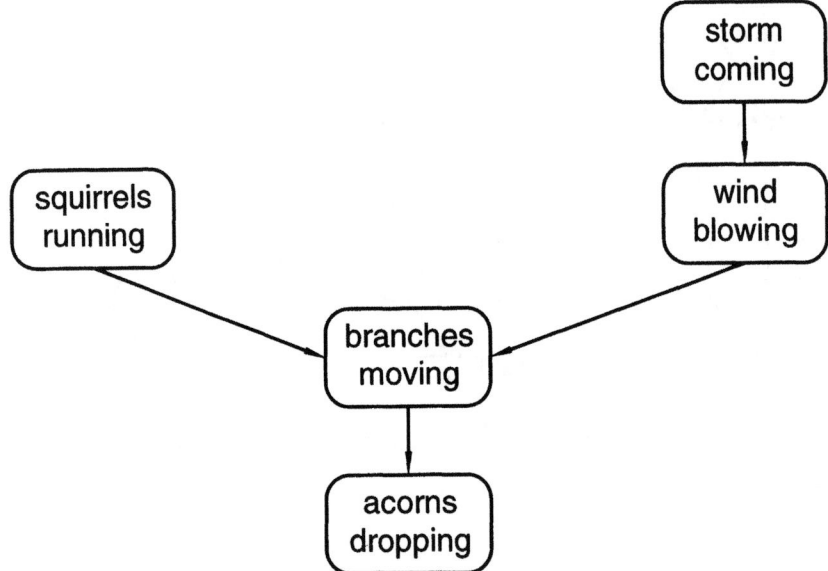

Fig. 2.3. A Bayesian net can be thought of as representing probabilities associated with causal relations. This Bayesian net causally relates five different events; prior and conditional probabilities (which form a key component of every Bayesian net) are not shown.

an index term represents the conditional probability that a hypertext node refers to that concept given that the node contains the index term. A query in this model is a conjunction of propositions that a hypertext node contains particular terms; the output is a list of probabilities (one for each document) that the query is satisfied given that the document in question has the desired content.

Frisse and Cousins [18, 13] implement a hypertext system based on a Bayesian net index in their DYNAMIC MEDICAL HANDBOOK system. In this system, the Bayesian net represents a hierarchical organization of terms that might be found in the nodes of the hypertext. The conditional probabilities of the net, which initially represent even probabilities, can be modified based on reader feedback. The resulting Bayesian net is tailored to the user's interests.

Bayesian nets also form the basis for Savoy and Desbois' two–level model [46]. Their model uses a Bayesian net to represent relationships between the nodes of the hypertext. A user of their system chooses terms of interest in the currently selected node. The system uses these terms as hints about how to update the Bayesian net. The updated net is then used to retrieve relevant documents. Thus, the hypertext reader is able to manipulate the link structure of the hypertext through modifications to the ancillary structure. The adaptive behavior displayed by the DYNAMIC MEDICAL HANDBOOK and by the Savoy and Desbois systems is especially advantageous in highly–interconnected, multi–author hypertexts.

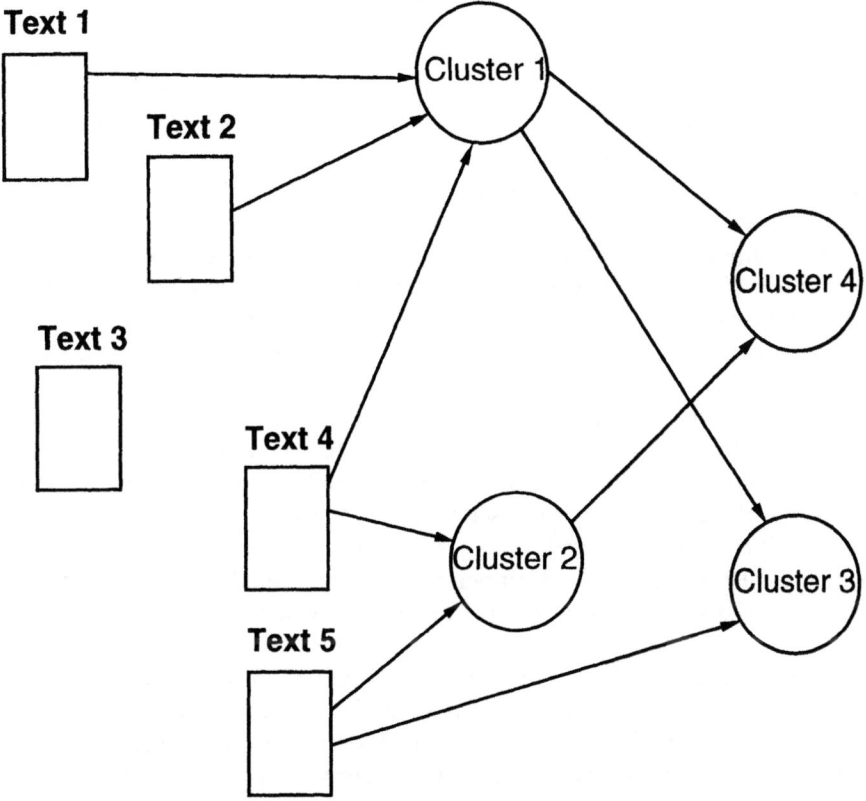

Fig. 2.4. In a *clustering model*, groups of nodes are aggregated to form supernodes, called *clusters*. Clusters may themselves be aggregated to form higher–level clusters.

2.3 Clustering Models

A variety of hypertext models augment the set of nodes with clustering information—information about which nodes are closely related to one another in a given context. These clustering models differ from the above two–level models in that the secondary structure they use is not a formalized representation model that one might study in its own right. Nonetheless, these models do contribute significant power to the hypertext system. Figure 2.4 depicts a generic clustering model.

Clusters as Secondary Structures. Casanova *et al.* [9] define a formal model for augmenting a hypertext with clustering information. Their model, which they call the *nested context model*, augments a hypertext with *context nodes*; these nodes are used to group sets of nodes, including other context nodes. Context nodes can be nested to any depth. The nested context model also includes formal models for presentation of and navigation through the augmented hypertext. The model is effectively a reference model; no implementation is discussed.

More than one type of cluster might prove valuable in a hypertext system. For example, Thüring *et al.* [52] augment hypertext with three types of organizational nodes: *structure nodes*, which are basic composites of other nodes without traversal restrictions; *sequencing nodes*, which allow the author to specify a particular node traversal sequence; and *exploration nodes*, which aggregate a set of nodes for arbitrary traversal, but which restrict entry and exit to a single access point.

One important use of clustering information is to provide pictorial representations of a user's location within a hypertext. Such graphical interfaces have been explored by a variety of researchers. Trigg [54] for example allows the hypertext author to create *guided tours*, which are graphs of paths through the hypertext which are displayed for reader perusal. In a more automated approach, Utting and Yankelovich [56] provide automatic generation of both global and local maps in the WEB VIEW system. Gloor [24] introduces the idea of a *CYBERMAP*, which is a small map of the hypertext that is constantly displayed as the user traverses the hypertext. To control the complexity of the map, nodes are partitioned into groups of related nodes called *HYPERDRAWERs*. Maintenance of a user model is cited as being crucial to the selection of a set of HYPERDRAWERs that are useful to the user.

The CANTO hypertext data model [33] augments a hypertext with 'concept nodes,' which contain key phrases for the identification of the content of the hypertext nodes. These concept nodes serve to cluster content nodes along taxonomic lines. This use of clusters is shown to increase the speed with which users can find information of interest, while correspondingly decreasing user disorientation and frustration.

Clustering Algorithms. The systems described above show how clustering information can be used to augment the power of a hypertext system. To be practical though, such clustering information must be derived automatically. Botafogo and Shneiderman [7] present algorithms for clustering the nodes of a hypertext. They are interested in finding aggregates of closely related nodes. A *compactness* metric, a function of the average distance between two nodes in the hypertext, is used as the basis for their algorithms' determinations; the lower the average distance, the higher the compactness. A *semantic cluster* of a hypertext is defined to be a subgraph of the hypertext with a higher compactness than that of the entire hypertext. Two algorithms are presented for organizing the nodes of a hypertext into semantic clusters: a biconnected components algorithm for hypertexts with undirected links, and a strongly connected components algorithm for those with directed links.

Crouch *et al.* [7] use *agglomerative hierarchic clustering* [57] to cluster documents for a hypertext system. In this method, each document starts out in a cluster by itself. The two clusters that are most similar (according to some similarity metric) are then aggregated into a single cluster. This process is repeated until a single cluster remains. This pattern of clusters forms a tree that can be browsed by the hypertext reader.

Hara *et al.* [26] suggest an approach to clustering called *Aggregation Clustering with Exceptions* (ACE). In this approach, the graph underlying the hypertext is partitioned into a hypergraph representing the clusters, together with an exception graph which represents the difference between the hypergraph and the original graph. Because calculation of an optimum ACE solution is NP–complete, a heuristic algorithm based on the Kernighan–Lin Algorithm [28] is used.

Automated link construction is the creation of links between related nodes by automated content comparison. Because automated link construction methods often invoke some form of node clustering during execution, they are closely related to the approaches described in this section. Automated link construction is discussed in Section 3.2.

3. Procedural Two–Level Models

A procedural two–level model of hypertext is one that eschews direct links in favor of a process that is invoked when an attempt is made to traverse a link. Procedural models have also been called *query–based browsing* [12], *link resolution* models [25, 53], *generalized link* models [6] and *intensional* models [17]. In a sense, every hypertext model is a two–level procedural model, because some notion of process is always required to traverse a link. However, the focus in this section is on two–level models that have an algorithmic rather than a data structure emphasis.

In a procedural two–level model, two flavors of dynamic link are possible. In the first, the target node exists, but the connection from the source node to the target node does not exist until the link generation process is invoked. In the second, neither the connection to the target node nor the target node itself exists until the attempt to traverse the link is made. Because the details of dynamic node generation rely heavily on the subject matter of the hypertext, I will consider only the generation of links here (irrespective of whether the target node exists).

A reference model is "a structured description of some domain that can be used to compare existing implementations in that domain, design new implementations, and...map out possible areas for standardization and show their relation to one another" [35, p. 9]. A number of hypertext reference models have appeared in the literature [21, 22, 25, 30]. By and large though, they skirt the issue of how links connect nodes. The Dexter model [25] includes provision for a procedural model. Direct links are handled by reference to 'Unique Identifiers':

> Every component has a globally unique identity which is captured by its unique identifier (UID). UIDs are primitive in the model, but

they are assumed to be uniquely assigned to components across the entire universe of discourse (not just within the context of a single hypertext). The accessor function of the hypertext is responsible for "accessing" a component given its UID, i.e., for mapping a UID into the component "assigned" to that UID. [25, p. 102]

A UID can thus serve as a direct link. Computed links are handled in the model through reference to a 'resolver function;' such a function takes a component specification as its argument and resolves it to a UID. This resolver function is thus the Dexter model's analogue to an ancillary procedural component.

Many procedural models have at their roots research in Information Retrieval (IR). Savoy [45] provides a general introduction to the use of Information Retrieval techniques in hypertext. He also presents an evaluation methodology for the comparison of search techniques. In the following subsections, I first discuss links that are generated on–the–fly. I then survey current methods for automated link construction. These latter techniques differ from dynamic link techniques in that they are applied to an entire corpus; the resulting links are conventional static links. While they do not fall strictly under the rubric of two–level procedural models, systems that do automated link generation are close enough to computed link systems to be included in this survey.

3.1 Computed Links

A **computed link** is a hyperlink that does not exist until a user tries to traverse it. When such an attempt is made (perhaps by clicking on an anchor), a process is generated to compute the target of the link. Furuta and Stotts [21] distinguish three types of processes that might be generated during link traversal: finite processes that require no user input, finite processes that are controlled in part by user input, and continuous processes.

Bieber [4, 5] suggests a generic model for two–level procedural hypertext, which he demonstrates in the MAX system. Bieber's goal is to allow existing systems to be smoothly integrated into a hypertext environment. To that end, he constructs rules for translating the output of the underlying system into a hypertext structure; these rules are called *bridge laws*. Each bridge law is a first–order predicate logic sentence relating particular actions the reader might take in the hypertext system interface with operations of the underlying system. When the reader performs some action, MAX searches its database of bridge laws for laws that match the action. Each applicable bridge law will generate one or more links; the reader may then select the link of greatest interest.

Marshall [31] divides the integration of a hypertext system with an external system into three types: data/content–based integration, in which the external application conforms to the hypertext system's anchoring protocol, thereby allowing external information to be treated as if it were part of the system; tool/node–based integration, in which link traversal corresponds to the retrieval of information from the application; and display/window–based integration, in which the hypertext system simply launches the application. In Marshall's terminology then, MAX provides data/content–based integration for systems that have no awareness of their own participation in a hypertext system.

Another general procedural model is suggested by Tompa *et al.* They view a hypertext as "a collection of documents and link–resolving components" [53, p. 119]. They present an architecture that serves as a framework for procedural models. In their model, each procedure that is able to resolve links registers a specification of the keys it accepts with a central link resolution handler. When a reader selects an anchor, the anchor is translated into a key which is then matched against the registered specifications. For each specification that is matched, a corresponding process is invoked to generate the actual link.

Pearl [38] introduces the Sun LINK SERVICE to handle distributed hypertext links under an open systems approach. The LINK SERVICE provides a link registry that binds keys to applications. An application that can display a particular node identifies itself to the LINK SERVICE, and passes a key representing the node; this key can then be used to retrieve the node. Using this architecture, a system can easily provide computed links by initiating a computation to find the desired node or nodes upon the receipt of a key.

This sort of architecture that maps from a stylized key to a node has gained enormous popularity in the WORLD WIDE WEB (WWW) [60]. WWW provides a syntax for keys called a *Uniform Resource Locator* (URL) [3], together with a protocol called *Hypertext Transfer Protocol* (HTTP) [34] for requesting the node corresponding to a key from a remote host. While a URL can specify a static link to a node, it can also be used to submit a query to an arbitrary program. Thus, WWW seamlessly merges static and dynamic links in a single hypertext model.

3.2 Automated Link Construction

A number of researchers have addressed the problem of automated link construction. While the links that result from such an approach are conventional static links, and all possible links are usually created *en masse*, these approaches nonetheless need to be considered in the context of two–level procedural models.

Chang [10] developed the HIENET system to provide user input to the automated link generation process. In the HIENET system, readers are allowed to create links. The system then infers a *Link Profile* that describes the user–created links, and attempts to instantiate new links that match the profile. When a reader adds a link from node A to node B for example, the system automatically adds links from all the nodes that are similar to node A to all

the nodes that are similar to node B. The similarity measure is drawn from
Salton's vector space model [43]; the similarity of two nodes is defined as a
vector inner product, where the vector terms are the term frequency inverse
document frequency (*tfidf*) of those words in the node whose term frequency
is closest to the median term frequency. In this way, HIENET is able to create
only links that are likely to be of interest to the reader.

Allan and Salton [2, 44] describe another approach to automated document linking based on the vector space model. They also use *tfidf* to cluster documents. They then divide each document into small pieces (typically
paragraphs) and perform clustering analysis at this more local level; doing
so helps to resolve ambiguities and eliminates connections that are based on
superficial similarities. The resulting clustering information can be used to
extract several types of links, including links that suggest a shift in topic,
links that indicate a superset/subset relationship between two documents,
and links that connect collections of related topics.

The main competitor to the vector space model in Information Retrieval
is the Boolean query model. The QUERIES–R–LINKS (QRL) system [12]
provides a hypertext–like interface to a Boolean query system. Users of the
system are allowed to highlight words of interest in the displayed text. If a
logical AND operation is desired, words may be connected with lines. The
results indicate that Boolean queries are easier for users to formulate using
this approach than with a conventional Boolean query language, although
the complexity of the queries that can be formulated is not yet up to the
level of such languages.

Another technique that is enjoying a revival in Information Retrieval and
related fields is *n*–gram analysis. An *n*–gram is simply a length *n* subsequence
of the characters in a text. Pearce and Nicholas [37] present a model of
text linking based on *n*–grams. In their model, a cosine measure is used to
associate nodes that have similar *n*–gram profiles. One of the most promising
features of this technology is its robustness in the face of misspellings and
other forms of text degradation. Pearce and Miller [36] explore the scalability
of the approach in a dynamic hypertext environment.

4. Conclusions

The power of a two–level model of hypertext comes from the separation of
the appearance of a link from the link's underlying structure. Because of
this added layer of abstraction, two–level models can provide solutions to a
variety of classic problems with hypertext. Beyond their applicability to the
problems enumerated in Section 1.2, two–level models have been applied to
the problems of hypertext linearization, document reuse, user disorientation,
access control, document corruption, hypertext complexity, and hypertext
reorganization.

Two–level models of hypertext have applicability to a variety of extensions to the basic idea of hypertext. These include:

- *Adaptive hypertext systems.* An adaptive hypertext system is one that attempts to gauge the needs of the reader and dynamically reconfigure some aspect of the hypertext to meet those needs. A two–level model can facilitate user adaptation by allowing modification of its ancillary structure. Inference on many common ancillary structures is both well–studied and well–behaved; adaptive hypertext systems can be simplified by taking advantage of these properties.
- *Distributed, multi–author hypertext systems.* In hypertext systems that are distributed across sites and across authors (as is the World Wide Web, for example), it is difficult to control and manage the links that are created between nodes. Two–level models provide hope for establishing a degree of order and uniformity to the link structure of such systems.
- *Hypermedia systems.* Hypermedia systems tend to have great difficulty in assigning semantics to non–textual objects. When a media object is attached to an ancillary structure in a two–level model, it can then derive semantics from that ancillary structure.

These are but a few of the benefits that two–level models of hypertext bring to bear on current problems in hypertext system design. Because of their inherent advantages, many more examples of two–level models will emerge in the years ahead.

Acknowledgement. This work was sponsored in part by a National Aeronautics and Space Administration Summer Faculty Fellowship.

References

1. Robert Akscyn, Donald L. McCracken, and Elise Yoder. KMS: A distributed hypermedia system for managing knowledge in organizations. *Communications of the ACM*, 31(7):820–835, July 1988.
2. James Allan and Gerard Salton. The identification of text relations using automatic hypertext linking. In James Mayfield and Charles Nicholas, editors, *Proceedings of the Workshop on Intelligent Hypertext*, 1993.
3. Tim Berners–Lee, ed. *Uniform Resource Locators.* http://www.w3.org/pub/WWW/Addressing/URL/, 1994.
4. Michael Bieber. Issues in modeling a "dynamic" hypertext interface for non-hypertext systems. In *Hypertext '91 Proceedings*, pages 203–217. Association for Computing Machinery Press, 1991.
5. Michael Bieber. Automating hypermedia for decision support. *Hypermedia*, 4(2):83–110, 1992.
6. Michael P. Bieber and Steven O. Kimbrough. On generalizing the concept of hypertext. *MIS Quarterly*, 16(1):77–93, March 1992.

7. Rodrigo A. Botafogo and Ben Shneiderman. Identifying aggregates in hypertext structures. In *Hypertext '91 Proceedings*, pages 63–74. Association for Computing Machinery Press, 1991.

8. Ronald J. Brachman and James G. Schmolze. An overview of the KL–ONE knowledge representation system. *Cognitive Science*, 9(2):171–216, 1985.

9. Marco A. Casanova, Luiz Tucherman, Maria Julia D. Lima, Jose L. Rangel Netto, Noemi Rodriguez, and Luiz F. G. Soares. The nested context model for hyperdocuments. In *Hypertext '91 Proceedings*, pages 193–201. Association for Computing Machinery Press, 1991.

10. Daniel T. Chang. HieNet: A user–centered approach for automatic link generation. In *Hypertext '93 Proceedings*, pages 145–158. Association for Computing Machinery Press, 1993.

11. Eugene Charniak. Bayesian networks without tears. *AI Magazine*, 12(4):50–63, 1991.

12. Nipon Charoenkitkarn, Jim Tam, Mark H. Chignell, and Gene Golovchinsky. Browsing through querying: Designing for electronic books. In *Hypertext '93 Proceedings*, pages 206–216. Association for Computing Machinery Press, 1993.

13. George H. Collier. Thoth–II: Hypertext with explicit semantics. In *Hypertext '87 Proceedings*, pages 269–289. Association for Computing Machinery Press, 1987.

14. Jeff Conklin and Michael L. Begeman. gIBIS: A hypertext tool for exploratory policy discussion. *ACM Transactions on Office Information Systems*, 6(4):303–331, October 1988.

15. W. Bruce Croft and Howard Turtle. A retrieval model for incorporating hypertext links. In *Hypertext '89 Proceedings*, pages 213–224. Association for Computing Machinery Press, 1989.

16. Donald B. Crouch, Carolyn J. Crouch, and Glenn Andreas. The use of cluster hierarchies in hypertext information retrieval. In *Hypertext '89 Proceedings*, pages 225–237. Association for Computing Machinery Press, 1989.

17. Steven J. DeRose. Expanding the notion of links. In *Hypertext '89 Proceedings*, pages 249–257. Association for Computing Machinery Press, 1989.

18. M. E. Frisse. Searching for information in a hypertext medical handbook. *Communications of the ACM*, 31:880–886, 1988.

19. Mark E. Frisse and Steve B. Cousins. Information retrieval from hypertext: Update on the dynamic medical handbook project. In *Hypertext '89 Proceedings*, pages 199–212. Association for Computing Machinery Press, 1989.

20. Richard Furuta and P. David Stotts. Programmable browsing semantics in Trellis. In *Hypertext '89 Proceedings*, pages 27–42. Association for Computing Machinery Press, 1989.

21. Richard Furuta and P. David Stotts. A functional meta–structure for hypertext models and systems. *Electronic Publishing—Origination, Dissemination and Design*, 3(4):179–205, November 1990.

22. Richard Furuta and P. David Stotts. The Trellis hypertext reference model. In Judi Moline, Dan Benigni, and Jean Baronas, editors, *Proceedings of the Hypertext Standardization Workshop*, pages 83–93. National Institute of Standards and Technology, 1990. NIST Special Publication 500–178.

23. Franca Garzotto, Paolo Paolini, and Daniel Schwabe. HDM—a model for the design of hypertext applications. In *Hypertext '91 Proceedings*, pages 313–328. Association for Computing Machinery Press, 1991.

24. Peter A. Gloor. CYBERMAP: Yet another way of navigating in hyperspace. In *Hypertext '91 Proceedings*, pages 107–121. Association for Computing Machinery Press, 1991.

25. Frank Halasz and Mayer Schwartz. The Dexter hypertext reference model. In Judi Moline, Dan Benigni, and Jean Baronas, editors, *Proceedings of the Hypertext Standardization Workshop*, pages 95–133. National Institute of Standards and Technology, 1990. NIST Special Publication 500–178.

26. Yoshinori Hara, Arthur M. Keller, and Gio Wiederhold. Implementing hypertext database relationships through aggregations and exceptions. In *Hypertext '91 Proceedings*, pages 75–90. Association for Computing Machinery Press, 1991.

27. Michael J. Hu and Peter Kirstein. An intelligent hypertext system. In James Mayfield and Charles Nicholas, editors, *Proceedings of the Workshop on Intelligent Hypertext*, 1993.

28. B. W. Kernighan and S. Lin. An efficient heuristic procedure for partitioning graphs. *Bell System Technical Journal*, 49(2):291–307, February 1970.

29. Ammar Kheirbek. A two–level hypermedia model based on conceptual graph theory. In James Mayfield and Charles Nicholas, editors, *Proceedings of the Workshop on Intelligent Hypertext*, 1993.

30. Danny B. Lange. A formal model of hypertext. In Judi Moline, Dan Benigni, and Jean Baronas, editors, *Proceedings of the Hypertext Standardization Workshop*, pages 145–166. National Institute of Standards and Technology, 1990. NIST Special Publication 500–178.

31. Catherine C. Marshall. A multi–tiered approach to hypertext integration: Negotiating standards for a heterogeneous application environment. In Judi Moline, Dan Benigni, and Jean Baronas, editors, *Proceedings of the Hypertext Standardization Workshop*, pages 167–177. National Institute of Standards and Technology, 1990. NIST Special Publication 500–178.

32. James Mayfield and Charles Nicholas. SNITCH: Augmenting hypertext documents with a semantic net. *International Journal of Intelligent and Cooperative Information Systems*, 2(3):335–351, 1993.

33. Charles K. Nicholas and Linda H. Rosenberg. Canto: A hypertext data model. *Electronic Publishing—Origination, Dissemination and Design*, 6(2):93–113, June 1993.

34. Henrik Frystyk Nielsen and Jim Gettys. Http—hypertext transfer protocol. http://www.w3.org/pub/WWW/Protocols, 1997.

35. H. Van Dyke Parunak. Reference and data model group (RDMG): Work plan status. In Judi Moline, Dan Benigni, and Jean Baronas, editors, *Proceedings of the Hypertext Standardization Workshop*, pages 9–13. National Institute of Standards and Technology, 1990. NIST Special Publication 500–178.

36. Claudia Pearce and Ethan Miller. The TELLTALE Dynamic Hypertext Environment: Approaches to Scalability. In this volume.

37. Claudia Pearce and Charles Nicholas. TELLTALE: Experiments in a dynamic hypertext environment for degraded and multilingual data. *Journal of the American Society for Information Science*, 47(4):263–275, April 1996.

38. Amy Pearl. Sun's link service: A protocol for open linking. In *Hypertext '89 Proceedings*, pages 137–146. Association for Computing Machinery Press, 1989.

39. James L. Peterson. *Petri Net Theory and the Modeling of Systems*. Prentice–Hall, 1981.

40. M. Ross Quillian. Word concepts: A theory and simulation of some basic semantic capabilities. *Behavioral Science*, 12(5):410–430, September 1967. Reprinted in Ronald J. Brachman and Hector J. Levesque, editors, *Readings in Knowledge Representation*, pages 98–118. Morgan Kaufmann, 1985.

41. Roy Rada. Hypertext writing and document reuse: The role of a semantic net. *Electronic Publishing—Origination, Dissemination and Design*, 3(3):125–140, August 1990.

42. Wolfgang Reisig. *Petri Nets: An Introduction*. Springer–Verlag, 1985.

43. Gerard Salton. *Automatic Text Processing*. Addison–Wesley, 1989.
44. Gerard Salton and James Allan. Selective text utilization and text traversal. In *Hypertext '93 Proceedings*, pages 131–144. Association for Computing Machinery Press, 1993.
45. Jacques Savoy. Effectiveness of information retrieval systems used in a hypertext. *Hypermedia*, 5(1):23–46, 1993.
46. Jacques Savoy and Daniel Desbois. Information retrieval in hypertext systems: An approach using Bayesian networks. *Electronic Publishing—Origination, Dissemination and Design*, 4(2):87–108, June 1991.
47. Roger Schank and Robert Abelson. *Scripts, Plans, Goals and Understanding*. Lawrence Erlbaum Associates, Hillsdale, NJ, 1977.
48. S. C. Shapiro. The SNePS semantic network processing system. In N. V. Findler, editor, *Associative Networks: Representation and Use of Knowledge by Computers*, pages 179–203. Academic Press, 1979.
49. J. F. Sowa. *Conceptual Structures: Information Processing in Minds and Machines*. Addison Wesley Publishing Co., 1984.
50. P. David Stotts and Richard Furuta. Petri–net–based hypertext: Document structure with browsing semantics. *ACM Transactions on Information Systems*, 7(1):3–29, January 1989.
51. P. David Stotts and Richard Furuta. Dynamic adaptation of hypertext structure. In *Hypertext '91 Proceedings*, pages 219–231. Association for Computing Machinery Press, 1991.
52. Manfred Thüring, Jörg M. Haake, and Jörg Hannemann. What's Eliza doing in the Chinese Room? Incoherent hyperdocuments—and how to avoid them. In *Hypertext '91 Proceedings*, pages 161–177. Association for Computing Machinery Press, 1991.
53. Frank Wm. Tompa, G. Elizabeth Blake, and Darrell R. Raymond. Hypertext by link–resolving components. In *Hypertext '93 Proceedings*, pages 118–130. Association for Computing Machinery Press, 1993.
54. Randall H. Trigg. Guided tours and tabletops: Tools for communicating in a hypertext environment. *ACM Transactions on Office Information Systems*, 6(4):398–414, 1988.
55. Randall H. Trigg and Mark Weiser. TEXTNET: A network–based approach to text handling. *ACM Transactions on Office Information Systems*, 4(1):1–23, 1986.
56. Kenneth Utting and Nicole Yankelovich. Context and orientation in hypermedia networks. *ACM Transactions on Information Systems*, 7(1):58–84, January 1989.
57. E. M. Voorhees. *The Effectiveness and Efficiency of Agglomerative Hierarchic Clustering in Document Retrieval*. PhD thesis, Department of Computer Science, Cornell University, Ithaca, New York, 1985.
58. Weigang Wang and Roy Rada. A semantic net for reusable hypertext. In James Mayfield and Charles Nicholas, editors, *Proceedings of the Workshop on Intelligent Hypertext*, 1993.
59. Robert Wilensky. Some problems and proposals for knowledge representation. In Janet L. Kolodner and Christopher K. Riebeck, editors, *Experience, Memory, and Reasoning*, pages 15–28. Lawrence Erlbaum Associates, New Jersey, 1986.
60. World Wide Web Consortium. About the world wide web. 1996. http://www.w3.org/pub/WWW/WWW

The TELLTALE Dynamic Hypertext Environment: Approaches to Scalability

Claudia Pearce[1] and Ethan Miller[2]

[1] U.S. Department of Defense
[2] University of Maryland Baltimore County

Summary. Methods and tools for finding documents relevant to a user's needs in document corpora can be found in the information retrieval, library science, and hypertext communities. Typically, these systems provide retrieval capabilities for fairly static corpora, their algorithms are dependent on the language for which they are written, *e.g.* English, and they don't perform well when presented with misspelled words or text that has been degraded by OCR (optical character recognition) techniques. In this chapter, we present the TELLTALE system. TELLTALE is a dynamic hypertext environment that provides full-text search from a hypertext-style user interface for text corpora that may be garbled by OCR or transmission errors, and that may contain languages other than English by using several techniques based on *n*-grams (*n* character sequences of text). In this chapter, we identify methods and techniques that we have applied to the *n*-gram data structures. We also discuss algorithms that we used to enhance the scalability of the TELLTALE Dynamic Hypertext System.

1. Introduction

Knowledge workers of many kinds, from scientific researchers, to reporters, office workers, and others, all need to process large growing collections of textual documents on a daily basis. This environment is characterized by changing corpora that may contain text that deviates considerably from standard English. Office workers must sift through a morass of electronic information such as electronic mail, optically scanned documents, and other machine-readable text. International business must also be capable of processing multiple languages, sometimes within the same document. Text may be corrupted through faulty transmission, translation, or optical character recognition. Unfortunately, traditional tools for finding information in text are geared primarily for one language (and often are restricted to one domain within that language) and are not well suited to corrupted data.

Contemporary full text search tools fall into two major categories: *traditional text retrieval* and *hypertext*. Traditional text retrieval tools process and scan text corpora against which users can pose queries [20]. Queries can range from highly-structured Boolean queries to completely-unstructured natural-language queries. Query results in traditional systems can consist of an unordered set of documents – as is the case in most commercial systems – or a ranked list of documents presented in decreasing order of relevance. Hypertext provides a somewhat different method of accessing the underlying corpus [17]. Access to related items of information is provided through a navigational-style interface in which a user selects highlighted areas of text in a document which then causes related information to be presented to the user. Types of links (*e.g.* associations from one document to another) can vary, but an underlying collection of linked segments of text is essential.

Each category of tool, traditional text retrieval and hypertext, has its strengths and weaknesses. For example, traditional text retrieval tools often contain many language dependent features such as stop word lists and stemming algorithms. In addition, these traditional text retrieval tools often use the roots of all non-stop words as index terms. The reader is referred to Croft [5] and Salton [20, 118-146] for descriptions of traditional systems. This process provides variability in the endings of words in a document but not in the roots of the words. Hypertext tools are traditionally of the static-corpus, hand-generated variety [12, 16] or, as in many newer versions, incorporate traditional text retrieval tools [6, 13, 7, 1] and are subject to the same problems as traditional text retrieval tools. Hypertext has the advantage of providing an intuitive user interface that allows users to jump from one document to related documents that have been selected solely on the basis of the text in the original document. This is in sharp contrast to traditional full text retrieval which relies on complex query languages.

TELLTALE draws on the strengths and addresses the weaknesses of both technologies to provide a dynamic hypertext environment using new variations on traditional full text retrieval. With this marriage of technologies and the incorporation of unique techniques to build in tolerance to garbles and to remove language dependencies, TELLTALE is a versatile full-text retrieval and dynamic hypertext tool. The purpose of this chapter is to provide an overview of the TELLTALE dynamic hypertext environment and its dynamic linking methods, to describe how language independence and garble tolerance are achieved in those linking methods, and to illustrate recent efforts to enhance TELLTALE's scalability for large document collections. Section 2. provides an overview of the TELLTALE Dynamic Hypertext Environment. The design and development of a TELLTALE-like research platform for testing a variety of scalability issues is covered in Sections 3.. The chapter concludes with a discussion of related efforts and future work in Section 4..

2. TELLTALE – A Dynamic Hypertext Environment

TELLTALE provides dynamism in its approach to full text retrieval in three ways. First, TELLTALE provides dynamism in selection of the *anchor* (selected area of text used as the source of links to other related portions of text) which allows users complete flexibility in their search for information. Second, the choice of link computation by the user at run-time provides another area of dynamism. By giving users a choice of link computation, they can select the choice most appropriate to their needs at the moment. Third, by actually calculating the link at run-time, the system can incorporate any new data that has been added since starting the system. The actual links are computed dynamically, not manually generated for a specific corpus. This combination of link type selection, anchor selection, and link computation serves as the basis for relating and querying the full text of documents in an underlying corpus. These dynamic mechanisms allow users to pose questions about the underlying corpus using a passage of text, to investigate the relationships between documents through navigation, and to browse a dynamic corpus.

The bases for the dynamic linking capabilities in TELLTALE are enhanced versions of the traditional statistically-based information retrieval tools. To overcome any dependence on a particular language, *e.g.* English, and to build in tolerance to spelling errors, we use *n-grams*, n-character sequences of text, in our statistically-based tools to supply some of the needed robustness. This use of n-grams, along with unique scoring techniques, provides the required robustness for garble tolerance and language independence.

Since anchors provide explicit visual cues for users, specialized highlighting tools are included in TELLTALE so that users can readily identify meaningful information in a hypertext without explicit anchor points. So that the highlighting tools in TELLTALE are also garble resistant and language independent, n-gram-based techniques are used in these tools as well. Two types of highlighting tools are provided in TELLTALE. First, *topic* highlighting is provided which highlights the n-grams contained in the anchor that occur in a selected target document (a document that resulted from traversing a link). The effect of the topic highlighting is to provide users with quick visual recognition of words and phrases from the anchor that are present in a target document while allowing for variability in spellings and endings. Second, a *statistical* highlighting technique, based on a technique by Cohen [3], is provided which highlights words and phrases that contain n-grams that occur more frequently than statistically expected based on a large sample. The effect of this statistical highlighting is to provide the gist of a selected target document.

In this section we discuss the mechanics of TELLTALE's linking mechanisms and the features of its user interface. A more complete discussion of TELLTALE's highlighting techniques can be found in Pearce's dissertation [18]. In Section 2.1 we discuss the n-gram approach used in TELLTALE as well as three dynamic linking mechanisms based on this n-gram approach. In Section 2.2 we discuss the TELLTALE user interface.

2.1 Dynamic Link Types Using n-grams

Partial character sequences of length n extracted from documents, called n-grams, have been used in several automatic document indexing schemes in several systems [10, 23, 26, 8]. Zamora [26] uses trigram analysis for spelling error detection. Damashek [8] uses n-gram analysis for similarity scoring with multiple languages and robustness against misspellings. These

n-gram approaches vary in the choice of n, the process for extracting n-grams, and the statistics stored about n-grams. Some n-gram approaches extract all unique n-grams in words, but ignore cross-word boundaries [26, 21]. Other approaches keep statistics on n-grams at various start positions within words [21]. A further variation on n-gram generation is to include inter-word spaces so that n-grams spanning words can be monitored [25, 2]. Damashek's method finds all unique n-grams in a document including inter-word spaces. This can be referred to as the *sliding n-gram* approach since a document can be easily scanned for all its unique n-grams by sliding an n-byte window over the text. Language independence is achieved by using all unique n-grams in a document and corpus when building document representation vectors. This process replaces the keyword stemming commonly used in traditional information retrieval systems [20] and eliminates other language-dependent features such as stop word lists. Robustness to errors in spelling is gained because of the redundancy introduced with the sliding n-gram approach, which identifies all unique n-grams in a document. Since not all characters in a word will typically be included in each n-gram that contributes to a word, considerable flexibility is built into the approach. In addition to the overlap provided by the sliding n-gram approach, Damashek's weighting scheme is unique in that it removes commonality among documents by generating an "average" document from the full corpus and then removing "average" n-gram weights from individual n-gram weights in a document. This has the effect that n-grams covering stop words and other common words are weighted less highly than n-grams covering other words. In contrast to the complete coverage of the sliding n-gram approach of Damashek, Mah [10] collects high-frequency bigrams and trigrams to be maintained as indexes, then combines these bigrams and trigrams to locate specific words and phrases. Low frequency bigrams and trigrams are not used so that the size of the index remains small. As a result, Mah's approach does not have the same level of coverage of characters and inherent robustness as does Damashek's. Cavnar's method tracks inter-word boundaries by maintaining all bigrams and trigrams in each line of a document, but misses inter-line boundaries [2]. Yannakoudakis' method [25] collects n-grams containing spaces at word endings only.

Sliding n-gram analysis serves as the basis for the three dynamic linking methods in TELLTALE: Similarity links, Lookup links, and Disambiguated Lookup links. The Similarity link is a method of linking documents based on the closeness of two document's respective vocabularies. Documents are represented by a vector of weights representing the contributions of various n-grams. Similarity is calculated by computing the cosine of the two vectors of n-gram frequencies. The Lookup link is a method of linking documents based on the percentage of the unique n-grams contained in an anchor string that actually occur in a document. The Lookup link can be thought of as a fuzzy string match. It is, as its name implies, a *lookup* of certain n-grams.

The Disambiguated Lookup link is a method of linking documents based on a combination of the above two link types. Specifically, the Similarity link is used to provide context and the Lookup link is used to find specific strings. This effectively disambiguates the context in which the search string is used. In Sections 2.1.1, 2.1.2, and 2.1.3 the three methods of calculating dynamic links in TELLTALE are described. A more complete discussion of the implementation details can be found in Pearce [18].

2.1.1 Similarity Link. The weighting scheme in Damashek's method [8] – the basis for the Similarity link – uses counts of each unique n-gram in the corpus and in each document. To provide these counts, a histogram is maintained for all unique n-grams in each document and in the corpus as a whole. Consider, for example, the following passage of text. To reduce the character set size, punctuation, special characters, and numerics have been removed (only the 26 lower case letters of the alphabet and the space remain) for the purpose of n-gram detection and accumulation.

> ...expert systems can be used in many different types of prob-
> lem areas places where expert systems make an important difference
> include ...

Choosing $n = 5$, the first several 5-grams are "exper", "xpert", "pert ", "ert s", and "rt sy". Notice that these same 5-grams occur again later in the passage, adding to their respective histogram counts.

For fast access we internally store this histogram of n-grams as a hash table of n-grams, using each n-gram as an access key. A *hash table* is a file organization in which records in the file are divided into a collection of numbered buckets. Assignment of records to buckets is determined by a function that transforms the value of a key in each record into a bucket number. This transformation function is called a *hash function*. With proper choice of hash function, storage of records is evenly distributed among the buckets. The hash function used in TELLTALE is based on the ASCII values of the characters in each n-gram. TELLTALE's hash function is described in Pearce [18] and a full description of hashing can be found in Knuth [15]. A collision list of unique n-gram occurrences is maintained in each bucket of the hash table. Tied to each unique n-gram is a list of documents in which that n-gram occurs, along with a count of how often it occurs in each document. For the English alphabet, there are 27^n possible n-grams. However, for any given document, relatively few of these will be represented. An upper bound on the number of unique n-grams in a document of size m is $m - n + 1$. Through experimentation, it has been found that 80,000 to 100,000 hash table buckets for 5-grams are sufficient to ensure relatively short collision lists — fewer than five elements on average — for corpora over forty megabytes in length.

In calculating the similarity of two documents, n-grams are used as index terms. The weight of each term is the difference between the count of a given n-gram for a document, normalized by the document's size, and the average normalized count over all documents for that n-gram. This provides a weight for each n-gram in a document relative to the average for the collection. For example, given the histogram count, $c_{i,k}$, of n-gram k in document i, the total n-gram count, m_i, in document i, and the average normalized count, a_k, of n-gram k over all documents, a document is represented as a vector $d_i = (d_{i,1}, d_{i,2}, \cdots)$ where the individual elements, $d_{i,k} = c_{i,k}/m_i - a_k$, have been normalized and the n-gram's average value removed. This is the same as dividing a document's vector by the document's total n-gram count and subtracting the corpus' *centroid* — the vector composed of the average weight for each n-gram in the corpus. The similarity between document vectors d_i and d_j is then calculated as the cosine of the two representation vectors,

$$SIM_c(d_i, d_j) = \frac{\sum_{k=1}^{t}(d_{i,k} \cdot d_{j,k})}{\sqrt{\sum_{k=1}^{t} d_{i,k}^2}\sqrt{\sum_{k=1}^{t} d_{j,k}^2}}. \qquad (2.1)$$

The numerator in Equation 2.1 is the dot product of the vectors d_i and d_j, representing documents i and j respectively. The denominator in Equation 2.1, the product of the sum of squares of each term in the respective vectors, is used to normalize the result. The average n-gram vector can be calculated by maintaining a running total for each n-gram and document size as documents are scanned. Scores computed using this approach range from -1 to 1.

Similarity links provide a mechanism for linking similar documents. This result is achieved because documents about the same subject tend to use the same vocabulary. In TELLTALE, vocabulary consists of n-grams that make up the words, not the words themselves. Queries are processed in the same manner as documents in the corpus. In TELLTALE, complete documents be scored not only against queries, but against any selected areas of text. The selected area of text becomes the anchor of the link and the anchor is treated as a new "document" to be scored against all other documents. To make this computation efficient, TELLTALE's implementation reuses certain terms in the Similarity link score [18]. The effect of the Similarity link computation is that of an associative table of contents. The user provides a sample of the "content" of interest and the hypertext engine supplies a list of relevant documents by using the Similarity link computation. The hypertext system then presents the user with a uniquely tailored selection of the corpus based on her information need.

2.1.2 Lookup Link. The hash table construction for holding the histogram of n-grams and document references discussed in Section 2.1.1 can be used as an inverted index into the document collection. To compute a Lookup link, the n-grams from the selected query phrase are first parsed, then each unique n-gram is hashed to find the documents in which it is contained. In other words, we "look-up" every unique n-gram in the hash table to find documents in which it occurs. If all of the n-grams of a query appear at least once in some document, then that document has a high probability of containing that query phrase. Also of interest are documents that contain lexically close matches of the word or phrase in the anchor. Thus, instead of looking only for documents in which all of the n-grams from the query phrase are present, those containing some percentage of the query n-grams, say 50 percent, are also selected. With this approach, some documents that do not contain the specified phrase will be selected, resulting in false hits. Those documents were selected, however, because they contained at least half (or some other percentage chosen by the user) of the unique n-grams present in the query. Precision is sacrificed for recall since with degraded text (text with many spelling errors), relevant documents would be overlooked if the required percentage was too high.

The Lookup link functionality can be expressed mathematically as the following asymmetric binary similarity score:

$$SIM_l(q, f_i) = \frac{\sum_{k=1}^{t}(q_k \cdot f_{i,k})}{\sum_{k=1}^{t} q_k} \tag{2.2}$$

where q is the query or link anchor, f_i is the ith document in the corpus, t is the total number of unique n-grams in the corpus, and q_k and $f_{i,k}$ are binary values, 0 or 1, representing whether the query and document, respectively, contain n-gram k at least once. The numerator is the dot product of query and document representation vectors in which binary values are used in the weighting instead of the more precise weighting used in the Similarity link. This score is asymmetric since one cannot reverse the order of the query, q, and document, f_i, without possibly getting a different score. The score is geared specifically toward the query since the denominator reflects only n-grams from the query.

The Lookup link associatively and robustly indexes documents. It is associative in the sense that pointers or offsets to specific locations in the text are not used in the hash table as they are in other inverted file indexing schemes. Instead, the lookup is based purely on whether a document contains various n-grams and not on direct pointers to exact locations where the specified information resides. In contrast to the Similarity link scoring, the Lookup link provides a method for finding a word or phrase that may not have sufficient weight to perform well as a query when using the Similarity link. As a side effect, this technique will bring up documents on a variety of topics that happen to contain a percentage of the requisite n-grams in the lookup query. Additionally, the Lookup link provides users with a "browsing" tool. It lets the user examine the senses and contexts in which a term is used while tolerating varied spellings.

2.1.3 Disambiguated Lookup Link. Disambiguated Lookup links provide a way to narrow the scope of either a Similarity link or a Lookup link by combining the two methods. The Lookup link is designed to find documents that contain strings closely matching the anchor of the Lookup link. For example, "dolphin" (or some close variation) can be used in different contexts in different documents. One document might use "dolphin" in the context of a football team, while another document might use it in the context of large aquariums. In the Disambiguated Lookup link, the current document is used to provide context for disambiguating the many senses of a word or phrase such as "dolphin." Conversely, from a collection of documents that result from a Similarity link, *i.e.* documents on a given topic of interest, Disambiguated Lookup links can select documents within the set of interest that contain a specific word or phrase. This refinement procedure can be thought of as an AND operation. Mathematically, the set of documents retrieved from a Disambiguated Lookup link can be thought of as the intersection of the set of documents selected from the Similarity link and the Lookup link. Given $SET_l = \{d_i | SIM_l(q, d_i) > threshold_l\}$ and $SET_c = \{d_i | SIM_c(q, d_i) > threshold_c\}$ for a query q we represent the disambiguated set as:

$$SET_d = SET_c \bigcap SET_l \qquad (2.3)$$

The threshold values, $threshold_l$ and $threshold_c$, are left to the discretion of the user; lowering thresholds improves recall at the expense of precision, while raising the threshold has the reverse effect. Based on *ad hoc* experimentation, it has been found that a good value for $threshold_l$ is approximately .5, or 50 percent when translated from the range $[0, 1]$ to a percentage, and a good value for $threshold_c$ is approximately .2, or 60 percent when translated from the range $[-1, 1]$ to a percentage.

It should be noted that all of the dynamic link methods described here produce a set of documents instead of a single document. The set of documents selected is based on the values of the score of a document versus the query (*i.e.* anchor). The documents that pass the established threshold are then ranked in descending order of score.

2.1.4 Link Retrieval Performance. Pearce has shown TELLTALE to be an effective retrieval tool for both clean and degraded data [18, 19]. The reader is referred to these works for a complete description of retrieval performance analysis for TELLTALE's linking methods.

2.2 Hypertext Interface Overview

Figure 2.1 shows the basic blocked window design of TELLTALE. Figure 2.1 illustrates five window areas. The area in the bottom left-hand corner is a writable area in which a user can place any selection of text to be used as a query (link anchor) either by typing into the area, by dropping in selected text from other windows, or by loading text from a selected file. This area is labeled "**Topic Text**" and it serves as a location from which the user can pose an initial query. Such an initial query provides the user with a potentially relevant set of documents and provides an entry point into the corpus. The user chooses the type of dynamic query computation from either the "**Lookup**" or "**Score**" buttons located below the **Topic Text** window.

The "**Browse List**" button allows users to save lists of interesting queries. **Lookup** computes a Lookup link and **Score** computes a Similarity link. The choice selected for the calculation in the example pictured in Figure 2.1 was **Lookup**. The **Topic Text** area can be used at any time, but is particularly effective when a user starts the environment and loads new data. In this case, the **Topic Text** area serves as an entry point into the system after data has been processed. The window on the lower right, titled "**Pearce Lookups**," displays a ranked list of documents resulting from the query. In the figure, documents are ranked as a result of the Lookup link computation. The **Pearce Lookups** window is also used to rank and list documents that are the result of a **Score** (Similarity link) computed from the **Topic Text** area. A slider bar underneath this window allows the user to adjust the threshold of scores for documents retrieved. The values on the slider bar range from zero to 100 percent where 100 percent indicates complete similarity and zero indicates no similarity. The upper left-hand window, labeled "**Main Text**," displays the selected document, in this case the contents of the document whose identifier is highlighted in the **Pearce Lookups** window. The document displayed is an Associated Press document from the TIPSTER data corpus [14]. In the window labeled "**Damashek Documents**" in the upper right-hand corner of the interface is a list of documents similar to the document found in **Main Text** using the Similarity link. This list is updated every time the document in the **Main Text** changes. The **Damashek Documents** window is accompanied by a slider bar as in the **Pearce Lookups** window. The slider controls the threshold of similarity. The middle window on the right-hand side is used to display words of statistical significance called **Cohen Words**. Statistical highlighting gives the user a quick survey of the contents of a document. When the statistical highlighting is activated, words and phrases containing important n-grams are highlighted within the document in the **Main Text** window, in addition to being listed in the window labeled "**Cohen Words**." In Figure 2.1 the highlighting of the **Cohen Words** within the text in the **Main Text** window has been turned off to enable the anchor selection of "Bekaa Valley." In the true spirit of hypertext, the user can select any phrase of any length from the **Main Text** window to be used as the anchor of a dynamic link illustrated by the selection of "Bekaa Valley." A pop-up menu, activated by anchor selection and mouse click, in the middle of the **Main Text** window provides the selections of dynamic link computations, Similarity, Lookup, and Disambiguated Lookup for the next link operation. This and other features of the TELLTALE interface are covered at length in Pearce [18].

2.3 Text Highlighting Techniques

As discussed earlier in this section, the dynamic hypertext environment provides two types of highlighting techniques. Topic highlighting is activated in Figure 2.2. Topic highlighting emphasizes any n-grams in the topic text that

Fig. 2.1. TELLTALE user interface with highlighted anchor and hypertext selection window.

are present in the main text. By highlighting n-grams, some variability in spellings is accommodated. For example, in Figure 2.2, portions of "Israeli", "Israel's", and "Arab-Israeli" are highlighted in response to the topic text "israel". Statistical highlighting (Cohen words) is activated in Figure 2.3. In this example, words and phrases containing high scoring n-grams, based on Cohen's statistic, are highlighted. The effect of this highlighting is to provides the reader with a quick gist of the document's content. With a quick glance, the user can determine whether or not the read a document in more detail. The reader is referred to Cohen [3] for a complete description of statistical highlighting calculations and to Pearce [18] for the variation on Cohen's highlights used in the TELLTALE prototype.

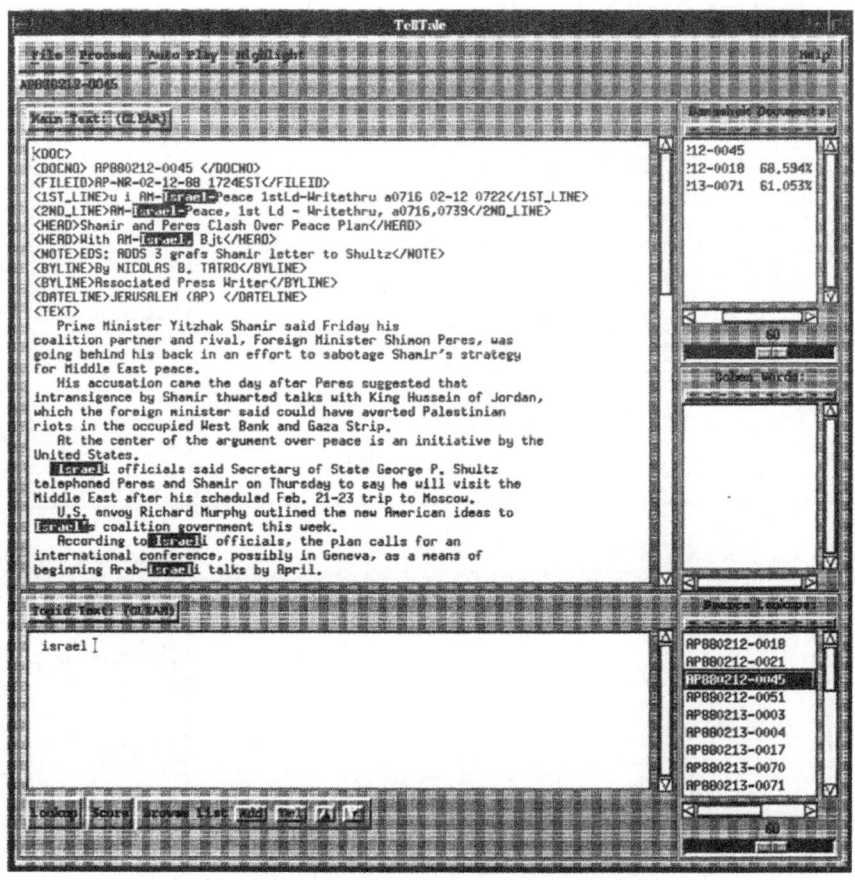

Fig. 2.2. TELLTALE user interface with topic highlighting.

2.4 Multilingual Text

TELLTALE is multilingual in several senses. First, TELLTALE is multilingual because the algorithms used in TELLTALE are independent of any specific language texts to be analyzed or displayed. Second, TELLTALE is multilingual because it has the ability to display a variety of fonts, thus allowing languages to be displayed in their native scripts. Figure 2.4 shows the TELLTALE interface displaying Russian text extracted from an Internet newsgroup. The Russian displayed in this example was encoded as 8-bit ASCII using a KOI Cyrillic font encoding. By using the upper 128 values of the possible 256 available values in the full 8-bit ASCII encoding, fonts such as the KOI Cyrillic allow both English (Roman alphabet stored in the lower 128 bits of ASCII along with numbers and special characters) and Cyril-

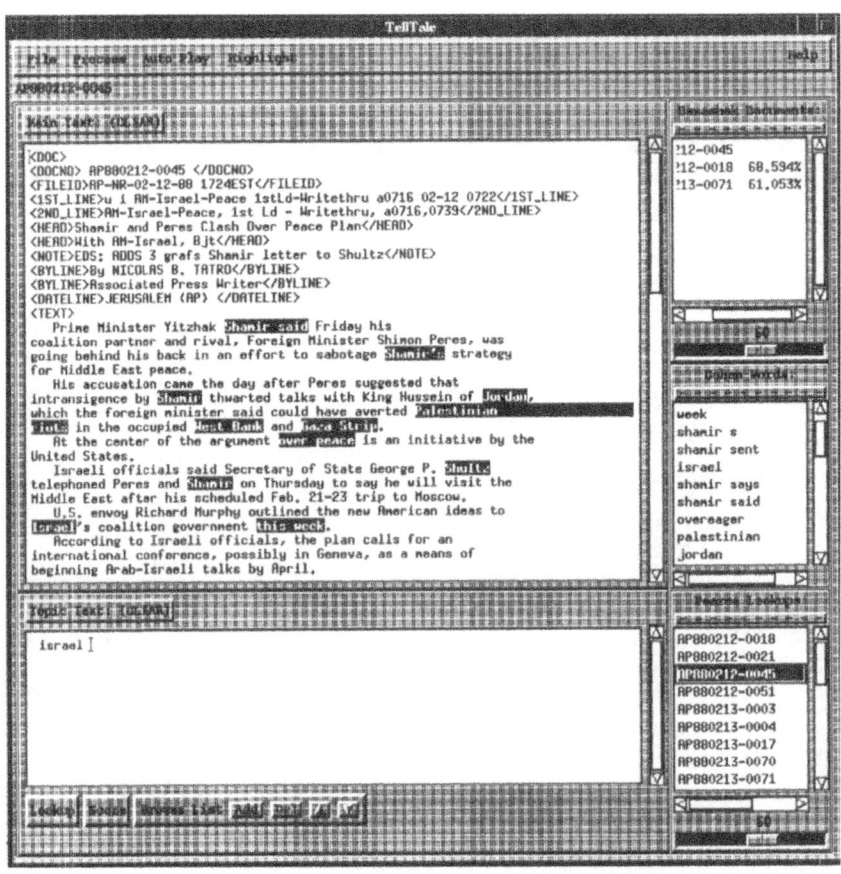

Fig. 2.3. TELLTALE user interface with statistical highlighting of *n*-grams.

lic (stored in the upper 128 values) to be displayed alongside of one another. Since TELLTALE's linking and highlighting algorithms are based on *n*-grams and not on words, the algorithms are not effected by the language used.

TELLTALE's original implementation did not contain the ability to display different language fonts. However, implementation of this new capability has proven to be very simple. Only minor changes in the interface were required and virtually all of the scoring and highlighting algorithms remained unchanged. In future implementations we hope to include a more comprehensive multilingual capability that incorporates 16-bit encoding standards (*e.g.* UNICODE [4]) to enable the processing and display of languages that require much larger coding schemes, such as Japanese.

Precision/recall analysis of the link types with multilingual data was not conducted due to the lack of available test data and relevance judgments for

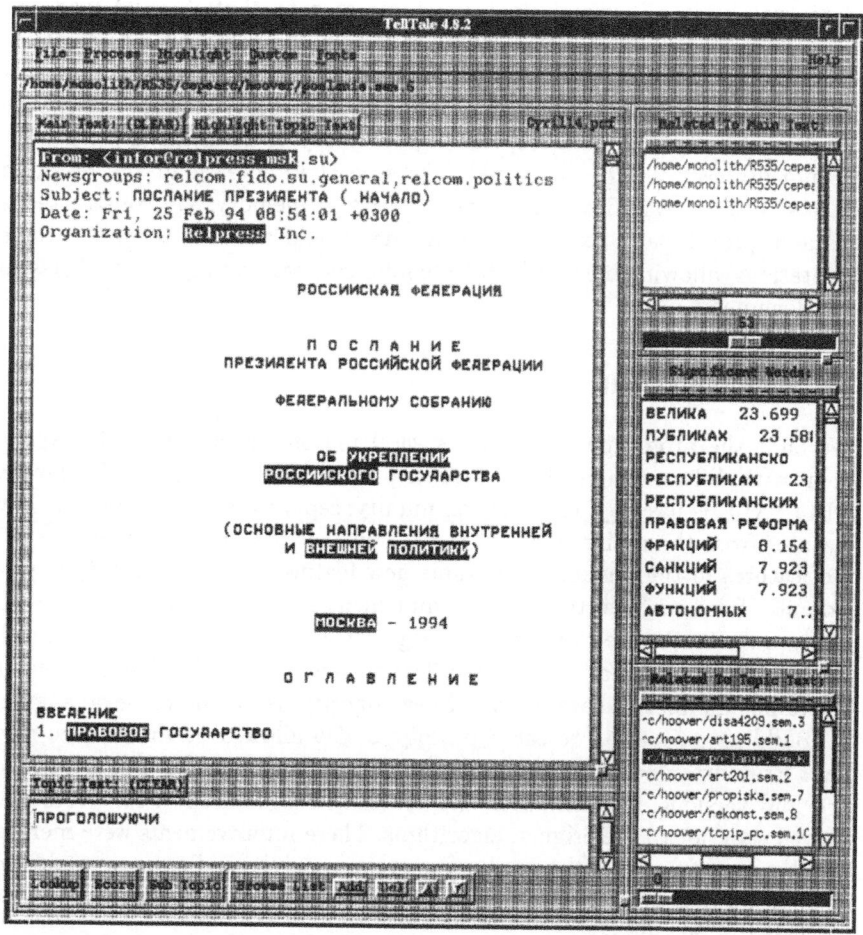

Fig. 2.4. Russian document from an Internet newsgroup displayed in KOI encoding of the Cyrillic alphabet.

multilingual data. Damashek, however, has conducted a number of tests with the sliding n-gram approach (the basis for our Similarity link) to demonstrate that languages can be sorted and identified using this approach [9].) Further experiments with multiple languages will be conducted as appropriate data sets become available.

3. Scalability Research Platform

The original TELLTALE prototype, while favorably viewed by users for its interface style, characteristics, and performance with several megabytes of data, was limited, however, in the volume of data that it could load and score. Users of this prototype were limited by the memory constraints of their workstation since TELLTALE precomputed (at startup) the similarity of each document in the corpus to every other document. This process is both lengthy and memory-intensive; starting up a copy of TELLTALE with 4,000 documents each 1 KB long could take several minutes, and the resulting data structures would consume over 32 MB of memory. We constructed a research prototype to explore methods that would allow us to bypass these limitations, allowing TELLTALE to handle corpora containing 10^9 bytes in 10^6 documents.

3.1 Prototype Goals

We built the prototype system for several reasons. First, we could experiment with different algorithms in a non-production environment. Currently, TELLTALE is used by a sizable community; separating the creation of new features from the maintenance of the current version allowed us to "break" old features in the pursuit of desirable new features. Using a prototype version also freed us from the need to implement a full user interface. As with many projects, the user interface is a large part of the code. Eliminating much of this code would make the system less suitable for production use, but it would not hamper the evaluation of new algorithms for the retrieval engine.

Building a separate research prototype also allowed us to evaluate new data structures and algorithms without necessarily including the baggage of previous versions. In some cases, the new methods we used in the prototype proved superior to the original algorithms. These improvements were merged into the next version of the production system. Additionally, we were able to implement new algorithms and data structures that supported scalability, as discussed in Section 3.2.

Our research prototype had one major feature not present in the production version — it was built using a `Tcl` (Tool Command Language) interpreter [22]. The `Tcl` interface allowed us to quickly build a graphical interface using `Tk` [22]. While this interface lacked some functionality present in TELLTALE, it was sufficient for our purposes and was implemented quickly. The `Tcl` interface has another major benefit, though. Since `Tcl` is a command language, the prototype could be controlled directly through scripts. This allowed researchers to write batch scripts to test the prototype's performance without having to use the graphical interface. Since the only interface to the indexing engine was through `Tcl`, we were guaranteed that the scripts would have the same effects as the equivalent commands selected through the graphical interface.

3.2 Data Structures

The research prototype includes three main data structures. Each keeps information about a particular type of "object" within the system. The object types are n-grams, documents, and files. As with TELLTALE, each file contains one or more documents, and each document contains one or more n-grams. Rather than build our own data structures from scratch, we used classes from the GNU libg++ class library. The data structures are built using hash tables; libg++ hash table classes include automatic table resizing as well as standard operations such as insertion, deletion, access, and traversal.

As Figure 3.1 shows, the three main data structures in the prototype are interconnected; they may be used to find the documents that contain an n-gram or to locate the file that contains a document. Absent is a similarity matrix that provides the similarity for any two documents in the corpus relative to the centroid. This matrix is absent for several reasons. First, it occupied too much memory — space which could be better spent storing other data structures. Second, it required a lot of time to precompute. Computing the similarity of all documents against a single document is not too time consuming; however, it becomes very expensive when done for each document. Scalability is the third reason for this change. The prototype could not assume that all documents would be fully read in when the program was started because doing so would require too much time just to convert files into n-grams; thus, it would be impossible to compute the matrix. Even if the matrix could be computed, it would be far too large to reside in memory — the matrix would require 500 MB for just 50,000 documents.

The central data structure in the prototype is the n-gram hash table. This table contains an entry for each unique n-gram in the corpus; this entry contains information such as total count for the n-gram as well as data necessary for similarity calculations. In addition, each n-gram may have a list of postings — one for each document that contains one or more occurrences of a particular n-gram. Our experiments using 5-grams showed that the 40 MB Wall Street Journal corpus contained just over 250,000 unique n-grams. In the same corpus, we found that a document with k n-grams had more than $k/2$ unique n-grams. As a result, the n-gram table required fewer than 8 MB to store the per-n-gram information, but would have required nearly 200 MB to store all of the n-gram postings. For large corpora, the prototype's memory limitation arises largely from n-gram postings rather than the n-gram hash table itself.

The document table contains one entry for each input document. It holds statistics such as document size and location (via pointer to the file table) for each document. It also contains per-document information used to quickly compute document similarities; the algorithm used is detailed in Section 3.3. This data structure uses fewer than 100 bytes per document. While this presents little difficulty for corpora of fewer than 50,000 documents, it may

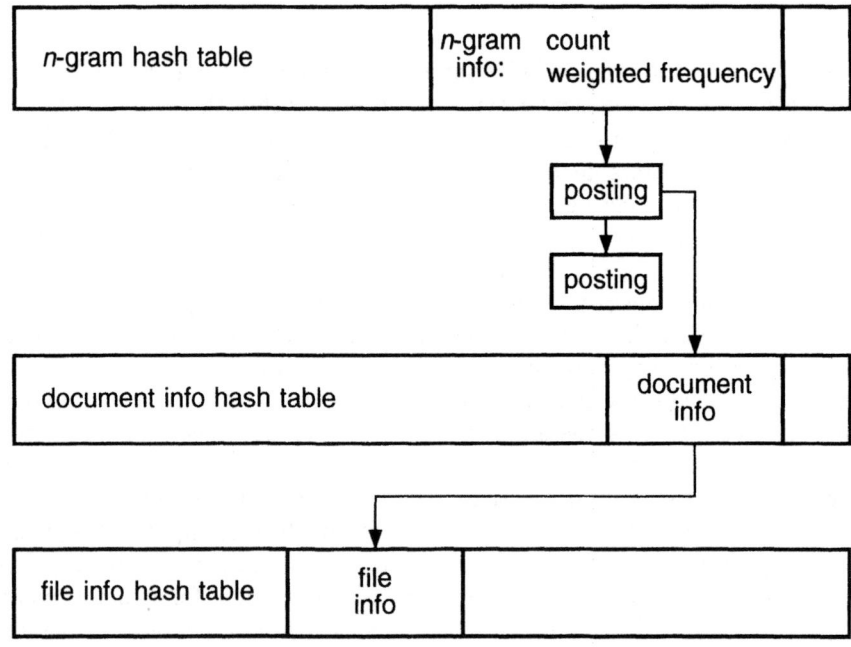

Fig. 3.1. Data structures in the TELLTALE research prototype.

require some modification to accommodate a corpus of one million documents.

The file table serves as an interface between the document "world" of the TELLTALE prototype and the file "world" of the Unix file system. Since each file may contain hundreds of documents, we decided to store per-file information such as file name separately; this provided a large savings in memory usage by allowing document hash table entries to hold a pointer to a "file" rather than keep all the file information themselves. While the table uses about 100 bytes per file, this cost is minimal even for a one gigabyte corpus containing 20,000 files of 50 KB each.

As we discovered, the most space-intensive portion of the prototype was the postings list. Thus, this is the data structure whose size must be reduced when the prototype is scaled to larger corpora. Solutions to this problem are discussed in Sections 3.4 and 3.5.

3.3 Algorithms Used

The TELLTALE research prototype used the same basic algorithms for similarity used in the production version, as detailed in Section 2.1.1. However, the calculation method differed from that in the production version. TELL-TALE precomputed all of the pairwise document similarities at startup, placing the results into a large matrix. The prototype, on the other hand, computes as little as possible when documents are read in. It postpones most of the similarity computation until it is actually needed.

The prototype must maintain both per-n-gram and per-document information to allow it to quickly compute the similarity between two documents. We can rewrite Equation 2.1 as

$$SIM_c(d_i, d_j) = \frac{\sum_{k=1}^{t}(x_{i,k}x_{j,k} - x_{i,k}a_k - x_{j,k}a_k + a_k^2)}{\sqrt{\sum_{k=1}^{t}(x_{i,k} - a_k)^2}\sqrt{\sum_{k=1}^{t}(x_{j,k} - a_k)^2}} \tag{3.1}$$

where $x_{i,k} = c_{i,k}/m_i$. The only part of this sum that must be recomputed for each query document is the sum of $x_{i,k}x_{j,k}$. However, this product is zero unless *both* values are non-zero, i.e., if both documents contain the n-gram in question. Similarity computations can thus be done on the fly by taking a single trip through the hash table and keeping a running total of this product for each document. This product is then combined with precomputed values for $\sum_{k=1}^{t} x_{i,k}a_k$ computed for each document i, $\sqrt{\sum_{k=1}^{t} x_{i,k}^2}$ computed for each document i, and $\sum_{k=1}^{t} a_k^2$. These values only change when new documents are added to the centroid, and are not recomputed for every similarity computation. Instead, they are figured the first time a user requests a similarity computation after the centroid has been modified.

By separating the similarity calculations into two parts, the prototype provides the user with better performance. Documents can be scanned in at the rate of approximately 100 KB/sec on a Sparc-10, allowing a 4 MB corpus to be "digested" in 40 seconds. The precomputations previously mentioned require an additional 30 seconds, bringing the total startup time for a 4 MB corpus to just over one minute. Then, additional similarity computations take around 5-10 seconds. To further enhance performance, we added a small cache of similarity vectors; this permits users to get instant response when requesting a similarity computation they had done recently.

3.4 Scaling Experiments

Exploring ways to scale TELLTALE was one of the main reasons for building the prototype. We considered several mechanisms that would allow TELL-TALE to handle multi-gigabyte corpora. These algorithms included reduction of the meta-data associated with the corpus, and distribution of the corpus across several cooperating processors.

Our experiments to date have focused on the second method for scaling TELLTALE: distributing the meta-data and processing across several processors. As mentioned in Section 3.2, the postings list occupied the largest fraction of memory in the TELLTALE prototype, while the corpus centroid was considerably smaller. By not keeping a postings list for each document, a single processor running the prototype could compute the centroid for a far larger corpus than it could index. This centroid could then be distributed to several CPUs, each of which maintains the postings list for a subset of the documents in the corpus.

We modified the `Tcl` interface to the TELLTALE prototype using the `dp` package [11], which allows `Tcl` applications to communicate via Unix sockets. This package allowed `Tcl`-controlled applications to act as servers that could receive commands, process them, and return responses in a way similar to Unix RPC. This process was entirely transparent to the application; only the client sending commands knew that they were being sent over a socket. This modification allowed us to write clients that did not include the TELLTALE prototype back end. Since their sole purpose was to send commands to TELLTALE servers, the clients did not need any TELLTALE-specific code.

We used 40 MB of articles from the *Wall Street Journal* for our experiments. First, we generated the corpus centroid (for 5-grams) on a single Sparc 10; this procedure processed about 100 KB of data per second, requiring 400 seconds to digest the entire corpus. The centroid was then written to disk. We then started prototypes on several different machines, and loaded the entire centroid into each one. Next, each machine read in a subset of the documents from the corpus, generating the necessary postings lists. Since each instance of the prototype was only responsible for a portion of the 40 MB corpus, they were able to fit the postings list in memory. Because each server used the corpus-wide centroid, its response to a similarity query against a piece of text was the same as if it had contained the postings list for the entire corpus. Of course, this method only worked because the "base" document had a postings list on each server – thus, each server generated such a list for the query text as part of the query processing.

Using this structure, a client was able send similarity queries to each of the servers and merge the responses. This method gave the same results as if the query were processed by a single instance of the prototype with a very large corpus. Because of the parallelism, though, the per-node memory requirement was reduced, as was the response time for the query. Our preliminary experiments showed the reduction in response time to be linear with the number of processors, though the reduction in memory usage was less than linear because of the overhead of storing the centroid multiple times.

We have not yet run experiments on reducing the size of the postings list; possible directions for this work are discussed in Section 3.5.

3.5 Future Prototype Experiments

The `dp` package allows TELLTALE to handle larger corpora by distributing them across several workstations. However, it does not increase the capacity of a single computer. To address this problem, we are pursuing three different approaches, each of which would allow a single workstation running TELLTALE to manage hundreds of megabytes of textual data. Combining single-node scaling with **dp** will allow a TELLTALE system to perform similarity computations over a corpus with a gigabyte or more of text.

The most obvious approach to indexing large amounts of text is to move the hash table from memory to disk. While a workstation memory is usually smaller than 100 MB, multi-gigabyte disks are both common and inexpensive. Storing the hash table on disk will allow a single workstation to index 200 MB of text using approximately 1.5 GB of disk, at a 1996 cost of under $400. Since the basic data structures remain unchanged, this approach will produce the same similarity results as TELLTALE would get using an in-memory hash table. The only possible drawback is poor performance — computing similarity would involve reading the entire hash table "bucket" for each n-gram in the query. While many buckets will be small, others (for example, " the ") may require reading several megabytes of data. Retrieving the on-disk data and processing it will likely require several minutes; however, this is the only one of the three methods that is guaranteed to generate the same list of linked documents as the original TELLTALE system did.

The second method to improve TELLTALE's scalability is to build the in-memory hash table using a subset of the n-grams from each document. Many of the n-grams in a document do not help to distinguish it from other documents in a corpus, either because they are too common or because they only occur a few times in the entire corpus. By eliminating the postings for these n-grams, we can reduce the amount of memory used by the hash table. In addition, n-grams that overlap might be removed because they convey little additional information. Reducing the number of postings from 1000 to 50-100 per document will shrink the hash table's memory usage by a factor of 10-20, increasing the number of documents that can be indexed by the same factor. However, this reduced hash table cannot be used to generate similarity scores because similarity depends on *all* of the n-grams in a document. Thus, this method will use two passes. The first pass will use the reduced hash table to find documents that are likely to be relevant. This pass will have high recall, but low precision. The second pass will increase precision by scanning in *all* of the n-grams for each document identified in the first pass and computing their similarity to the query text. So long as the centroid is that of the full corpus, the similarity values computed will be the same as if the similarity had been computed over the entire corpus. However, the first pass may miss some documents that should have been included near the top of the similarity list. This approach should be faster than the first method, but it may be less accurate — finding good algorithms for choosing n-grams for the reduced hash table and selecting appropriate documents in the first pass will be crucial to ensuring results similar to those of TELLTALE with a full in-memory hash table.

Using signature vectors [24] to characterize documents is the final method we will be using. Each document will have a long (2 Kbit or more) bit vector associated with it. Bits in this vector will be set by hashing n-grams to find an offset. As with the reduced hash table method, we must choose the n-grams that are appropriate for storing in this vector. Since the vector will require a fixed space regardless of how many bits are set, more n-grams can be in this list. With a 2 Kbit vector, the n-gram list might contain 20,000 entries. This allows more n-gram postings to be associated with each document at the cost of reduced precision. As with the reduced hash-table approach, this method will make two passes over the corpus. The low-precision first pass will identify documents "likely" to be interesting, and the second pass will proceed as for the reduced hash table. Since the first pass is not precise to begin with, the slight reduction in precision from signature vectors should not cause too many problems, and the increase in recall from storing more n-grams per document may reduce the number of documents that need to be identified for the second pass.

The three approaches will be compared in two areas: difference in results from in-memory TELLTALE, and performance. Since the disk-based hash table will produce the same results as the original TELLTALE implementation, it can be used as the benchmark for the other two approaches. The result of these experiments will show the tradeoff between speed and accuracy for the three approaches.

4. Summary and Conclusions

TELLTALE is a hypertext tool that dynamically computes links between related items of text using novel full text search techniques. TELLTALE's uses sliding n-gram based indexing and scoring techniques to provide robustness to degraded text and to remove dependencies on language. Linking mechanisms in TELLTALE tolerate high error rates (up to 30 percent of the characters), outperforming existing systems in its tolerance to high character error rates. TELLTALE is versatile and truly dynamic in the selection and calculation of links. A combination of three link types, Similarity, Lookup, and Disambiguated Lookup, provide the user with a collection of methods from which he can choose based on his immediate need. The dynamism in TELLTALE's link computation and link selection methods is augmented by link anchor selection and novel highlighting techniques. These dynamic linking and highlighting capabilities work together to give the TELLTALE dynamic hypertext environment its navigational and browsing capabilities. In addition to the high resistance to garbles provided by TELLTALE's linking and highlighting mechanisms, these mechanisms also provide TELLTALE with the necessary robustness to analyze and display multiple languages. Further, TELLTALE's navigation and browsing tools provide additional value and capability to that provided by traditional full text search and retrieval techniques. Finally, the ability to tolerate degraded and multilingual text in TELLTALE represent capabilities not shared by traditional full text retrieval tools.

Acknowledgement. Special thanks go to Marc Damashek for the invention of the sliding *n*-gram scoring technique which is so prominently featured in the TELL-TALE dynamic hypertext system; to Jonathan Cohen for his work on *n*-gram based highlights and his numerous insightful comments during the course of this research; to Tom Nelson who slaved over the code for the original TELLTALE prototype; and to Bill Rye for his many speedups and enhancements to the production version of TELLTALE.

References

1. M. Aboud, C. Chrisment, R. Razouk, F. Sedes, and C. Soule-Dupuy. Querying a hypertext information retrieval system by the use of classification. *Information Processing and Management*, 29(3):387–396, 1990.
2. W. B. Cavnar. N-Gram-Based text filtering for TREC-2. In Donna Harman, editor, *Proceedings of TREC-2: Text Retrieval Conference 2*, Gaithersburg, MD, 1993. National Institute of Standards and Technology.
3. Jonathan Cohen. Highlights: Language- and domain-independent automatic indexing terms for abstracting. To appear in JASIS, 1995.
4. The Unicode Consortium. *The Unicode Standard: World Wide Character Encoding*. Addison-Wesley, Redwood City, CA, 1992.
5. W. B. Croft and R. Thompson. I^3R: A new approach to the design of document retrieval systems. *Journal of the American Society for Information Science*, 38:389–404, 1987.
6. W. B. Croft and H. Turtle. A retrieval model for incorporating hypertext links. In *Hypertext '89 Proceedings*, pages 213–224. ACM Press, November 1989. Pittsburgh, PA, Nov 5-8.
7. Donald B. Crouch, Carolyn J. Crouch, and Glenn Andreas. The use of cluster hierarchies in hypertext information retrieval. In *Hypertext '89 Proceedings*, pages 225–237. ACM Press, November 1989. Pittsburgh, PA, Nov 5-8.
8. Marc Damashek, 1995. U. S. Patent Number 5,418,951.
9. Marc Damashek. Gauging similarity with N-Grams: Language-independent categorization of text. *Science*, 267:843–848, 10 February 1995.
10. R. D'Amore and C. Mah. One-time complete indexing of text: theory and practice. In *Proceedings 8th International ACM Conference on Research and Development in Information Retrieval*. ACM Press, 1985.
11. The dp package for Tcl/Tk. Available for ftp from ftp://aud.alcatel.com/tcl/extensions/tcl-dp3.3b1.tar.gz.
12. Douglas C. Engelbart and W. K. English. A research center for augmenting human intellect. In *Proceedings of the Fall Joint Computer Conference*. AFIPS Press, Montvale, NY, 1968.
13. Mark E. Frisse and Steven B. Cousins. Information retrieval from hypertext: Update on the dynamic medical handbook project. In *Hypertext '89 Proceedings*. ACM Press, November 1989. Pittsburgh, PA, Nov 5-8.
14. Donna Harmon, editor. *TREC-2- Text REtrieval Conference-2*. National Institute of Standards and Technology, August 1993.
15. Donald E. Knuth. *Sorting and Searching*, pages 561–562. Addison Wesley, 1973.
16. Theodor H. Nelson. Managing immense storage. *BYTE*, 13(1):225–238, January 1988.

17. Jakob Nielsen. *Hypertext and Hypermedia.* Academic Press, San Diego, CA, 1990.
18. Claudia E. Pearce. *A Dynamic Hypertext Environment Through n-gram Analysis.* PhD thesis, University of Maryland Baltimore County, 1994.
19. Claudia E. Pearce. Dynamic hypertext links for highly degraded data in telltale. In *Fourth Annual Symposium on Document Analysis and Information Retrieval,* pages 89–106. Information Science Research Institute, University of Nevada Las Vegas, University of Nevada, 4505 Maryland Parkway, Box 454021, Las Vegas, Nevada 89154-4021, 1995.
20. Gerard Salton and Michael McGill. *Introduction to Modern Information Retrieval.* McGraw-Hill Book Company, 1983.
21. C. Y. Suen. *n*-gram statistics for natural language understanding and text processing. *IEEE Transactions on Pattern Analysis and Machine Intelligence,* PAMI-1(2):164–172, 1979.
22. Brent B. Welch. *Practical Programming in Tcl and Tk.* Prentice-Hall, Inc., 1995.
23. P. Willette. Document retrieval experiments using indexing vocabularies of varying size. II. hashing, truncation, diagram and trigram encoding of index terms. *Journal of Documentation,* 35:296–305, December 1979.
24. Ian H. Witten, Alistair Moffat, and Timothy C. Bell. *Managing Gigabytes.* Van Nostrand Reinhold, 1994.
25. E. J. Yannakoudakis, P. Goyal, and J. A. Huggil. The generation and use of text fragments for data compression. *Information Processing and Management,* 18(1):15–21, 1982.
26. E. M. Zamora, J. J. Pollock, and A. Zamora. The use of trigram analysis for spelling error detection. *Information Processing and Management,* 17(6):305–316, 1981.

Domain Model Based Hypertext for Collaborative Authoring

Weigang Wang[1], Claude Ghaoui[2], Roy Rada[3]

[1] GMD-IPSI, Dolivostr. 15, D-64293, Darmstadt, Germany
[2] CMS, Liverpool John Moores University, Liverpool L3 3AF, U.K.
[3] EECS, Washington State University, Pullman, WA 99164-2752, U.S.A.

Summary. Domain information models reflect the common structural and semantic characteristics of information organization in particular domains. This chapter describes the creation of a domain model based hypertext and the experiences gained in using such semantic net based systems. Experiences indicate that the use of semantic nets for representing domain model based hypertext can enhance hypertext organization and can maintain the structural and semantic consistency of the documents created in a collaborative environment. An active management document defined with such a model can facilitate the coordination of an authoring team. The structured hypertext feature of such a system can facilitate the automatic construction of HTML; hence the methods advocated in this paper for structuring and managing collaborative hypertext are directly applicable to the World Wide Web.

1. Introduction

The authoring of large technical documents is typically a collaborative process. To improve the performance of the process, tools for establishing shared information organization models and tools for coordinating the team effort are needed.

A semantic net is a knowledge representation scheme consisting of a directed graph in which concepts are represented as nodes, and relations between concepts are represented as links [13]. The analogy of a semantic net to hypertext is straightforward and has long been recognized [3, 18]. While most hypertexts can be seen to have a semantic net underlying them, the hypertexts most explicitly related to semantic nets are the ones with typed or named nodes and links. An *unconstrained semantic net* corresponds to a general hypertext system with arbitrary link types that are free from constraints. A *constrained semantic net* corresponds to a hypertext system whose typed links can only be used between allowable node types. When node types and link types are defined according to particular domain concepts and relationships between these concepts, the constrained semantic net becomes a domain model based semantic net. With such a semantic net, shared information organization models can be maintained by the hypertext system irrespective of changes to the semantic net.

Collaborative authoring tasks involve high levels of uncertainty and ambiguity, and therefore require coordination. Rice, Woljslaw, and Malone

[24, 31, 14] define Coordination Theory as the body of principles describing how actors can work together harmoniously, performing activities which are directed towards some ends or goals. Many coordination processes require that a decision be made and accepted by a group. Group decisions, in turn, require members of the group to communicate in some form [16]. This communication requires that messages be transported in a language that is understandable to both. Different collaborative authoring systems provide different mechanisms that facilitate coordination. Examples include providing shared views that increase the awareness of individuals and groups, and defining roles and activities [4]. The *domain model based hypertext* can be used as a communication channel for coordination, because it can not only create shared information organization models, but can also communicate the content, the structure, and the associated information of the models. In our approach, in addition to using the established structure of the targeted document products as a means for coordination, a coordination plan is defined and maintained; this plan is an active document that supports granular coordination requirements which are difficult to handle by a computer system alone without human facilitation.

Section 2 describes the use of semantic nets to represent domain information models. A traversal-based document composition method is described, and examples of the rules that maintain the models are given. Section 3 presents experience gained from using semantic net based collaborative hypertext systems. Section 3.1 describes an authoring experience with two similar semantic net base hypertext systems, one with constraints and the other without. This experience shows the value of computer assistance in maintaining high level structural and semantic consistency of the underlying semantic nets. In Section 3.2, a coordination plan is defined to support authoring and publishing. This experience shows how to define a plan document as an active management tool for coordinating co-authoring tasks. Section 3.3 describes the automatic construction of hypertext documents for the World Wide Web. Section 4 discusses the implication of this research for the World Wide Web.

2. Domain Model Based Semantic Nets

Similar to semantic modeling in the database field [17], creation of a domain model based semantic net has the following components:

- domain analysis to produce a domain model, which depicts the domain concepts and relations between these concepts;
- semantic net representation of the domain model (defining node types and link types);
- creation of rules to govern the description (creation and manipulation) of the semantic net; and
- creation of operators for manipulating the semantic net.

2.1 Domain Analysis

The goal of domain analysis for information organization is to derive a domain information model that depicts the domain concepts and relations between these concepts. The application domain for this work is technical document preparation with intensive reuse of existing documents. For effective reuse, information needs to be well organized [23]. In a library, an indexing language (a thesaurus or a classification scheme) plays a key role in organizing thousands of documents and in facilitating the retrieval of the documents [12]. A table of contents helps readers and writers visualize the structure within a document. The headings of the tables of contents constitute a granular indexing of the contents under them, thus helping users to pinpoint the relevant document sections.

A thesaurus is a set of concepts in which each concept ('preferred term') is associated with 'non-preferred terms' (synonyms of the preferred term) and a few basic relations among concepts. These relations are defined by international standards [11] and include 'narrower than' (NT), 'used for' (UF) and 'related to' (RT) relations. A term is a word or sequence of words that refers to a concept. A document can be viewed as an analogue to thesaurus, headings in a document can be seen as concepts, the containment relation between a section and its subsections is a kind of 'NT' relation, and the cross-reference relation is a kind of 'RT' relation. Annotations can be added to make a comment or to initiate a discussion (i.e., to comment on a comment).

In the above model, the hierarchical (or multi-hierarchical) relation of the thesaurus and the table of contents constitute a backbone of a structured hypertext, while other cross-reference (referential) relations are attached to the backbone to form a network. The linking semantics in this model are reflected in the correct use of these relations between the concepts that bear them. The structural and semantic knowledge defines a domain model for organizing information in an understandable and meaningful way.

2.2 Semantic Net Representation

A semantic net can be used as a unifying representation for a single document or for a library of documents. to do so, nodes can be classified by the semantic concepts they represent into:

- thesaurus node types (such as 'preferred term' and 'non-preferred term'),
- document node types (such as 'section'), and
- annotation node types (such as 'comment').

Link types used with the above node types include:

- thesaurus organizational links (such as 'NT'),
- document organizational links (such as 'document'),
- annotation organizational links (such as 'comment'), and

– referential links (such as 'RT' and 'see also').

For guiding the traversal of a semantic net, link types are grouped into two main categories [3]:

– organizational links, which include the above first three types of links representing hierarchical and multi-hierarchical containment relations among concepts; and
– referential links, which include all kinds of cross-reference links.

Most technical documents follow a logical structure. A composition schema based on such logical structure is particularly useful for the traversal of a semantic net. The bases of the composition schema are the separation of nodes from their contents and the classification of links into organizational and referential links. While the referential links have no structural restrictions, the organizational links should form a rooted weighted DAG (Directed Acyclic Graph) [10].

With the semantic net representation, a document is composed of a hierarchical backbone together with the referential links attached to the hierarchy. It is constructed by a variant depth-first traversal algorithm. The traversal program starts with a given node, from which it goes along organizational links (by default) to produce the hierarchical backbone. The traversal algorithm differs from a standard depth-first traversal, in that a node is allowed to be visited more than once. This allows the creation of multi-hierarchies using organizational links between existing nodes. The schema can provide users with static composites (stable documents) by applying its default traversal options, and it can also help to generate dynamic composites by allowing users to specify various traversal options.

2.3 Rules and Operators

To maintain the consistency of the semantic net, rules governing its description are needed. Two classes of rules are defined:

– graph-based rules for enforcing structural constraints; and
– semantics-based rules for enforcing semantic constraints.

Structural constraints concern the 'shape' formed by organizational links; in this model the shape is constrained to be a rooted weighted DAG. Example of graph-based rules are 'a node must be created together with an organizational link'; 'an organizational link between two existing nodes can be created, only if no cycle is to be created organizational links'; and 'when the last organizational link to a node is to be deleted, the DAG structure rooted from the node and all other links attached to the sub-DAG must be removed'. Semantic constraints concern the 'meaning' of semantic net; this is reflected in the consistent use of semantically typed links between allowable semantically typed nodes. A semantics-based rule is defined as a triplet of (source-node-type, link-type, target-node-type). For example, the rule (preferred term, NT, preferred term) specifies that the organizational thesaurus link 'NT' can only be used between two nodes representing thesaurus 'preferred terms'.

The operators on the semantic net can be generally classified into two categories: semantic net manipulation operators and semantic net presentation operators. Semantic net manipulation operators include the creation, copying, modification, and deletion of nodes, contents, links, and documents. Semantic net presentation operators include the generation and display of hierarchical views and semantic net views, and filtered views. Through enforcement of the rules, structural and semantic constrains can be maintained after applying any operators to the semantic net.

3. Experiences

Two prototype systems, one named MUCH (Many Using and Creating Hypertext) [22] and the other named RICH (Reusable Intelligent Collaborative Hypermedia) [28] have been implemented using similar semantic net models described above. In both systems, the semantic nets are presented to users with a hierarchical view browser. The hierarchical view browser has a fold-unfold outline window on the left hand-side, and a content window on the right-hand side. MUCH has no constraints on linking and uses a depth-first traversal algorithm to generate hierarchies from the underlying network. The default traversal goes along links of any type. On the other hand, RICH uses the domain model based semantic net with linking constraints and with a variant depth-first traversal algorithm. Its default traversal goes along organizational links.

In the next three subsections, three authoring experiences are described: one for creating a hypertext document with the two systems and another for using a shared document to coordinate the collaborative authoring tasks. All the users (authors) in these two cases are computer scientists. The third subsection describes the construction of hypertext documents in HTML with the RICH system.

3.1 Creating Multi-hierarchical Hypertext Documents

Four people were asked to prepare a multi-faceted plan document. One group of two people used the MUCH system and the other group of two people used the RICH system. The requirement for the plan document was that it should have a multi-hierarchy structure as its backbone and many referential links attached to the hierarchies. Each hierarchy emphasizes a facet of the plan of a research organization, such as 'People', 'Groups', and 'Roles'. 'Groups' are decomposed into several subgroups for different tasks, such as 'Research

Group', 'Tool Group', and 'Publish Group'. 'People' take different 'Roles' and work in subgroups.

The group that used MUCH faced many problems and failed to produce the required plan document. They found the creation of the multi-hierarchies in the MUCH system to be difficult, especially in a collaborative authoring environment. They realized that creating or deleting a link between two existing nodes might lead to radical consequences (different outline views). The document they finally created has only one hierarchy.

The group used the RICH system successfully produced the required multi-faceted document. First, they created a main hierarchical structure with the default organizational document links. Then they used organizational links to create multi-hierarchy structures. Finally they added referential links among the hierarchies and completed the hypertext document (see Fig. 1). In the hierarchical view browser (shown in the upper left-hand corner of Fig. 1), different headings at the top level can be unfolded for different perspectives. In the semantic net browser (shown in the lower left-hand corner of Fig. 1), it can be seen that the "Software Reuse" paper has multiple incoming links; this indicates that the paper was co-authored by Rada and Wang, published in Software Engineering Journal, and relates to a hypothesis on software reuse and hypertext.

Fig. 3.1. A Hypertext Document for Research Management

Users may not understand the algorithm used by the MUCH system, but even those who understand the algorithm may not appreciate its use for composing hypertext documents. They typically try to predict the outline traversed from a small network; this approach can easily fail when the number of nodes increases or when multiple users modify the network at the same time. With the RICH system, the default traversal algorithm always presents users with stable hierarchical views. This is what users expected. Also with the RICH system, when creating a new node or creating a link between two existing nodes, both the general graph-based rules and the domain linking rules will be checked. If a violation is detected, a warning message will be displayed (see Fig. 2), and the operation will be aborted. In Fig. 2, the warning on the left-hand side is given when a graph-based rule is violated. The warning on the right-hand side is given when a semantics-based rule is violated. In this way, the consistency of the underlying semantic net is maintained.

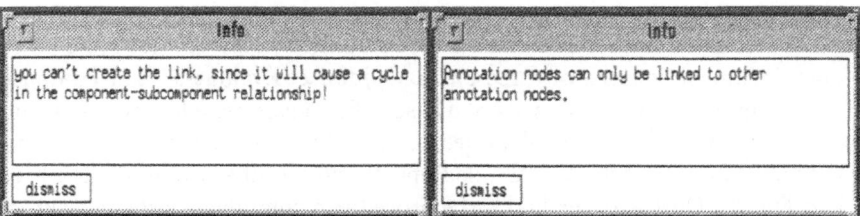

Fig. 3.2. Warning Messages

3.2 The Support of Coordination

A total of fifteen people worked on authoring three textbooks with the MUCH system [6]. They were divided into three teams, one team for each textbook. The work aimed to produce two forms of each textbook: hypertext and paper. The three books are: 'Software Reuse', 'Interactive Media', and 'Developing Educational Hypermedia'. In the following, they will be referred to as the 'Reuse Book', the 'Media Book' and the 'Education Book' respectively.

Some members of the authoring teams played both managerial and authoring roles. The three teams formed a 'book publishing group'. The members of the authoring teams had different expertise and experiences. For each team, the major author was informally recognized to be in charge of his team. The director divided the work into several subtasks, outlined time schedules and distributed the work among the members. The topics of the three books were partly related and overlapped. A 9-month period was planned for completing the books.

In this task, some issues, which would require coordination, were expected to arise. The following are some examples:

1. Due to the overlapping expertise and experiences, authors are expected to be asked to contribute to different textbooks, on parts relevant to their knowledge.
2. Authors need to organize and understand their individual work in relation to that of the group.
3. Conflict is likely to occur, not only at preplanned locations and times, but also unpredictably as two or more authors work on shared parts of a document.
4. There is a need to coordinate the merging of individual contributions, while maintaining consistency, coherence, and overall quality.
5. there is a need to check that plans and progress match long-term and short-term goals, keeping up with time-schedules.

On such a scale, it is dangerous to rely entirely on collaborator's good will for completing a satisfactory work. This scenario conveys the complexity of the authoring task at hand, which motivated the definition of the coordination plan.

A coordination plan is defined and maintained in the MUCH system. The plan document consists of three parts: Guidance, Evaluation and Feedback.

Guidance is mapped to a set of five specifics: goals, people, roles, schedules and procedures. Goals, people, roles and schedules are defined and entered in the form of two reports: the 'Guide Report' and 'Feedback Report' (see Fig. 2 and Fig. 3). On the other hand, the procedures component provides authors with guidance on how to perform certain tasks, like authoring, linearization and handling reuse. It may also provide guidance for handling other problems, like maintaining coherence and consistency, and reducing redundancy. Any other issues that are relevant to the task at hand may be defined as part of the 'procedures' component.

Evaluation part includes defining standard criteria and a mechanism for systematic evaluation of progress and quality. Evaluation is used to determine whether achievement is consistent with long term and short term goals. It is mapped to a set of two specifics: the first comprises criteria for evaluating 'progress' in terms of meeting time schedules and matching goals, and the second comprises criteria for evaluating 'quality of content'.

Feedback is a necessary condition for goal setting to work. Regular evaluation is usually expected to provide regular feedback that includes precise directions for what to do next. Feedback is mapped to a set of three specifics: the first and second specifics, like those of the evaluating criteria, provide feedback on progress and quality issues. The third provides feedback on specific problems, and suggests alternate solutions. The Problem-Solution component stores any outstanding problems, their causes and possible solutions.

In addition to providing goals-people-roles-schedules, the coordination plan included a contingency plan for coping with changes in personnel, duties, and commitments. Guidance on procedures for authoring included directions on handling problems. Authors were provided with a list of criteria for quality

mucha Outline Window	mucha Display Window
mucha Document Coordination More...	mucha File Search/Spell Font Justify Region Title Page Media More...

Hierarchical Browser | Info | Update | Mail | Week_3rd_June_94

Left panel (Hierarchical Browser):

```
much
 * activities
    * administration
    * research management
    * publishing group
       * management reports
          Week 9th Sept
          Week  26th Aug94
          Week 12th Aug 94
          Week 29th Jul 94
          Week 18th Jul 94
          Week 17thJune 94
        " Week 3rd June 94
        * Week 20th May 94
        * Week 6th May 94
          Week 22April 94
        * Week 1 April 94
        * Week 18 March 94
          Week 4 March 94
        * Week 18th Feb 94
        * Week 4th Feb 94
        * Week 21st Jan. 94
        * Week 7th Jan 94
```

Right panel (Display Window):

The CoRe Organisation – Objectives Sheet		
Group Name:	Books Publishing	
Group Guide:	Claude Ghaoui	
Date:		3 Jun 1994
Objectives from Last Meeting	Name	Completed?
Books: Reuse: fix Printing problems,	Mick	yes
review and send to Intellect on 26/5	Claude	yes
OSCAR: complete new changes,	Roy/Renata	yes
print and send to 2 publishers.	Claude	yes
Drawing Book: Revised Introductions,	Claude	yes
sent Revised Intro to Elizabeth Stone,	Claude	yes
sent email of all updates all editors.	Claude	yes
Writing Book: contacted Morgan and	Claude	yes
he replied (see note below).		
G&H Book: complete changes	Roy	ask Roy?
Med–Multi: format the book to Intellec	Claude/Helen	not yet
CD: collect video material from WWW	Claude	yes
get people's permission to publish:–	Claude	
MM94:		
send update info for Author Kit	Claude	yes
Objectives for Next Meeting		Name
G&H Book:finish all changes–concise outline.		Roy

Fig. 3.3. Guide Report

mucha Outline Window	mucha Display Window
mucha Document Coordination More...	mucha More...

Hierarchical Browser | Info | Update | Mail | feedback

Left panel (Hierarchical Browser):

```
much
 * activities
    * administration
    * research management
    * publishing group
       * management reports
          Week 9th Sept
          Week  26th Aug94
          Week 12th Aug 94
          Week 29th Jul 94
          Week 18th Jul 94
          Week 17thJune 94
        * Week 3rd June 94
        * Week 20th May 94
          feedback
        * Week 6th May 94
          Week 22April 94
        * Week 1 April 94
        * Week 18 March 94
          Week 4 March 94
        * Week 18th Feb 94
        * Week 4th Feb 94
        * Week 21st Jan. 94
```

Right panel (Display Window):

Were objectives of previous 2–week period met?
No (but due really to the large number of objectives outlined). But considerable progress has been made in getting most of the planned books nearer to publication.
****
Are 2–week objectives producing measureable deliverables?
Very much so. e.g. the Reuse book is now very close to matching Intellect's format requirements.
****
Do 2–week objectives match 4–month objectives (every guide report should list its 4–month objectives)?
Obviously so. 4 month objective to publish all books, this is slowly (but surely) being realised.
****
Is there a good match from objectives to roles and from roles to staff?
Maybe yes, however, there appears to be a lot of emphasis on Claude doing tasks herself (this is apparently unavoidable at this stage).
****
Is staff morale good?
Let's just say the work is being done. The group is under quite a lot of pressure with all 5 of its projects at critical stages.
****
* On the McGraw–Hill side:
  Haynes has agreed with the intros. but nothing from Saul. Would you please suggest a revision to the two remaining intros. —- J
  send intros to McGraw–Hill by end of this week and then communicate regularly with Elizabeth Stone to assure that book is moving smoothly.
* The Expertmedia book is less critical for now.
* The three critical books are the Reuse, OSCAR, and Peopleware ones.

Done.

Fig. 3.4. Feedback Report

control [30]. This helped in conducting a systematic evaluation and receiving regular feedback. The three books authored with the guidance of this coordination plan were successfully published by different publishing houses [21, 20, 19].

However, as far as the semantic net model is concerned, contrary to the expectations of the builders of the MUCH system, the users did not exploit the ability to type semantic links [29]. Typically authors used the default link type regardless of their semantic intentions. When a link type other than the default type was chosen, that choice was often inconsistent with the way another user would label a similar link. The system has proven to be useful for authoring conventional documents. Authors were not practically able to produce hypertext documents. These experiences from another angle provide justification for the domain model based approach for creating hypertext.

3.3 Construction of HTML Documents

The RICH system is suitable for writing documents with markup languages, such as LaTeX and groff. As the World Wide Web (WWW) becomes more and more popular, one of the applications of the system is to create documents in HTML. Because the high level document logical structure is handled by the system, there is no need for authors to add markup (such ¡h1¿ and ¡h2¿) on headings. Another benefit of not hard-coding heading tags in node name or contents is that it enables nodes (and their sub-hierarchies) to be moved (or copied or shared) within or among documents in the authoring process. The heading tags will be automatically added when a tree of nodes is exported as a document. Referential links (cross-references) to related information can be added into node contents in URL (or UID) format.

To generate a HTML document, users can select a starting node as the root of the document, and select one of the exporting options:

1. a single file with level headings. This option produces a document suitable for printing a paper copy,
2. a single file with level headings and a table of contents pointing to the corresponding sections. This option is for the presentation of small documents,
3. a set of files, each as a node of the produced document, presented in a design similar to the Emacs-Info pages [26]. In addition to the content of the node, the top of each page contains the title of the node, and pointers to upper, previous, and next nodes in the document. At the bottom of the page there is a list of headings pointing to sub-sections. In addition, a toc page (table of contents) is also generated. This option is for the presentation of documents such as manuals that are not supposed to be read from beginning to the end.
4. a set of files, similar to those in the third option. The difference is that, instead of indicating a breadth-first walk-through (as used in Emacs-Info), the 'next' and 'previous' pointer here are used for sequential reading

(i.e. indicating a depth-first walk-through). This is for the presentation of documents such as books that are likely to be read from the beginning to the end.

All these options are implemented with different (or variant) traversal programs upon the same underlying semantic net. For instance, the first two options correspond to a depth-first traversal, while the last two options correspond to a combination of depth-first and breadth-first traversals. Other options can be added for new presentation designs.

Authoring HTML documents with the system, users can not only generate HTML documents in their chosen presentation designs, but they can also make use of all its support for collaborative authoring.

4. Discussion

How should hypertext be structured? In Intermedia [8], a node is supposed to be a document; while in most hypertext systems, such as Textnet [27] and NoteCards [9], a node is often a part of a document. Some of hypertext authoring systems sharply constrain the types of links that can be used, while others impose minimal constraints. KMS [1], Augment [5], Guide [2] encourage the use of hierarchical link types. Xanadu [15], NoteCards, Hyper-Card [7], HyperTies [25], and Intermedia do not favor a constraint on links. They allow any link types, and allow a link to connect any node to any other node. However, most of these free linking systems provide some constructs for creating hierarchical structures. Examples are the 'filebox' of NoteCards and the 'toc' node of Textnet.

The World Wide Web (WWW) does not differentiate between organizational and referential links; links are not typed at all. The World Wide Web project argues that documents do not necessarily have an overall structure. It aims to allow information to be gathered from authors who may be no more expert than their readers. But this freedom, especially without distinguishing organizational links from referential links, may be disadvantageous when automatic composition mechanisms for collecting a group of related nodes are required. For instance, the currently WWW cannot support the printing of a group of nodes as a single document. Programs that fetch a group of related files from WWW often ends up with a large collection of files, most of which may be irrelevant. With hypertexts growing large in volume and more cooperative in user interaction, the importance of an overall hierarchical indexing structure becomes evident. The typical examples from the WWW are the provision of internal document structure (indicated by heading tags of HTML) and the provision of various indexing pages and home pages.

A semantic net is a reasonably straightforward knowledge representation scheme which has a limited logical expressiveness but a substantial intuitive appeal. While other representations, such as general object-oriented ones, might be more flexible, they are not as readily created and manipulated on the surface by naive users. The capability of representing a domain model by a semantic net can improve hypertext organization and reusability. The key to achieving this is to apply a set of rules to govern the creation and manipulation of a domain model based semantic net. In this chapter, a method for constructing such a semantic net has been introduced. By incorporating rules, an unconstrained semantic net can be converted into a constrained semantic net, and a constrained semantic net can be used to create a domain model based semantic net. In this way, the flexibility of a general hypertext system and the intelligent aid of an expertext system can be bridged. With the domain model based semantic net, the shared information organization models can be maintained irrespective to changes to the semantic net. The structured hypertext model of the RICH system provides a promising unifying representation for small-volume hypertext (a single document) and large-volume hypertext (a library of documents).

Collaborative authoring challenges the designers of authoring technology. Although patterns of collaboration vary across groups and contexts, a joint creation of complex documents normally involves considerable social and intellectual complexity. Socially, it requires that group members establish shared goals, divide tasks among themselves keeping in mind goals of others, and resolve questions of authority within their group. Intellectually, it requires that group members establish shared goals and common understanding. They must also solve high-level writing problems such as deciding on a document structure that is consistent with their goals. To meet these social and intellectual challenges, the group must adopt procedures for enabling it to launch work, circulate and discuss drafts, review and revise each others' work, and make sure that individual work fits when incorporated into a unified whole. All of these activities require effective coordination and planning, which this chapter tackles by defining and maintaining a coordination plan together with the targeted document produces.

Although the World Wide Web has become very popular as an information sharing and browsing system, as a platform for collaborative authoring; it lacks structural constructs and its stateless network protocol does not easily support the development of group awareness mechanisms. The work presented in this chapter may provide some insight into the incorporation of structural constructs into WWW-like systems, and the coordination of collaborative authoring tasks with management related information stored as hypertext documents.

References

1. R. Akscyn, D. McCracken, and E. Yoder. KMS: A distributed hypermedia system for managing knowledge in organizations. *Communications of the ACM*, *31*, 7, pages 820–835, 1988.

2. Peter J. Brown. Turning ideas into products: The guide system. *Hypertext '87*, pages 33–40, November 1987.
3. J. Conklin. Hypertext: An introduction and survey. *Computer, 20, 9*, pages 17–41, September 1987.
4. P. Dourish and V. Bellotti. Awareness and coordination in shared workspaces. In *Proceedings of the Conference on Computer-Supported Cooperative Work, Oct 31-Nov 4, Toronto, Canada*, pages 107–114, New York, 1992. ACM Press.
5. D. Engelbart. Authorship provisions in augment. In *IEEE Compcon Conference*, 1984.
6. C. Ghaoui. Authoring and linearizing hypertext for electronic and print publishing. *PhD Thesis*, May 1995.
7. G. Goodman and M. Abel. Communication and collaboration: Facilitating cooperative work through communication. *Office: Technology and People, 3*, pages 129–145, 1987.
8. B. J. Haan, P. Kahn, V. A. Riley, J. H. Coombs, and N. K. Meyrowitz. IRIS hypermedia service. *Communications of the ACM, 35, 1*, pages 36–51, January 1992.
9. F. Halasz. Reflections on notecards: Seven issues for the next generation of hypermedia systems. *Communications of the ACM, 31, 7*, pages 836–855, 1988.
10. F. Halasz and M. Schwartz. The dexter hypertext reference model. *Communications of the ACM, 37, 2*, pages 30–39, February 1994.
11. ISO. Guidelines for the establishment and development of multilingual thesauri. *ISO 5964*.
12. F. Lancaster. *Vocabulary Control for Information Retrieval*. Information Resources Press, Washington, DC, 1972.
13. F. Lehmann. Semantic networks. In F. Lehmann, editor, *Semantic Networks in Artificial Intelligence*, pages 1–50. Pergamon Press Ltd, 1992.
14. T. Malone and K. Crowston. What is coordination theory and how can it help design cooperative work systems? In *Proceedings of the Conference on Computer-Supported Cooperative Work, Los Angeles, Oct 7-10*, pages 357–370, New York, 1990. ACM Press.
15. T. Nelson. Virtual world without end. In *keynote to the CyberArts International conference*, 1990.
16. G. Olson and D. Atkins. Supporting collaboration with advanced multimedia electronic mail. In J. Galegher, R. E Kraut, and C. Egido, editors, *Intellectual teamwork: The Social and Technological Foundations of Cooperative Work*, pages 429–451. Hillsdale, NJ: Lawrence Erlbaum, 1990.
17. K. Parsaye, M. Chignell, S. Khoshafian, and H. Wong. *Intelligent Databases*. John Wiley and Sons, Inc., 1989.
18. R. Rada. Hypertext writing and document reuse: the role of a semantic net. *Electronic Publishing, 3, 3*, pages 3–13, 1990.
19. R. Rada. *Developing Educational Hypermedia: Coordination and Reuse*. Ablex Publishing, Norwood, New Jersey, to appear 1995.
20. R. Rada. *Interactive Media*. Springer-Verlag, New York, 1995.
21. R. Rada. *Software Reuse*. Intellect Books of Oxford, England for paperback and Ablex Publishing of New Jersey for hardback, 1995.
22. R. Rada, W. Wang, and A. Birchall. An expertext system for collaborative authoring. *Expert Systems with Applications, 5, 3/4*, pages 275–288, 1992.
23. R. Rada, W. Wang, H. Mili, J. Heger, and W. Scherr. Software reuse: from text to hypertext. *Software Engineering Journal*, pages 311–321, September 1992.

24. R. Rice and J. Huguley. Describing collaborative forms: A profile of the team-writing process. *IEEE Transactions On Professional Communication, vol. 37, no. 3*, pages 163–170, September 1994.
25. B. Shneiderman. User interface design for the hyperties electronic encyclopedia. In *ACM Hypertext'87 Proceedings*, pages 189–194, 1987.
26. R. Stallman. EMACS manual for TWENEX users. *AI Memo 555*, October 1981.
27. R. Trigg and M. Weiser. TEXTNET: A network-based approach to text handling. *ACM Transactions on Office Information Systems, 4, 1*, pages 1–23, 1986.
28. W. Wang. Semantic net based hypertext for authoring and reuse. *PhD Thesis*, 1995.
29. W. Wang and R. Rada. Experiences with semantic net-based hypermedia. *International Journal of Human-Computer Studies*, 1995. (expected to appear in the special issue on knowledge-based hypermedia).
30. K. Whittaker. *Systematic Evaluation: Methods and Sources for Assessing Books*. Clive Bingley Publishing, London, 1982.
31. C. Wojslaw. Teamwork and community. *IEEE Technology and Society Magazine, vol. 11, no. 4, Winter 1992/1993*, pages 23–27, 1993.

Information Retrieval, Information Structure, and Information Agents

Daniela Rus[1] and Devika Subramanian[2]

[1] Department of Computer Science, Dartmouth College, Hanover, NH 03755, USA
[2] Department of Computer Science, Rice University, Houson TX 77005, USA

Summary. This paper presents a customizable architecture for software agents that capture and access information in large, heterogeneous, distributed electronic repositories. The key idea is to exploit underlying *structure* at various levels of granularity to build high-level indices with task-specific interpretations. Information agents construct such indices and are configured as a network of reusable modules called structure detectors and segmenters. We illustrate our architecture with the design and implementation of smart information filters in two contexts: retrieving stock market data from Internet newsgroups, and retrieving technical reports from Internet ftp sites.

1. Introduction

The proliferation of information in electronic form and the development of high-speed networking make the problem of locating and retrieving information in vast electronic environments one of the grand challenges of computer science. Examples of electronic corpora include repositories of newspapers and technical reports, data from high-energy physics experiments, weather satellite data, and audio and video recordings. Examples of tasks that query and manipulate these electronic collections include content-based retrieval of technical reports, access of documents via citations, summaries of stock prices from archives, and retrieval of temporal weather patterns from a weather database. The goal of *information capture and access* (ICA) is to organize and filter electronic corpora guided by user-specified tasks. We organize data by acquiring partial models that associate task-level content with information, which in turn facilitates location and retrieval. Our research goal in this paper is to develop methods for solving the ICA problem and to provide a computational paradigm for *customizing* this process in heterogeneous, distributed repositories.

A diverse collection of tools like Wais, Smart, Gopher, Archie and Mosaic [Kah, SM, SEKN] have been developed for information capture and access. Information capture tools like Gopher and World Wide Web (WWW) provide hierarchical and networked organization of data, but they require substantial manual effort to build and maintain. Information access over Gopher and WWW is via manually hard-wired hyperlinks and keyword search. In addition, existing automated search engines take little advantage either of non-textual cues in electronic data or of other underlying structures. Consider the task of finding papers on cognitive theories of practice substantiated by human data. A word-based query involving the keywords `cognitive, theory, practice`, and `data` produces hundreds of papers, only a small fraction of which are actually relevant. The problem is that in a database of psychology papers these keywords occur frequently in varying contexts. Thus, the precision value for the search is low. A better automatic filter can be constructed by exploiting knowledge about conventions of data representation. For example, the fact that experimental data is generally presented in tables and graphs in technical papers can be used to substantially reduce the number of potentially relevant matches to the query. Cues like tables and graphs complement the textual content of documents. In addition, they generalize to other types of media (like video). Information retrieval tools need both textual and "structural" cues for query formulation, as well as for information capture and access.

We propose an approach to ICA that relies on *structural* cues to construct data indices at the appropriate level of granularity. We call this approach *structure-based information capture and access.*[1] The term structure refers to any pattern that is at a level of abstraction higher than the basic unit of data representation (e.g., characters and pixels). Patterns that exist in metadata (for instance in the hyperlink structure for a collection of documents) yield organization and semantic structures. Tables, figures, lists, paragraphs and sections are standardized, layout abstractions for documents. Theorems, lemmas, examples and counterexamples are content abstractions. These structures have evolved as conventions for organizing documents and can be exploited naturally as filters to select relevant data. In general, high-level structures are not immediately available, and computation is needed to reveal them.

We advance the theory that such structure is a natural basis for modularizing information search computations. Modularization supports the orthogonal processing of different data dimansions (sound, video, pictures, text, organization) and permits exploiting domain constraints to enhance performance. In this paper, we provide a framework for synthesizing *customized* information processing engines by assembling pre-fabricated modules that reveal and detect structure in data.

These pre-fabricated structure-detecting and revealing modules can be implemented as static programs. For distributed corpora, we claim that it is more advantageous to organize them as *transportable software agents.* Transportable agents can travel from machine to machine processing information locally, thus avoiding costly data transfers over congested networks. Our transportable agents navigate the Internet using reactive planning methods and a virtual yellow page system for guidance [RGK]. Agents, in addition

---

[1] Conventional word-based systems are also structure-based ICA systems. However, they exploit only one type of structure in the data.

to being transportable and capable to plan, can learn and make decisions autonomously.

We draw inspiration from robotics [Bro1, Bro2, Don, JR] to design information agents. The basic modules for physical robots are sensors and effectors. Our information agents are autonomous sensori-computational "circuits" comprised of a network of *virtual sensors* to detect, extract, and interpret structure in data and *virtual effectors* for transportation. This paper describes our agent architecture and the sensory modules required for processing information. These modules fit on our transportable agent platform called *Agent Tcl* [Gra, RGK, GKNRC]. Transportable agents are programs that can move through a network under their own control, migrating from host to host and interacting with other resources and agents. They are capable of sensing for network and software conditions and navigate driven by reactive plans. This is possible because an Agent Tcl agent is a program capable of suspending execution, moving to a different machine, and re-starting from the interruption point. For more details see [Gra, RGK, GKNRC].

Two types of sensori-computational modules are necessary for ICA: (1) structure detectors, which efficiently decide whether a block of data has a specified property (for example, "is this block of text a table?"); and (2) segmenters, which partition the data into blocks that are appropriate for the detectors. The modules are efficient, reliable in the presence of uncertainties in data interpretation and extraction, and fault tolerant. The modules are capable of tuning their performance parameters to the environment and task at hand.

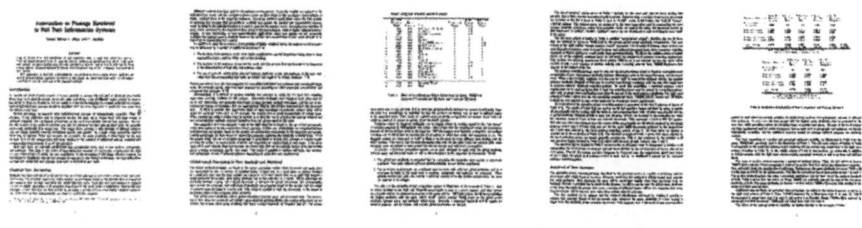

Fig. 1.1. A zoomed-out view of an article on Information Retrieval

We illustrate our approach to ICA with an example developed in full detail in the rest of the paper. Consider the task of finding precision-recall measures for a specific collection (such as the CACM) from a scanned archive of technical reports. Using knowledge that precision-recall numbers are contained in articles on information retrieval and are frequently displayed in tables, we

dimensional views (e.g., walk-throughs in 3D rooms). The major use of structure in their work is to summarize and present information to a user.

– *Mobile Robotics.* The analogy between mobile robots in unstructured physical environments and information agents in a rich multi-media data environments is not just metaphorical. We have observed [Bro1, Bro2] that the lessons learned in designing task-directed mobile robots can be imported to the problem of information capture and access. We were influenced in defining topology-based segmenters and structure detectors by the work of [Don, JR], who consider the problem of determining the information requirements to perform robot tasks using the concept of information invariants and perceptual equivalence classes.

2. Organizing Principles for Information Gathering Search Engines

For any specific information access query, no matter how complicated, we can write a special purpose program on top of existing tools to search for the answer. However, there is such great variety in the information landscape that it is impractical to provide a special search program for each possible query. This is because building each one from scratch takes a considerable amount of time and expertise. We are not arguing against the use of search engines specialized for specific query classes. We propose speeding up the process of building specialized search engines for classes of queries by recycling the computations they perform. This requires the recognition and reuse of significant computational modules; in particular, we need (1) a basis for the modularization and (2) schemes for combining the modules into complete search engines.

The basis for the modularization is structure at multiple levels of granularity in the electronic repository. By structure we mean any regularity or pattern present in the data. Word counts as used in traditional information retrieval are examples of statistical structure, and tables or graphs are examples of geometric structures. Sometimes structure is not apparent in raw data. In such cases, modules that segment and transform data to reveal underlying structure can lead to effective search algorithms.

We show that it is possible to synthesize special-purpose search algorithms by combining simple modules for detecting and filtering structure. Each module can be viewed as an operation in a calculus of search. The set of all modules together with the combination operators defines a high-level language for specifying search engines.

The desirable properties of segmenting and structure-detecting modules are:

– **Reliability.** Detectors and segmenters that rely on perfect data interpretation perform poorly. Consider for instance the design of a structure detector for tables. The general organization of a table is in rows and columns, but the actual table content and layout differ with each example. Tables with partially misaligned or missing records should be detected with a specified degree of accuracy and confidence. In this paper, we design structure detectors and segmenters to be robust in the presence of uncertainty in data representation and to have bounds of accuracy for data interpretation.

– **Efficiency.** The objective of information gathering is to find good answers in response to a user's query, as fast as possible. The data environment is so large that neither structure detectors nor segmenters can afford to look at every data item, so it is important to design these units efficiently. Our measures of efficiency are tuned to specific applications. We prove bounds on efficiency (typically time and space bounds) as a function of performance accuracy. For instance, we prove that our segmenter has complexity linear in the perimeter of the regions defined by a white space border of width d in a document (rather than in the area of these regions).

– **Error detection and recovery.** Modules should be designed to recover from errors in the segmentation and interpretation of data. Additionally, since our data is in a distributed, wide-area network, it is important that they detect and recover from network failures. This is typically accomplished by having each module be self-correcting—a lesson about the organization of complex systems that was discovered in the context of mobile robotics and insect intelligences [Bro1, Bro2]. Our designs incorporate task-specific error detection and recovery schemes.

A complex search is organized as a network of on-line computations. Each node in the network corresponds to a module; modules interact by sharing data. Our information agents are: (1) transportable across machines, (2) customizable to a user-specification, and (3) autonomous in decision-making.

In the remainder of this section we discuss details of designing modules (segmenters and detectors) and organizing them as information search engines.

2.1 Segmenters

Segmenters partition data at the appropriate grain size for structure detectors. The table detector expects information to be broken up into pieces at the paragraph level; this is generated by a paragraph segmenter described later in this section.

We model granularity shifts in the descriptions of the data using concepts from topology [Mun]. A topology over a set S is a set of subsets of S that are collectively exhaustive—the union of the subsets yields S. A topology is closed under the operations of union and finite intersection. The coarsest description of a data collection W, where the only distinction made is between W and the rest of the world, is called a trivial topology and consists of two subsets of W—W itself, and the null set $\emptyset$.

2.1.1 An Example: Segmenting Documents. Given a pixel array of a document, the segmenter's goal is to partition the document into regions that capture its layout. This problem has two parts: determining where the regions are, and classifying them according to their layout structure. Examples of regions are titles, text blocks, pictures, tables, captions, *etc.* In what follows, we present an algorithm for finding specific regions of layout structure.

Definition 2.3. *Let B be a polygonal partition of the document. A border of width d is the set $Border(B, d) = B \oplus S_d^1 - B$. Every element of $Border(B, d)$ is a white space.*[3]

A document is treated as a pixel array. Intuitively, a border of white space of width d exists around a polygonal region B in the document if we can roll a coin of diameter d around the region. We define an inclusion relation between polygonal partitions S_1, S_2 in a document; in particular we say that S_1 is included in S_2, denoted $S_1 \subset S_2$, if every pixel in S_1 is also a pixel of S_2.

Definition 2.4. *A layout region B relative to a border of width d in a document D is a document partition for which $B \cup Border(B, d) \subset D$, and there is no region $B' \subset B$ with this property.*

This definition identifies borders around both convex and non-convex document partitions. It cannot, however, identify rings of white space contained entirely within a region. Note that the geometric definition of a border is parameterized on d, the width of the border. It allows us to construct a hierarchical model of the document layout without relying on a predefined set of document features like sections, captions, *etc.* The levels of the hierarchy are defined by different values of d. That is, we can partition document into regions at different grain sizes according to the border of white space that can be drawn around them. For example, if the task is to partition the front page of The New York Times into blocks, values of $d > 0.2$ inches extract the entire title, while values of $d < 0.1$ inch separate each character of the title into its own block. If we are given a set of characteristic d values for a document, we can segment that document into regions for each d value. The region topology generated with d_1 is a refinement of the region topology generated with d_2 if $d_1 < d_2$. Thus a collection of d values defines a totally ordered set of region topologies for a document. The coarsest element in the set consists of one region: the entire document. The ith element of the set contains regions relative to a border width of d_i. The $i + 1^{th}$ element is constructed recursively by refining the regions found in the ith partition with a (smaller) d value of d_{i+1}. Each topology is computed by rolling coins of successively smaller sizes through the maze of white spaces in a document.

---

[3] $A \oplus B = \{a + b \mid a \in A, b \in B\}$ is the Minkowski sum of sets A and B. S_d^1 is a circle of diameter d.

Notation:
$C = \{\langle v, b\rangle\}$ denotes the critical vertex list
where v denotes an (x, y) location in the pixel array
and b is a sweep direction
(1 for horizontal and -1 for vertical).
R denotes the list of vertices for the new regions.
O denotes the list of vertices for the input region.
d denotes the border width.
p is the pixel array for region O.
Input: d, O, p.

Initialization: $C = (\langle o, 1\rangle)$, for some $o \in O$.
$R = O$.
While $C \neq \emptyset$ **do**
    begin
        $\langle v, b\rangle = pop(C)$;
        sweep p from v in direction b looking for
        runs of white space r longer than d bounded by vertices v_1 and v_2.
        For each v_i that has not been visited along b,
        $C = C \cup \{\langle v_i, -b\rangle\}, R = R \cup \{v_i\}$.
    end

Fig. 2.2. The Perimeter Tracer for the Block Segmentation Algorithm for a given border width d. The regions are determined by connecting vertices found by the algorithm.

The block segmentation algorithm in Figure 2.2 finds regions by detecting borders of width d. It traces the perimeters of identified regions. Its computational complexity is $O(p)$, where p is the number of pixels that do not occur in any of the identified regions. For each region, the algorithm examines a number of pixels linear in the perimeter of the region, rather than its area. For dense documents, like lead pages of a newspaper, this is a significant reduction in complexity.

Proposition 2.1. *The perimeter tracing algorithm identifies polygonal partitions that are unions of axis-parallel rectangular regions with borders of width d as specified in Definition 2.4. For a pixel array of size $m \times n$, it identifies regions by examining no more than $O(p)$ pixels, where p is the number of pixels that occur outside identified regions.*

The restriction to unions of axis-parallel rectangles is due to the sweeping strategy employed by the algorithm. The size d of the border width has to be chosen carefully for the algorithm to perform well, *i.e.*, for the number p of pixels examined to be significantly smaller than mn. With a border width equal to the inter-character spacing, the algorithm examines every pixel, similar to existing area-based methods, and generates the finest region topology of the document.

How reliably does the algorithm identify meaningful blocks in a scanned document? The accuracy of the block partitions is a function of the d values made available to the block segmenter. Significant d values, denoting the width of white spaces between logical units like paragraphs and sections, extract partitions of the document at the paragraph and section level, respectively. These spacings can be provided by a user or estimated by the system using random sampling of regions of the document. The correctness of our block segmentation scheme relies on regularities in the environment of documents—in particular, the fact that documents are typeset with some standard conventions. Most documents have a rectangular layout produced with a finite set of fonts. Each font size has a characteristic spacing between lines and characters. Our algorithm relies on the following generic typesetting rules. A superset of these conventions are in [NSV].

1. Printed lines are roughly horizontal.
2. The base lines of characters are aligned.
3. Word spaces are larger than character spaces.
4. Paragraphs are separated by wider spaces than lines within a paragraph, or by indentation.
5. Illustrations are confined to rectangular frames.

Suppose the inter-paragraph spacing is d_p, and we supply the algorithm with a d value of $d_p \pm \epsilon_p$, where $0 \leq \epsilon_p \leq d_p$. How likely are we to extract paragraphs in the scanned document using the block segmenter? The answer to this question is determined entirely by the data and not the algorithm. If d values in the interval $[d_p - \epsilon_p, d_p + \epsilon_p]$ are not associated with other "natural" logical units of the document, our algorithm will correctly produce a partition of the document at the paragraph level. The algorithm is robust in environments where significant d values are spaced more than ϵ_p apart. A more formal statement of this intuitive analysis of robustness requires the formulation of layout models of scanned documents. A formal robustness analysis is presented in the next subsection for a structure detector that operates on paragraph-level regions in an ASCII document.

The algorithm, as presented in Figure 2.2, assumes that there is no noise in the data and that we can reliably detect borders. In particular, on any sweep line, horizontal or vertical, we assume that we can find clean runs of white pixels of length larger than d. In reality, runs of white pixels are polluted by black pixels that occur at random locations. For instance, letters like f, g, j, p, q, and dots on i's protrude into the white space around a region. We associate a tolerance parameter ϵ_d, with every d value. ϵ_d represents the number of black pixels that can be ignored in the detection of a run of white pixels of length d. The tolerance ϵ_d should be chosen in direct proportional to the value of d. Metaphorically speaking, we treat each coin of size d as a bulldozer that can push ϵ_d or fewer black pixels out of the way.[4] In our

---

[4] We thank Jim Davis for this idea.

implementation of the block segmenter, we experimentally determined these values for documents drawn from the scanned technical report archive at Cornell.

2.2 Structure Detectors

Structure detectors are programs that can decide whether a block of data has a specified property P. An example for text blocks is the property of being a table or a graph.

Definition 2.5. *A structure detector is a computable function* $s : \tau(W) \rightarrow 2^{\tau(W)}$ *defined on a topology* $\tau(W)$ *to a* discrete *subset* $t(W)$ *of that topology, such that* $t(W)$ *has the property* P.

A structure detector s for a property P is *correct* if it finds all the subsets of $\tau(W)$ that satisfy P. A structure detector s for property P is *robust* if whenever it recognizes $t(W)$, it recognizes all its ϵ-perturbations.

2.2.1 An Example: Detecting Tables. *Webster's Seventh Dictionary* defines a table as a *systematic arrangement of data usually in rows and columns for ready reference*. Implicit in this definition is a *layout* component and a *lexical* component: the data is organized in columns of similar information. Consider the structure in Figure 2.3: the records are two lines long, the columns in the second line of a record do not align with the columns in the first, some columns extend into adjacent ones, and there are lexical irregularities in its records. In spite of these imperfections, the layout and lexical structures are clear, and we identify the structure as a table. Our goal is to create a structure detector that checks for column and content structure while tolerating irregularities to within specified error bounds.

The measure for the column layout of a block of text is given in terms of a data structure called the *white space density graph* and denoted by WDG. Let B be a block of text of n rows and m columns and $w : \{c \mid c \text{ is a character }\} \rightarrow \{0, 1\}$ with $w(space) = 1$ and $\forall c \neq space, w(c) = 0$.

Definition 2.6. Vertical structure: *The* white space density graph *of B is a polygonal line* WDG $: [0, m] \rightarrow [0, 1]$ *defined by points* WDG$(i) = \frac{1}{n} \sum_{j=0}^{n} w(B_{i,j}), \ 0 \leq i \leq m$.

Figure 2.5 shows the WDG associated with the table in Figure 2.3.

Definition 2.7. Deviations in vertical structure: *Given an error tolerance* ϵ_v, *a block of text has* column structure *if it occurs between two successive local maxima above* $(1 - \epsilon_v)$ *in the* WDG.

Each local maximum is a candidate column separator. A candidate column is a real table column only when it has corresponding horizontal lexical structure. We are far from being able to identify row structure based on semantic content, but semantic uniformity in rows is highly correlated with lexical uniformity. We exploit this correlation in the design of a table detector that is robust in the presence of layout imperfections.

The process of discerning lexical structure is facilitated by the presence of non-alphabetic characters. For example, it is easy to recognize that the entries of the sixth column in Figure 2.3 represent similar information, since they have a very regular and distinct lexical pattern. In distinguishing lexical structure, we identify the following equivalence classes of characters: alphabetic, numeric, and special (each special character is in its own class). Let $c_0, c_1, \ldots, c_n$ denote the columns of a table. We use regular expressions for generalizing the contents of a column. The table in Figure 2.3, all items in the sixth column (the meeting times) can be described by the following conjunctive regular expression $NN : NN$, where N is a symbol denoting a number and : is a special character. The *lexical description* of a column c_i is a non-trivial regular expression r_i that describes the smallest possible language that includes all elements of c_i. The regular expression $r_1 + \cdots + r_n$ is a *trivial* generalization of a given set of the elements $r_1, \ldots, r_n$; otherwise it is *non-trivial*.

Definition 2.8. Horizontal structure: *Consider the columns $c_1 \ldots c_n$ of a block of text satisfying Definition 2.7, and consider the lexical descriptions $r_1 \ldots r_n$ of these columns. This text also has row structure if and only if the language described by $r_1 r_2 \ldots r_n$ is non-empty.*

100a	Introduction to Computer Programming	4	Lec1 TR	9:05	Ives 120
	Wagner		Lec2 TR	11:15	Ives 120
100b	Introduction to Computer Programming	4	Lec1 TR	9:05	Olin 255
	Van Loan		Lec2 TR	11:15	Ives 110
101	The Computer Age	3	TR	1:25	Upson B17
	Segre				
102	Intro Microcomputer Applications	3	Lec1 TR	10:10	RR 105
	Hillman (Ag. Engr.)		Lec2 TR	12:20	RR 105
108	A Taste of UNIX and C	1(4wk)	MWF	3:35	Olin 255
	Glade	su			

Fig. 2.3. A Schedule of the Introductory Computer Science Courses

Now consider Figure 2.3, which has small irregularities in the lexical structure of the columns. To express this more rigorously, let M be a metric for string comparison (we use the Levenshtein metric [SK]). Given $\epsilon > 0$, two strings a and b are ϵ-similar if $M(a, b) \leq \epsilon_h$. We use ϵ_h-typings, defined below, of the regular expressions that correspond to the entries of a column in order to control the imperfections we allow in horizontal structure.

Definition 2.9. Deviations in horizontal structure: *Given $\epsilon_h > 0$ and a set of strings, an ϵ_h-typing is a division of the set into disjoint subsets such that any two strings in the same subset are ϵ_h-similar.*

Lexical typing for a table is done in two parts. Each candidate column is analyzed to determine a regular expression for its type. The alphabet of types is generated by ϵ_h-typing the column elements. The lexical type of the table is obtained by computing the minimum regular expression over the column types. This step in the algorithm allows for the occurrence of multi-line records in a table and for ϵ_h tolerance in the record units. A minimal ϵ_h-typing partitions the elements of the column in the coarsest possible way.

Input: A text block B, vertical tolerance ϵ_v, horizontal tolerance ϵ_h
Output: *true* if B is a table and *false* otherwise.

1. Form the WDG of the text block.
2. Find column separators of height $1 - \epsilon_v$ in the WDG. If none exist, the text is not a table, so quit; otherwise continue.
3. Perform an ϵ_h-typing on the regular expression representations of the entries of each column.
4. Find the lexical structure these typings imply, if any. If such a structure is found, the text is a table; otherwise, it is not a table.

Fig. 2.4. The Table Detection Algorithm

Figure 2.4 describes the table detection algorithm. An example application of this algorithm to the table in Figure 2.3 follows. The first step in the algorithm is to create the WDG associated with the table, by calculating the percentage of blank spaces in each column of the block. Figure 2.5 shows the WDG associated with the text in Figure 2.3. The second step is to look for column separators, *i.e.*, peaks in the graph of height at least $1 - \epsilon_v$. This graph has six high peaks that are associated with the rivers of white space flowing between the seven columns in Figure 2.3. In the third step, each candidate column is analyzed for lexical structure. If the column description patterns can be combined into a regular expression across the entire table, the block of text is a table; otherwise it is not.

We now analyze the robustness of the algorithm. Computing peaks in the WDG is quite easy. What is not obvious is how to determine a reasonable threshold value ϵ_h that robustly and efficiently filters tables from basic text. We measure efficiency as the cost of the actual computation, and the probability that base text is passed through unnecessary lexical analysis. One approach is to require the user to specify the value of ϵ_h using his knowledge about the data environment. Another approach is to have the algorithm statistically learn the value of ϵ_h by analyzing the WDG of tables identified by the user. A third solution does not rely on user assistance, but rather makes use of a probabilistic analysis of WDGs of basic text. The question we ask is: for a high peak value in the WDG, what is the probability that it corresponds to a true table column rather than a random distribution of spaces in basic-text? From this analysis, we extract a tolerance parameter that can be used as an absolute lower bound on ϵ_h for detecting tables with irregularities in layout.

The analysis makes the following assumptions:

- The average word length that occurs in text is known. For English, [KF] have determined that the average word length of distinct words is 8.1 characters, but of word occurrences in written text, it is 4.7 characters. For simplicity, we assume that in basic text the average word length is 4 characters.
- The blank spaces in base text are distributed independently. This is due to the fact that the lengths of words and of the spacing between them are variable, and their occurrences in a line of text are random. We have tested the independence of the distribution of whitespace by extensive experiments with *Splus* [Splus]. This independence assumption implies that the blank spaces of a line have a binomial distribution.[5]

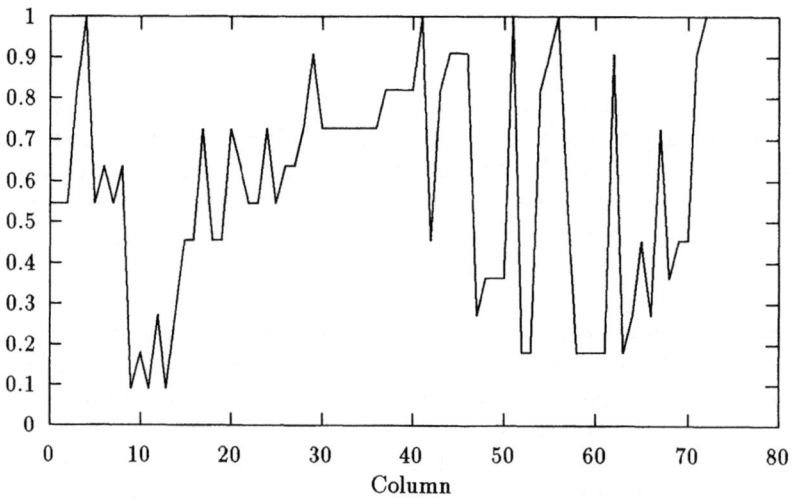

Fig. 2.5. A White Space Density Graph for Table 2

Let B be a block of text of n rows and m columns. Let p be the probability that a character c in a row is blank, and let $q = 1 - p$ be the probability that the character is non-blank.[6] Let WDG be the white space density graph for

---

[5] An interesting problem is to determine when the binomial distribution approaches a normal distribution; at present, we have no solution to this problem.

[6] An average word length of 4 characters yields $p = 0.2$ and $q = 0.8$.

B. Denote by WDG(k) the value for the kth column of B. Application of Chebyshev's theorem[7] yields:

Corollary 2.1. *If the absolute value of a peak in the* WDG *is greater than* $np + h\sqrt{npq}$, *the probability that the peak is an occurrence of basic text is at most* $\frac{1}{h^2}$.

In other words, by setting the peak threshold to $np + h\sqrt{npq}$, we ensure that with probability at least $1 - \frac{1}{h^2}$ the presence of any value above the threshold is a candidate column separator in a table. The user can specify required confidence in identifying columns $(\frac{1}{h^2})$, and we can calculate the peak threshold, since n, p, q and h are all known.

Better bounds of the probability of making a mistake when labeling a block of text as a table can be obtained by using the Hoeffding-Chernoff bounds for binomial distributions [Hoe, AV]:

$$Pr[X \geq (1 + \alpha)pn] \leq e^{-\alpha^2 \frac{np}{3}}. \tag{2.1}$$

The appropriate value for α can be found by setting $\alpha np = h\sigma$, where $\sigma = \sqrt{npq}$. It follows that $\alpha = h\sqrt{\frac{q}{np}}$, and for this value of α, Equation 2.1 becomes:

$$Pr[X \geq (1 + \alpha)pn] \leq e^{-\frac{h^2 q}{3}}. \tag{2.2}$$

For example, Equation 2.2 allows us to conclude that for an error of 0.001, $h = 4.6$. Chebyshev's theorem requires $h = 31$ for the same amount of error.

A block of text is a table if it has both vertical and horizontal structure. We now consider the complexity of lexical component analysis.

Proposition 2.2. *Finding the minimum* ϵ_h-*typing is NP-complete.*

Proof. Reduction to partitions into cliques.

Even though finding the minimum typing is a hard problem, a useful ϵ_h-typing can be found efficiently. An element is placed in a partition only if it is $\frac{\epsilon_h}{2}$-similar to the original element of that partition; when an element is encountered for which no such partition exists, it becomes the original element of a new partition.

The types of the entries of each column are assembled into the *type matrix*. A $m \times n$ type matrix is constructed for a block of text of m lines and n columns. If $t_{ij} = t_{i'j'}$ the data in row i and column j and the data in row i' and column j' are ϵ-similar. The type matrix for the table in Figure 2.3 is given in Figure 2.6. A GCD algorithm [BK] can be used to determine the type, if any, of the overall matrix and thus to decide whether the matrix represents a table. We provide for error tolerance in the typing of each column

---

[7] For any distribution with standard deviation σ, at least a fraction $1 - \frac{1}{h^2}$ of the measurements differ from the mean by amounts at most $h\sigma$.

$$\begin{bmatrix} t_1 & t_2 & t_4 & t_6 & t_8 & t_9 & t_{10} \\ t_0 & t_3 & t_0 & t_6 & t_8 & t_9 & t_{10} \\ t_1 & t_2 & t_4 & t_6 & t_8 & t_9 & t_{10} \\ t_0 & t_3 & t_0 & t_6 & t_8 & t_9 & t_{10} \\ t_1 & t_2 & t_4 & t_0 & t_8 & t_9 & t_{10} \\ t_0 & t_3 & t_0 & t_0 & t_0 & t_0 & t_0 \\ t_1 & t_2 & t_4 & t_6 & t_8 & t_9 & t_{10} \\ t_0 & t_2 & t_0 & t_6 & t_8 & t_9 & t_{10} \\ t_1 & t_2 & t_4 & t_6 & t_8 & t_9 & t_{10} \\ t_0 & t_3 & t_5 & t_0 & t_0 & t_0 & t_0 \end{bmatrix}$$

Fig. 2.6. Type Matrix For the Course Table

by supplying an error parameter ϵ_r. This parameter specifies the amount of "noise" in the pattern that defines the type of a column. For example, if $\epsilon_r = 0.2$, the type of the fifth column in Figure 2.6 is taken to be t_8; the two entries that are labeled as t_0 are treated as noise.

We have implemented this table detector that is robust with respect to layout imperfections and used it to build search engines for retrieval tasks whose answers are found in tabular form (see Section 2.2.2).

2.2.2 Experiments with the table detector. We have tested the performance of the table detector on several thousand articles culled from a number of Usenet news groups[8] over a period of a few weeks. Each article was partitioned into paragraphs and then filtered through the table detector. The results were compared with human labeling (as tables and nontables) of the same data. From a subset of the data consisting of messages in comp.biz.hardware, 711 segments were analyzed. The table detector correctly identified 147 out of the 151 tables labeled by a human. The parameter setting was $\epsilon_v = 10\%$, $\epsilon_h = 30\%$, and $\epsilon_r = 50\%$. The results of our experiments yielded 2.65% false negatives, and 2.95% false positives. For perfect tables (*i.e.*, tables with perfect vertical alignment and with uniform lexical structure) the recognition accuracy is 100%.

False negatives occur for imperfect tables when there is noise in the vertical alignment greater than the specified error limit, or when records (rows) are non-uniform. Also, false negatives occur when tables are embedded so that the text around them bias the vertical and/or horizontal structure of the block. Tables with multi-line headers where the ratio of the size of the header to that of the table exceeds the horizontal error tolerance are also misidentified. False positives occur when there is accidental alignment of blanks in a paragraph of text. This happens more frequently for short paragraphs (less than 5 lines).

We studied the sensitivity of the table detector on a data set consisting of 74 tables of very different formats. We counted the number of tables detected

---

[8] These groups include clari.tw.stocks, biz.comp.hardware, biz.jobs.offers, comp.benchmarks, alt.internet.news, and bionet.journals.contents.

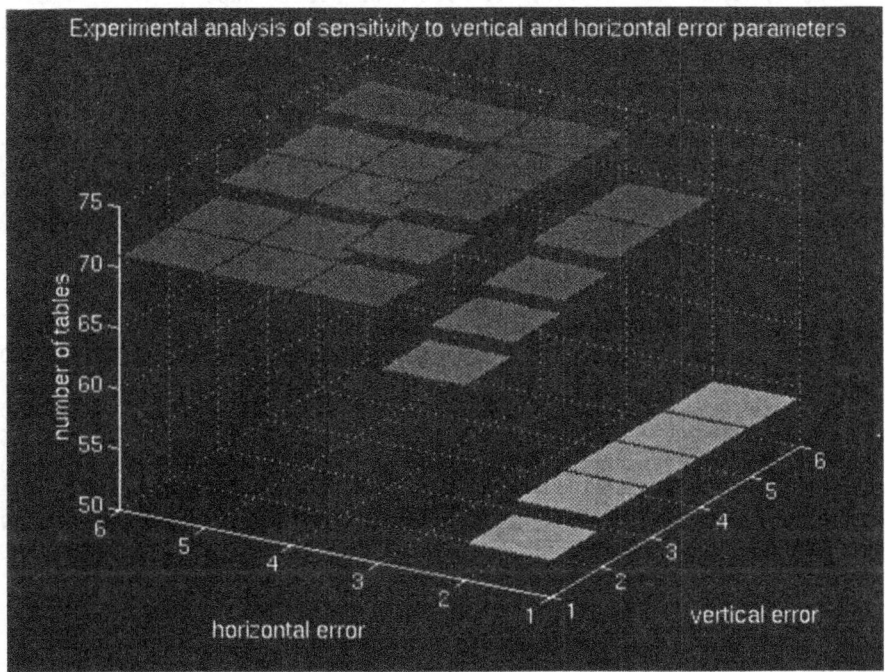

Fig. 2.7. The dependency of the performance of the table detector on ϵ_v and ϵ_h. The performance numbers are doubly encoded color and height: dark colors and high values along the x axis denote good performance.

by varying the vertical noise ϵ_v from 5% to 25% in increments of 5% and by varying the horizontal noise ϵ_h from 20% to 40% in increments of 5%. The results are plotted in Figure 2.7. The algorithm is much more sensitive to values of ϵ_v than of ϵ_h. The worst performance over the parameter range we studied was for $\epsilon_v = 5\%$ and $\epsilon_h = 20\%$: 53 out of 74 tables were recognized. The best performance was for $\epsilon_v \geq 15\%$: 73 out of 74 tables were recognized. The one table that was not detected had very irregular lexical content. Figure 2.8 shows the table that was not recognized and Figure 2.9 shows a complicated table that was recognized.

2.3 Assembly of Information Agents

Users assemble search engines from task specifications. In this section, we discuss how simple agents are constructed from available detectors and segmenters, and how complex agents can be built from simple ones. To synthesize an information agent for a given task, the user

```
Tape Backups:
    Conner/Maynard Int. 250Mb, QIC-80,1 FREE DC2120 tape        -> $170
    Colorado Internal 250Mb, QIC-80                             -> $180
    DC-2120 120/250Mb Tapes                                     -> $22
```

Fig. 2.8. An example of a figure with irregular lexical content that is not recognized by the table detector within the parameter range we studied. The first column consists of the entire text to the left of the "->". The lexical analysis failed on the first column due to the presence of many mixed special characters. If the text consisting of "250Mb, QIC-80" had lined up, the table would have been recognized. This mismatch problem is exacerbated by the fact that the table is short.

```
256k cache for all 486 boards                                  Add $25
    486DX2-66, 64k cache,    ""      ""   (Clock Doubler) (Intel CPU) -> $580
Local Bus Upgrades:
    VESA local bus ISA boards (2 VESA/ISA slots, 6 ISA slots)  Add $10
    486 Motherboard w/ NO CPU, 256k Cache                      -> $105
    486 VESA Local Bus Motherboard w/ NO CPU, 2 VLB, 256k Cache -> $120
    486 VLB w/NO CPU, 256k Cache, 2 VLB, ZIF, Pentium upgrdbl   -> $150
    486 VLB w/NO CPU, 256k Cache, 2 VLB, ZIF,US dsgnd,Pntm upgrdbl-> $160
Misc:
    486 CPU Heat Sink Fan (Clips on to any 486 CPU)            -> $15
```

Fig. 2.9. An example of a table with irregular lexical content and misalignment that was recognized by the table detector. This table has 20% non-whitespace in the first and last column separators and so a parameter setting with $\epsilon_v \geq 20\%$ is successful.

1. identifies a set of structures at different levels of detail that are relevant to the task, and chooses (or creates) detectors that can recognize these structures,
2. chooses segmenters that partition data at the right granularity for each detector,
3. composes the agent from these segmenter/detector pairs, and
4. interprets the computed data.

For example, to find precision-recall measures for the CACM collection from a given article, the designer uses knowledge that the answer to the query is found in tabular form. Since tables need to be identified, the relevant structure detector is the one introduced in Section 2.2.1. The segmenter that partitions the environment for processing by the table recognizer is the block segmenter in Section 2.1.1 with a border width parameter that filters paragraphs in the environment. Once tables are identified, they need to be further refined into rows by the block segmenter with the appropriate border width parameter. We compose the two segmenter/detector pairs (table level and row level) in series to extract rows of identified tables in the environment. Finally, the contents of each row have to be interpreted to obtain the precision-recall measures. This last step requires knowledge about the form of precision-recall measures.

2.3.1 Formalizing agents. We represent an agent in the language of *circuits* [BDG]. Asynchronous circuits are a useful engineering metaphor for assembling agents from detectors and segmenters. We draw upon the rich formal history of circuit theory to provide principled specifications of the computations that agents perform.

Definition 2.10. *An asynchronous agent circuit $A = (V, E)$ is a directed acyclic graph representation of a computation. The elements of V denote structure detecting or segmenting operations, and the edges in E denote data paths between the nodes. Each path in the graph is an alternating sequence of segmenters and structure detectors.*

We provide circuit descriptions for the modules introduced in the previous section. A structure detector is both a filter over data (e.g., a table detector picks out blocks that are tables) and a boolean function (e.g., a table detector checks whether a block is a table). The definition of a structure detector (Definition 2.5) specifies it as a predicate which can be viewed extensionally as the subset of a set or intensionally as a boolean function over a set. We rely upon the correspondence between these two representations of a predicate to define structure detectors as circuits.

Each structure detector (see Figure 2.10(a)) is composed of a combinational circuit that computes the predicate (denoted by the circle) and a latch (denoted by the square) that filters the data. The input to the structure detector is a stream of data. Both the latch and the combinational circuit receive the data at the same time. The combinational circuit checks whether the block of data has some property and uses this value as a toggle to release the data as output.

Complex detectors can be built from simple ones by using boolean operations of $\land$, $\lor$, and $\neg$ on the predicate components of the individual modules. Figures 2.10(b) and (c) show the composition operations.

A segmenter can also be described as a data-driven, asynchronous circuit (see Figure 2.10(d)). A segmenter is composed of a combinational circuit that computes a predicate, a data shredder, and a latch. The computed predicate determines where to place the "hyperplanes" for shredding data. The shredder physically partitions the data into units; this partition is converted into a data stream by the latch. Unlike structure detectors, we do not consider direct compositions of segmenters. This is because we view segmenters as preprocessors of data for detectors and we prefer to compose segmenter-detector pairs instead of composing segmenters. Thus, for example, if we wanted to segment a file into individual lines with two segmenter modules S1 and S2 where S1 segments a file into paragraphs, and S2 segments paragraphs into lines, we construct the path S1-id-S2 in the agent graph, where id is the identity structure detector.

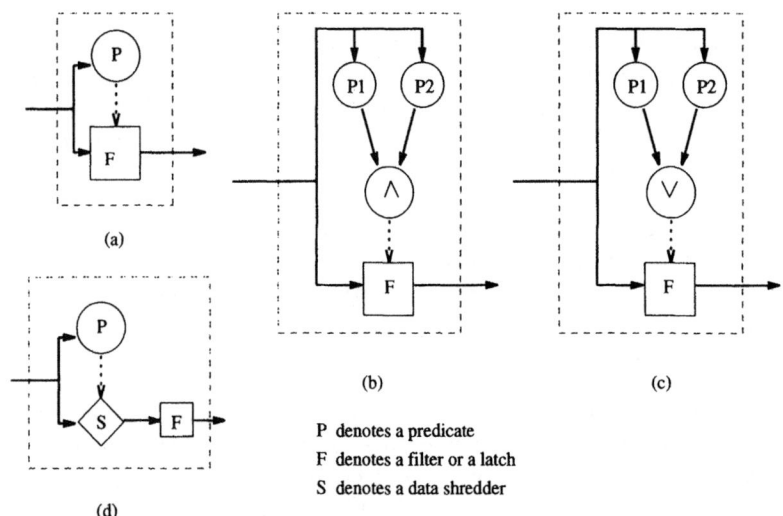

P denotes a predicate
F denotes a filter or a latch
S denotes a data shredder

Fig. 2.10. Circuits for structure detectors and segmenters.

Structure detecting and segmenting circuits are assembled into agent circuits by synthesizing a data flow graph. A detector and a segmenter can be connected in series in any order to form a simple agent. For this composition to make sense, we need the output topology of the first circuit in the series to match the input topology of the second circuit. For example, a table detector should be connected to a segmenter that partitions a document into blocks at the paragraph level. The constraints on matching topologies are type-theoretic and define minimal conditions for correct composition. We call the topology matching constraints *calibration* constraints. Calibration constraints ensure that data at the right granularity passes between the components.

Definition 2.11. *Simple agent: A simple agent is constructed from a segmenter* $S : \tau_1(W) \to \tau_2(W)$ *or a detector* $D : \tau(W) \to 2^{\tau(W)}$ *connected in series, denoted* $S \cdot D$, *such that the calibration constraint* $S(\tau_1(W)) = \tau(W)$ *holds. The series composition* $D \cdot S$ *can be constructed provided that* $\tau_1(W) = D(\tau(W))$.

This simple agent takes a partition $\tau_1(W)$ of the data and generates a subset of a refinement of $\tau_1(W)$ that satisfies s. We define two composition schemes for agents and identify calibration constraints on each scheme.

Definition 2.12. *Serial composition: An agent* $a_1 : \tau_{in1}(W) \to \tau_{out1}(W)$ *can be serially composed with an agent* $a_2 : \tau_{in2}(W) \to \tau_{out2}(W)$ *in that order yielding a new agent* $a : \tau_{in1}(W) \to \tau_{out2}(W)$ *constructed from the functional composition of* a_1 *and* a_2, *provided that the calibration constraint* $\tau_{out1}(W) =$

$\tau_{in2}(W)$ holds. We also require that the composition respect the alternation constraint between segmenters and detectors. We denote the composition $a_1 \bullet a_2$.

Definition 2.13. *Parallel composition: An agent* $a_1 : \tau_{in1}(W) \to \tau_{out1}(W)$ *can be composed in parallel with an agent* $a_2 : \tau_{in2}(W) \to \tau_{out2}(W)$, *yielding an agent* $a : \tau_{in1}(W) \to \tau_{out1}(W) \times \tau_{out2}(W)$, *provided the calibration constraint* $\tau_{in1}(W) = \tau_{in2}(W)$ *holds. We denote the composition* $a_1 \parallel a_2$.

If a_1 and a_2 are simple agents, then the above operation constitutes sharing of a segmenter. Parallel composition of two simple agents allows for different recognizers to operate on the same data partition. For instance, a table detector and a detector for recognizing graphs in text both employ paragraph level partitions.

2.3.2 Relating task and environment structure. The design of appropriate structure detectors and segmenters for a task relies on underlying assumptions about conventions for representing information in the data environment. Consider the task of designing an agent to help protein crystal growers access the latest information about the primary amino-acid sequence, solubility, and molecular weight of the protein they wish to crystallize. Such knowledge is available in databases (their number is growing rapidly) accessible by tools like WWW, Netscape, and Gopher. There are a number of programs available at various Internet sites to compute properties of the protein, *e.g.*, the isoelectric point, from knowledge of the primary amino-acid sequence. At this time, human crystal growers manually compile information available from these databases and perform conversions to get the data in a uniform framework to run protein simulation programs to get all the computed properties. This is a tedious task that can be automated with the construction of a search engine with knowledge about the forms in which this information occurs and with methods for recognizing and extracting it.

What structure detectors and segmenters are needed for this task? How do we systematically relate the computations they perform to the specific information that needs to be extracted? The designer uses knowledge that some biology databases store information in a relational format and others store them as an association list of property-value pairs. The segmenters for this engine partition the data environment into the known databases and within each database recognize and partition the data into a relational table or an association list (alist). The parametric alist segmenter has knowledge about association lists and how to recognize ϵ-perturbations of alists. So rigid formatting constraints on data are not needed for the proper recognition. By layering the segmenter detector pairs appropriately, the designer ensures that the right task-specific components are extracted.

2.3.3 Data interpretation. By data interpretation, we mean attaching meaning in task-specific terms to the computations being performed by each component. Interpretation need not, and in fact generally is not, done by the search engine. The designer ensures that the search engine maintains an invariant—the mapping between the results of computations (recall these are topologies) and the "meaning" of the extracted data. In the Stock Filter, discussed in the next section, the designer establishes a mapping between the structure extracted by the table detector and a "stock table"—the latter is a task-specific category, the former a geometric object. The mapping constitutes the interpretation of items in the rows as companies and stock prices, and items in the columns as high, low and closing values. The designer incorporates checks in each agent to ensure the integrity of this mapping between results of computations performed by the agent and their task-specific interpretations. There are two implementation choices for data interpretation. Interpretation can be procedurally encoded by the designer in structure detectors. Alternatively, interpretation constraints can be declaratively encoded and interpreted at run-time for the "parsing" or "filtering" of data. The tradeoffs between these two extremes in implementation choices can be evaluated using established methods for analyzing interpreted versus compiled code. While declarative encodings usually permit more flexible interpretation of data, compiled schemes are generally more efficient. Further examples of data interpretation are discussed in the context of the Stock Filter and the Bib Filter described in the following sections.

3. Example 1: Compiling Reports from Tabular Data

Consider the task of compiling a stock report for AT&T for a given period of time using an electronically archived collection of The New York Times. For each day in the given time interval, we can structure the task as follows:

1. We partition the paper into sections using the segmenter in Section 2.1 with the border parameter that characterizes sections in The New York Times.
2. We filter the business section from the paper (this is where the stock data is most likely to occur) by using a structure detector for section titles.
3. We partition the business section into blocks at the paragraph level, using the segmenter in Section 2.1 with the border parameter that characterizes paragraphs.
4. Since stock data in The New York Times is represented in tabular form, or in graphical form, we select the tables and graphs using the table detector and the graph detector.
5. We zoom into each table and graph to extract the specific information on AT&T.

We have implemented a smart filter that performs this operation on data coming through newsgroups (see Figure 3.1). The first level segmenter is a block segmenter that takes postings, one at a time, and produces its paragraph level partition. Two structure detectors follow it. One filters out the

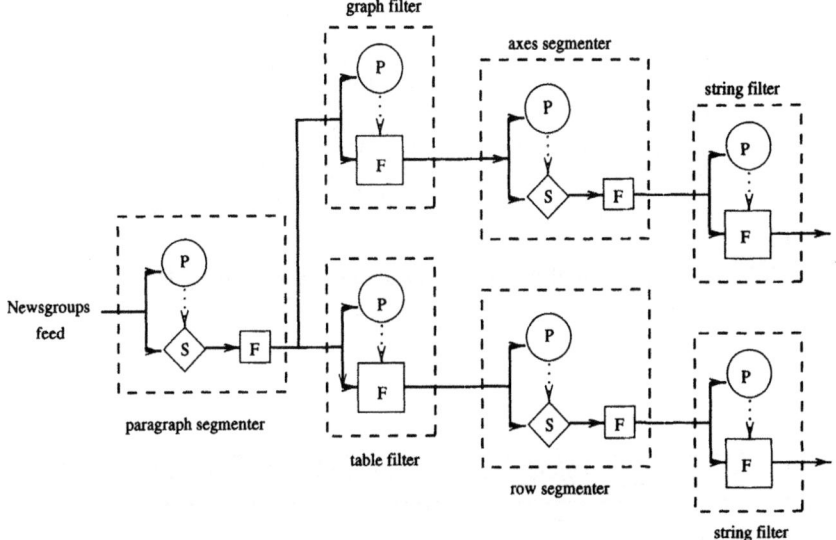

graph filter

axes segmenter

string filter

string filter

Newsgroups
feed

paragraph segmenter

table filter

row segmenter

Fig. 3.1. The circuit representation of a filter for compiling stock reports.

tables and the other filter out the graphs. The subset of paragraph blocks
that are recognized as tables are provided to a row segmenter, in order to
separate the records. The rows are individually passed to a string filter to
identify the AT&T records.

The data interpretation phase is complex. The filter makes no assumptions
about the format of the stock data other than that it is a table. The fields for
the high, low, and closing value have to be identified and extracted from the
record retrieved by the string comparator. If there is a header, the interpreter
scans it looking for the keyword "close" and determines the location of the
closing value in the record. If there is no header, the interpreter uses other
information about the format of the table. It uses the fact that stock market
tables usually contain three columns corresponding to high, low, and closing
values, and that the closing value is between high and low. This information,
which can be encoded as rules, can be used to identify the location of the
closing column.

We have implemented the Stock Filter for the data domain of Internet
newsgroups. Typical messages consist of a combination of prose and tables
that vary in format. This search engine extracts tables from a given list of
business newsgroups (an example of an extracted table is shown in Figure 3.2)
which are then searched for records labeled "ATT". An extracted record is
interpreted by a procedure attached to the table detector. The procedure
contains rules that define the High, Low, and Closing columns on a table of
stock data. Figure 3.3 shows the X-Window user interface for this filter, and
sample results for running this filter are given in Figure 3.4.

Issue	Notes	Dividend Ratio	P-E Ratio (100s)	Volume /Ask	High /Bid	Low /Current	Close	Change	Age
3Com	O			8200	34.00	33.13	33.25	-0.50	
AST	O			3905	15.00	14.00	14.00	-0.75	
ATT	N	1.32	20	13493	58.75	57.50	58.50	1.25	
Adaptec	O			9713	26.38	25.50	25.75	-0.63	
AdobeS	O	0.32		4622	45.00	43.00	43.38	-0.38	
AdvMicr	N		9	6039	23.38	22.75	23.25	0.13	
Aldus	O			1095	19.00	18.25	18.75	-0.13	
Alias	O			284	9.75	9.25	9.38	-0.13	

Fig. 3.2. A data segment of stock quotations extracted by the table detector from the newsgroup clari.tw.stocks (18 March 1993).

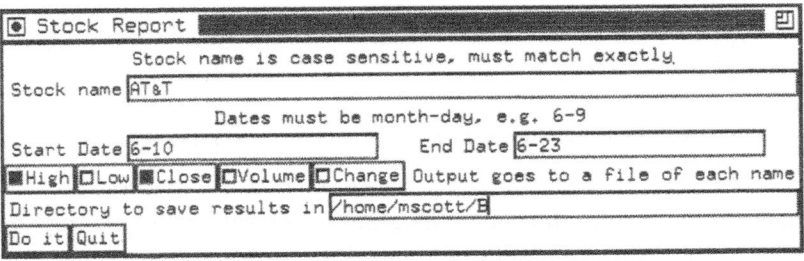

Fig. 3.3. The user interface of the stock filter.

We note that the Stock Filter can be used to retrieve any other type of information that is present in tabular form. In particular, we have instantiated the design in Figure 3.1 for the task of retrieving precision-recall measures for specific collections from our database of scanned technical reports on information retrieval. For the paper shown in Figure 1.1, a block segmenter detects paragraph blocks, and the table detector extracts the table in Figure 3.5. The three-line record of the table is further processed by string comparators to extract the actual measures. The same search engine can be used for any other retrieval task whose answer exists in tabular form, using appropriate data interpretation procedures.

4. Example 2: Automatic Information Gathering with Customized Indexes

With increasing amounts of heterogeneous distributed data, there is a need for tools that can autonomously obtain information with minimal human intervention. The complexity of the problem is in finding the location of

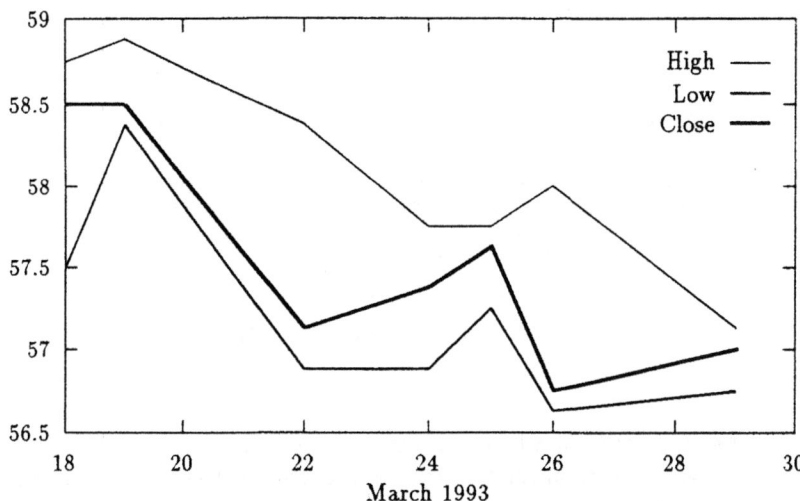

Fig. 3.4. Compilation of a stock report for AT&T over time, using the stock filter in the domain of newsgroups.

a document in a huge and unorganized world. It is impractical to look at every server in the world for every single query. Our idea is that once we have invested the effort to collect information relevant to a specific query, we remember the list of sites found, and use it to perform a selective search when asked another query from the same class.

For example, suppose you are interested in books in French; you would need to know the list of bookstores (physical and electronic) that carry French books. A roll call of bookstores would cluster the relevant sources. When you need a book in French, you would begin by checking with the stores in the computed cluster. Subsequently, when bookstores carrying French books open or close, you would want a way of adding or deleting them from the cluster. Our goal is to provide a facility for creating and maintaining clusters of information sources customized for specific query classes.

We have designed and implemented a search engine that actively finds and orders information sources containing technical reports about a given topic.[9] The engine is customizable by each user. For each topic of interest, a user invokes the engine to compute a cluster of relevant sites. Each node

---

[9] In the current implementation, queries are specified by listing keywords. Our selective search approach can be coupled with more sophisticated methods for query specifications. For instance, we can use the table detector for specifications involving tables.

Evaluation Parameters	3.Restricted Sentence Match	4.Output With Text Paragraphs	5.Full Text Section or
Retrieved Documents			
all queries	1106	1204	1345
Recall after 5 docs	0.4583	0.4834	0.5043
Recall after 15 docs	0.6667	0.7141	0.7631
Precision after 5 docs	0.7689	0.7867	0.8067
Precision after 15 docs	0.5022	0.5274	0.5519
11-point Average Precision	0.6920	0.7520 +9.7%	0.8198 +18.5%

Fig. 3.5. An extracted table from an information retrieval article.

in the cluster consists of a location and a tree of paths to directories within that site. The first time around, every site is examined to construct the initial list. In our previous example, every bookstore has to be polled to find out if it carries French books. Once constructed, the cluster is used to efficiently compute specific queries about the given topic. For example, given a cluster with sites that contain papers on the query class robotics, a specific query like the most recent version of the paper by Rodney Brooks on Cog can be answered by restricting the search to the given sites. Since the information landscape changes, the cluster is not a static entity. Updates to the cluster involve sites as well as paths within a site. We consider two methods for keeping the cluster current. The *lazy* method updates the cluster only when the answer to the specific query is not found in the current list. The *eager* method automatically adds new relevant servers as they become available. Both methods work incrementally.

We call the cluster of sites and paths at sites a customized index for a given query class. The customized index comprises part of the internal state of such an agent. It drives the physical navigation of the agent through the Internet. The index prunes away a large fraction of irrelevant sites. The cost for the pruning is paid by the first query in that class and amortized over all subsequent queries. Of course, this amortization is not valid if data changes so frequently as to make the index out of date as soon as it is created.

Bib Agent is built on top of the Alex [Cate] filesystem which provides users transparent access to files located in ftp-sites all over the world. Bib Agent can thus use Unix commands like `cd` and `ls` to navigate to the directories and subdirectories accessible by anonymous ftp. A structure detector collects the contents of each directory (using the `ls` Unix utility and a filter) and selects a subset of directories for the next set of navigators. These directories are processed in parallel. The Bib Agent has knowledge about the structure of anonymous ftp directories—for instance, it consults directories named **pub, papers**, or **users** but not **bin**. This task-specific knowledge is used to navigate autonomously as far as possible. At each node, the Bib Agent estimates the cost of its exploration by examining the number and size of its files and subdirectories. If the cost is above a threshold, the agent provides the user with the opportunity to help prune and prioritize its options.[10] If the user responds, the agent remembers the user preferences and uses them in the future.

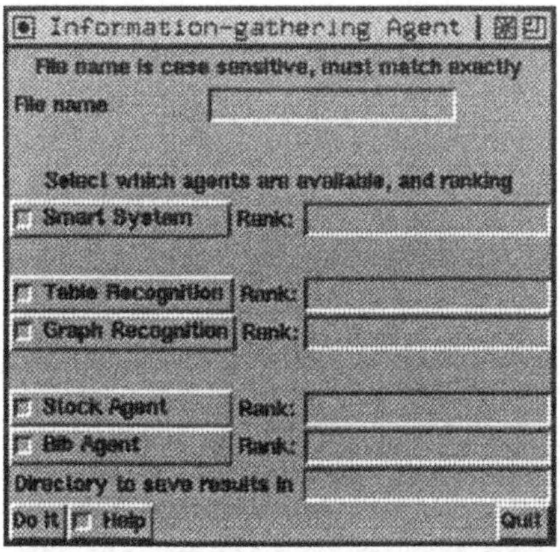

Fig. 4.1. The query window that serves as interface for our agents.

The directory tree at each site is traversed in a breadth-first manner. For each encountered file, Bib Agent establishes a type by examining the name and selects appropriate searching and displaying routines for that type (*e.g.*, ghostview for .ps files and mpeg-play for .au files, *etc*). A sample output from our implementation is shown in Figure 4.2.

Bib Agent is a learning agent that is transportable (through **ftp**). It incrementally constructs a road map of the Internet indexed by query classes. The road map consists of cached paths to information. These cached paths allow it to get to these locations more easily in the future. Bib Agent also customizes the cached paths from user input as it searches. Unsuccessful paths are pruned quickly by this approach, and a user can customize Bib Agent with his own preferences by showing it some examples.

The complexity of this agent arises from the considerable knowledge about the Unix file organization embedded in each structure detector in the tree. We illustrate this using an example from our existing implementation. When the agent for this task reaches the directory **/vol/alex/edu/mit/ai** it has a choice of seven large subdirectories to search. Our detector uses the README

---

[10] In our present implementation, a query window (see Figure 4.1) is displayed.

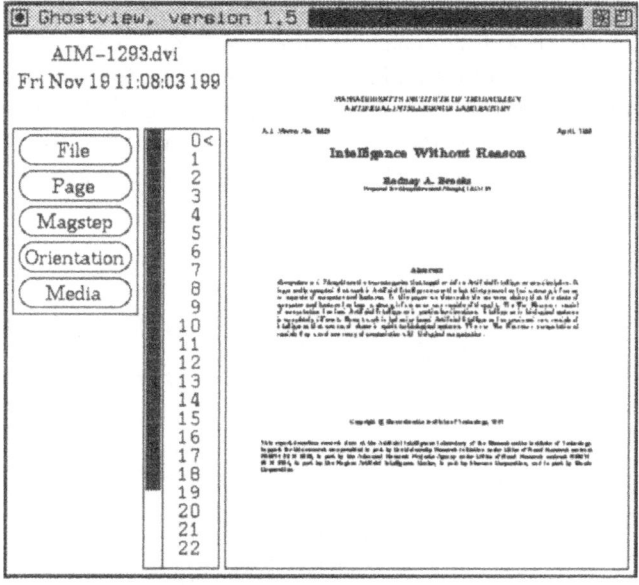

Fig. 4.2. This figure shows the document retrieven in response to a query for ai papers on *biological* models and systems. In response to this query, the agent navigated to the *mit/ai/ftp/ai-pubs/publications* directory. Once there, the agent did not know the local subdirectory structure. The agent prompted the user for help with selecting a subdirectory. The user's choice was between the *1991, 1992,* and *1993* subdirectories. The user selected 1993, and the agent returned the only paper with *biological* models in the abstract. The first page of this document is shown in this figure.

file to aid in the selection of a subset of subdirectories for further investigation. Bib Agent knows all the error messages of the Alex system and provides customized routines to handle them. In some cases, Bib Agent asks the user to help resolve an error message from Alex. For instance, Bib Agent knows about connection time-outs and will delay reconnecting to the site by a certain amount. If repeated timeouts occur, Bib Agent informs the user and asks for the next course of action.

4.1 Experimental Data

We have tested the performance of our Bib Agent by simulating a distributed collection. The test data consists of the Cornell computer science technical report library for the years 1968 through 1994. The technical reports are stored in various formats: text (abstract only), postscript, dvi, and HTML. We treat the reports from each year as belonging to a separate site. Within each site, reports are stored in a complex directory-subdirectory structure. Our agent automatically navigates through this world.

For each site, the Bib Agent performs a breadth-first search of the directory-subdirectory structure, examining all files that it encounters along the way using the search filter (*e.g.*, keywords) provided by the user. The path list computed for each site consists of all the paths to directories that contain files on the given topic.

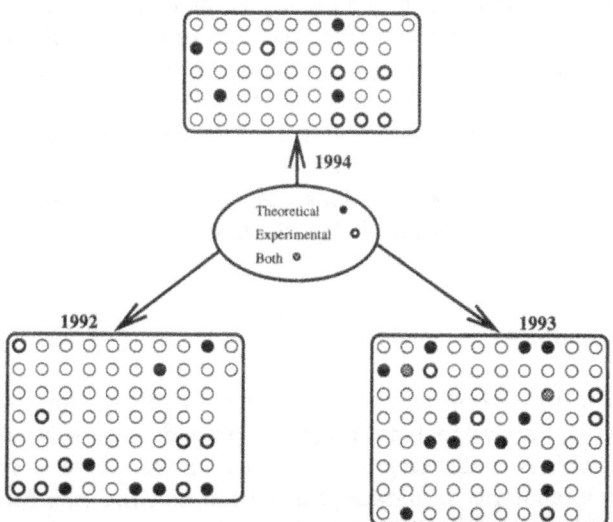

Fig. 4.3. The results from running the Bib Agent to cluster the Cornell technical reports on the query classes Theory and Experiments. The world consists of three distributed nodes, each containing technical reports from a different year.

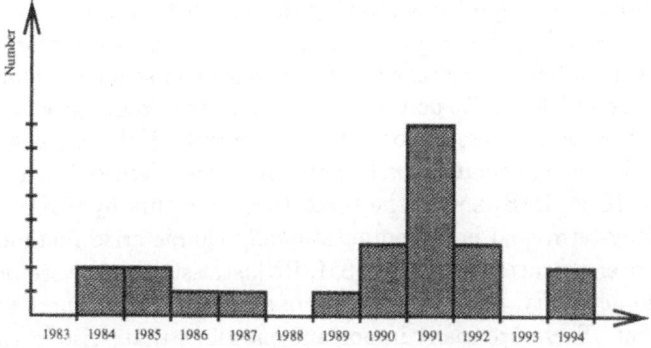

Fig. 4.4. The results of running the Bib Agent to collect papers on the ISIS project. The world consists of 12 distributed nodes, each containing technical reports from a different year.

Data from executing the Bib Agent is shown in Figures 4.3 and 4.4. In Figure 4.3 we show the cluster of papers that talk about theories (the filled bullets), experiments (the bold bullets), and both theories and experiments (the shaded bullets.) These clusters contain a small fraction of all the existing technical reports. Thus, a specific query, for example "theory and experiments in robotics at Cornell", quickly retrieves the paper that corresponds to one of the shaded bullets. Similarly, the ISIS cluster can be used for efficient retrieval as well as compiling statistics on the history of the ISIS group.

The present implementation of Bib Agent uses keyword query specifications. We can reconfigure the Bib Agent to process specifications involving tables by replacing the text (keyword) filters in our implementation by table filters. The easy construction of new variants of the Bib Agent is made possible by our modular construction kit of detectors and segmenters. We are currently working on an implementation of Bib Agent in Agent-Tcl with a World Wide Web interface. This will be provided to external users as a service of the Dienst Technical Report server [DL].

5. Discussion

Our goal is to develop and prototype a methodology for customizable information and access tools for large, distributed, heterogeneous information domains. This is challenging for many reasons: (a) there is a mismatch between the granularity of data representation and the task specification; (b) there is little agreement about how to specify general retrieval tasks; (c) the amount of data is too large for exhaustive search. Our hypothesis is that the structure that exists in electronic data at various levels of detail embodies implicit representational conventions, and that smart filters composed of structure detectors and segmenters that use this structure are a suitable computational paradigm for organizing the search for information.

The key technical challenge is association of content with information. By this we mean finding structural cues or substitutes for semantic information at different levels of detail. To do this, we need a formal framework for analyzing what information is necessary for performing a task. Such a framework, based on the notion of *information invariants*, has been discussed in the robotics context by [Don, DJR] and in the theoretical literature by [BK].

Our long-term goal is to computationally characterize methods such as statistics over character sequences [SM, PN], statistics over word occurrence, layout and geometry, and other notions of structure with respect to information content. There are many important questions that arise in the context of structure-based information retrieval, including:

- For a given class of ICA tasks and data repositories, what are the appropriate structural cues?
- What information is encoded by a given structure?

- What class of partial models can be constructed with a given segmenter?
- What class of ICA tasks is a given agent good for?
- Can we define a computational hierarchy of ICA tasks? That is, is there an order relation on the information necessary to solve various classes of tasks?

We advocate modular construction of smart filters from libraries of structure detectors and segmenters. These detectors and segmenters come with performance guarantees. For instance, the table detector can detect tabular information to within user-specified tolerance in row and column misalignments. Our scheme is suited for fast prototyping of customized information agents.

Our design philosophy is orthogonal to the philosophy behind large, general-purpose systems like WAIS, Archie, and Gopher. When is this design methodology more appropriate than others? To answer this question, we need a theoretical basis for characterizing ICA tasks and for measuring the effectiveness of alternate architectures on task classes. The notion of structure introduced in this paper is a first step toward characterizing tasks in an implementation-independent manner. We constructed a smart filter for the class of retrieval tasks whose answers can be found in tabular form. We used this filter to build a search engine for compiling stock reports and for finding precision-recall measures. Our current implementations of this engine have been tested on Internet newsgroups, Internet ftp sites, and on the CS-TR project.[11] We would like to provide our tools for smart filter construction to a much larger body of users and gather feedback.

Several criticisms can be levied against this task-directed information agent approach to ICA tasks.

1. *Task specification: at what level of detail do we need to specify tasks?* To specify a task we need to describe the desired information at a detailed enough level that an agent can locate and retrieve it from the environment. An analogy helps in clarifying issues in task specification. Suppose you want your maid to match all the socks in your laundry. You will probably tell her to "match the socks and put them away in my sock drawer". Now what does she have to know to do this? First, she needs to know that socks come in pairs and matching them means finding all pairs. Next, she needs to know where the laundry is in your apartment, and where socks are likely to be found (in the dryer, washer, under the bed, under the sofa cushions, in the fish tank, *etc.*). These constitute task-specific knowledge that the maid needs to accomplish the task. Some of the knowledge is essential to perform the task correctly and others aid in efficient accomplishment of the task. If your maid doesn't know what matching socks means, she will be unable to perform the task at all. If

---

[11] The CS-TR project a nation-wide effort to create an electronic library of computer science technical reports.

she doesn't know preferred locations of socks in your apartment, it will probably take her longer to do the task. It is useful to think of information agents as electronic maids; these agents give us sanitized views of information worlds. They accomplish important, routine tasks that we need done, but don't have the patience to do.

2. *Matching structures to tasks: how can we identify structures relevant to a task?* To design information agents we need to identify structures in the environment that can lead us to the required information for solving the task. These structures exist because humans use and design conventions for representing information. For instance, typesetting rules embodied in TEXhave standardized the visual appearance of technical papers. Structure can thus be used as a cue for task-level (semantic) content. Can one match structures to tasks in a general way, or is it going to reduce to 1001 special cases? Since this matching relies fundamentally on conventions for representing information, this question translates to one of characterizing these conventions. Such a characterization is outside the scope of this paper. Our hope is that as we construct more agents in our testbed environment of scanned technical reports, we will identify patterns in matching structures to tasks.

3. *Scale up: This approach may be good for simple ICA tasks, but does it work for more complex tasks?* In our framework, task complexity is characterized by how well understood the mapping between task and environmental structures is. We can view structure detectors as bandpass filters which extract information within specific frequency ranges. A library of structure detectors pulls out different bands of interest. Our library contains parametric structure detectors and corresponding segmenters for commonly occurring patterns in the data environment. We have demonstrated their use in the construction of agents for two useful task classes. Problems caused by heterogeneity and noise in data are solved by our approach. However ill-specified tasks still present a challenge.[12] Our focus in this paper has been to expand the class of tasks that can be solved to beyond those specified by keywords. Our approach supports the scaling of task classes to those specifiable and solvable by geometric or visual cues.

4. *Solution Complexity: When word-based indices work impressively well, why do we need high-level structures to extract information?* We do not suggest the supplanting of existing word-based methods by our structure-based techniques; rather, we envision their synergistic combination to

---

[12] Consider, for instance, John Hopcroft's test for a conceptual retrieval system "how does the Brown Computer Science Department's research budget compare with that of Cornell's"? Where is this information to be found? What are suitable indicators for this metric (other than the research budget itself)? This query highlights the fact that there is a tremendous amount of information about the environment that the designer needs to know up-front in order to solve information retrieval tasks.

provide rapid filtering in large text environments. For example, the ability to recognize the logical and layout structure of documents provides automatic support for the SGML-like markup of documents that text retrievers like SMART require. For non-text environments, structures based on geometry and other domains are necessary for content-directed retrieval of information.

We recognize that issues relating to how users specify structures associated with tasks, and the development of a broad query language, are important to make the agent approach user friendly, and its use wide spread. We hope that this paper will provide inspiration for such investigations.

In the end, how well our approach performs is an empirical question. Whether users of the information super highway prefer to build their own hot rods with a structure detector and segmenter kit, or take public transportation that serves all uniformly[13], will ultimately be judged by history.

Acknowledgement. We are very grateful to Charles Nicholas and James Mayfield for carefully reading earlier drafts and for making suggestions that helped us improve the paper considerably. Special thanks to James Allan, Javed Aslam, and K. Sivaramakrishnan for their careful reading of earlier drafts. Thanks go to Jim Davis, Bruce Donald, Dean Krafft, Chris Lewis, T. V. Raman, Jonathan Rees, Matthew Scott, Kristen Summers, and Rich Zippel for enlightening discussions.

Daniela Rus has been supported by the Advanced Research Projects Agency of the Defense Department under ONR Contract N00014-92-J-1989, by ONR Contract N00014-92-J-39, by NSF Contract IRI-9006137, and by ONR Contract N00014-95-1-1204. Devika Subramanian has been supported by NSF Contract IRI-8902721.

References

[AS] J. Allan and G. Salton, The identification of text relations using automatic hypertext linking, in *the Workshop on Intelligent Hypertext, the ACM Conference on Information and Knowledge Management*, November 1993.

[AV] D. Angluin and L. Valiant, Fast probabilistic algorithms for Hamiltonian circuits and matchings, *Journal of Computer and System Sciences* vol. 18, pp 155-193, 1979.

[BDG] J. L. Balcázar, J. Díaz, and J. Gabarró, *Structural Complexity I*, Springer-Verlag, 1992.

[Bel] N. Belkin and W. Croft, Information filtering and information retrieval: two sides of the same coin?, *Communications of the ACM*, vol. 35(12), pp. 29-38, 1992.

[BK] M. Blum and D. Kozen, On the power of the compass (or, why mazes are easier to search than graphs), in *Proceedings of the Symposium on Foundations of Computer Science*, pp. 132-142, 1978.

---

[13] at the lowest common denominator over usages

[Bro1] R. Brooks, Elephants don't play chess, *Design of Autonomous Agents*, ed. P. Maes, MIT/Elsevier, 1990.

[Bro2] R. Brooks, A robust layered control system for a mobile robot, *IEEE Journal of Robotics and Automation*, 1986.

[CG] J. Canny and K. Goldberg, A "RISC" Paradigm for Industrial Robotics, to appear, *Proceedings of the International Conference on Robotics and Automation*, 1993.

[Cate] V. Cate, Alex: a global file system, in *Proceedings of the Usenix Conference on File Systems*, 1992.

[CRD] P. Crean, C. Russell, and M. V. Dellon, Overview and Programming Guide to the Mind Image Management Systems, Xerox Technical Report X9000627, 1991.

[DL] J. Davis and C. Lagoze, Drop-in publishing with the World-Wide Web, in *Proceedings of the Second International WWW Conference*, pg 749-758, 1994.

[Don] B. Donald, Information Invariants in Robotics, to appear, *Artificial Intelligence*.

[DJ] B. Donald and J. Jennings, Constructive recognizability for task-directed robot programming, *Journal of Robotics and Autonomous Systems*, 9(1), 1992.

[DJR] B. Donald, J. Jennings, and D. Rus, Information Invariants for Cooperating Autonomous Mobile Robots, in *Proceedings of the International Symposium on Robotics Research*, 1993.

[EW] O. Etzioni and D. Weld, A softbot-based interface to the Internet, in *Communications of the ACM*, vol. 37, no. 7, pp. 72-76, 1994.

[FNK] H. Fujisawa, Y. Nakano, and K. Kurino, Segmentation methods for character recognition: from segmentation to document structure analysis, *Proceedings of the IEEE*, vol. 80, no. 7, 1992.

[GK] M. Genesereth, S. Ketchpel, Software agents, in *Communications of the ACM*, vol. 37, no. 7, pg 48-53, 1994.

[GGT] L. Gravano, H. Garcia-Molina, and A. Tomasic, The Efficacy of GlOSS for the Text Database Discovery Problem, Technical Report no. STAN-CS-TN-93-01, Computer Science Department, Stanford University, 1993.

[Gra] R. Gray, Agent Tcl, A transportable Agent System, in J. Mayfield and T. Finnin, editors, *Proceeedings of the CIKM Workshop on Intelligent Agents*, Baltimore, MD 1995. Also Technical Report PCS-TR95-261, Department of Computer Science, Dartmouth College, 1995.

[GKNRC] R. Gray, D. Kotz, S. Nog, D. Rus, and G. Cybenko, Mobile Agents for Mobile Computers, submitted to MOBICOM96. Also Technical Report PCS-TR96-285, Department of Computer Science, Dartmouth College, 1996.

[HP] M. Hearst and C. Plaunt, Subtopic Structuring for Full-Length Document Access, in *Proceedings of the Sixteenth Annual International ACM SIGIR Conference on Research and Development in Information Retrieval*, pp. 59-68, 1993.

[Hoe] W. Hoeffding, Probability inequalities for sums of bounded random variables, *Journal of American Statistical Association*, vot. 58, pp 13-30, 1963.

[HU] J. Hopcroft and J. Ullman, *Introduction to Automata Theory, Languages, and Computation*, Addison-Wesley, 1979.

[HKR] D. Huttenlocher, G. Klanderman, and W. Rucklidge, Comparing images using the Hausdorff distance, to appear, *IEEE Transactions on Pattern Analysis and Machine Intelligence*.

[HNR] D. Huttenlocher, J. Noh, and W. Rucklidge, Tracking non-rigid objects in complex scenes, Cornell University Technical Report TR92-1320, 1992.

[JB] A. Jain and S. Bhattacharjee, Address block location on envelopes using Gabor filters, *Pattern Recognition*, vol. 25, no. 12, 1992.

[JR] J. Jennings and D. Rus, Active model acquisition for near-sensorless manipulation with mobile robots, in *Proceedings of the IASTED Conference on Robotics and Automation*, 1993.

[Kah] B. Kahle, Overview of Wide Area Information Servers, WAIS on-line documentation, 1991.

[KC] R. Kahn and V. Cerf, *The World of Knowbots*, report to the Corporation for National Research Initiative, Arlington, VA 1988.

[KSC] H. Kautz, B. Selman, and M. Coen, Bottom-up design of software agents, in *Communications of the ACM*, vol 37, no. 7, pp. 143-145, 1994.

[KF] H. Kucera and W. Francis, *Computational Analysis of Present Day American English*, Brown University Press, Providence, RI, 1967.

[Les] M. Lesk, The CORE electronic chemistry library, Proceedings of the SIGIR, 1991.

[Mae] P. Maes, Agents that reduce work and information overload, in *Communications of the ACM*, vol 37, no. 7, pp. 31-40, 1994.

[MCFMZ] T. Mitchell, R. Caruana, D. Freitag, J. McDermott, and D. Zabowski, Experience with a learning personal assistant, in *Communications of the ACM*, vol 37, no. 7, pp. 81-91, 1994.

[MT*] M. Mizuno, Y. Tsuji, T. Tanaka, H. Tanaka, M. Iwashita, and T. Temma, Document recognition system with layout structure generator, *NEC Research and Development*, vol. 32, no. 3, 1991.

[Mun] J. Munkres, *Topology: A First Course*, Prentice Hall, 1975.

[NSV] G. Nagy, S. Seth, and M. Vishwanathan, A prototype document image analysis system for technical journals, *Computer*, vol. 25, no. 7, 1992.

[PN] C. Pearce and C. Nicholas, Generating a dynamic hypertext environment with n-gram analysis, in *Proceedings of the ACM Conference on Information Knowledge Management*, pp. 148-153, 1993.

[Rob] S. Robertson, The methodology of information retrieval experiment, *Information Retrieval Experiment*, in K. Sparck Jones, Ed., pp 9-31, Butterworths, 1981.

[RCM] G. Robertson, S. Card, and J. Mackinlay, Information visualization using 3D interactive animation, in *Communications of the ACM*, Vol. 36, No. 4, pp. 57070, 1993.

[RSa] D. Rus and D. Subramanian, Multi-media RISSC Informatics: Retrieving Information with Simple Structural Components, in *Proceedings of the ACM Conference on Information and Knowledge Management*, Nov. 1993.

[RSa] D. Rus and D. Subramanian, Customizing informaiton access, in *ACM Transactions on Information Systems*, vol. 15, no. 1, pp 67-101, 1997.

[RSb] D. Rus and K. Summers, Using whitespace for automated document structuring, in N. Adam, B. Bhargava, and Y. Yesha editors, *Advances in digital libraries*, Springer-Verlag, Lecture Notes in Computer Science 916, 1995.

[RGK] D. Rus, R. Gray, and D. Kotz, Autonomous and Adaptive Agents that Gather Information, in I. Imam editors, *Proceedings of the AAAI96 Workshop on Intelligent Adpative Agents*, Protland, OR, 1996.

[RGK] D. Rus, R. Gray, and D. Kotz, Transportable Information Agents, in *Proceedings of the First International Conference on Autonomous Agents*, Marina del Ray, CA, 1997.

[SM] G. Salton and M. McGill, *Introduction to Modern Information Retrieval*, McGraw-Hill, New York, 1983.

[SB] G. Salton and C. Buckley, Improving retrieval performance by relevance feedback, *Journal of American Society for Information Science*, vol. 41(4), pp. 288-297, 1990.

[Sal] G. Salton, *Automatic Text Processing: the transformation, analysis, and retrieval of information by computer*, Addison-Wesley, 1989.

[SK] D. Sankoff and J. Kruskal, *Time warps, string edits, and macromolecules: the theory and practice of sequence comparison*, Addison-Wesley, 1983.

[ST] M. Schwartz and P. Tsirigotis, Experience with a Semantically Cognizant Internet White Pages Directory Tool, *Journal of Internetworking Research and Experience*, March 1991.

[SEKN] M. Schwartz, A. Emtage, B. Kahle, and B. Neuman, A comparison of Internet discovery approaches, *Computer Systems*, 5(4), 1992.

[TSKK] Y. Tanosaki, K. Suzuki, K. Kikuchi, and M. Kurihara, A logical structure analysis system for documents, *Proceedings of the second international symposium on interoperable information systems*, 1988.

[TA] S. Tsujimoto and H. Asada, Major components of a complete text reading system, in *Proceedings of the IEEE*, vol. 80, no. 7, 1992.

[WS] D. Wang and S. Srihari, Classification of newspaper image blocks using texture analysis, *Computer Vision, Graphics, and Image Processing*, vol. 47, 1989.

[WCW] K. Wong, R. Casey, and F. Wahl, Document Analysis System, *IBM Journal of Research and Development*, vol. 26, no. 6, 1982.

[Splus] User   Manual,   *Splus   Reference   Manual*,   Statistical Sciences,Inc.,Seattle,Washington, 1991.

[CACM93] *Communications of the ACM*, vol. 36, no. 4, 1994.

Springer
and the
environment

At Springer we firmly believe that an international science publisher has a special obligation to the environment, and our corporate policies consistently reflect this conviction.

We also expect our business partners – paper mills, printers, packaging manufacturers, etc. – to commit themselves to using materials and production processes that do not harm the environment. The paper in this book is made from low- or no-chlorine pulp and is acid free, in conformance with international standards for paper permanency.

 Springer

Lecture Notes in Computer Science

For information about Vols. 1–1253

please contact your bookseller or Springer-Verlag